Development And African Philosophy

Development And African Philosophy

✦

A Theoretical Reconstruction of African Socio-Political Economy

Francis O. C. Njoku

iUniverse, Inc.
New York Lincoln Shanghai

Development And African Philosophy
A Theoretical Reconstruction of African Socio-Political Economy

iUniverse, Inc.

For information address:
iUniverse, Inc.
2021 Pine Lake Road, Suite 100
Lincoln, NE 68512
www.iuniverse.com

ISBN: 0-595-32949-7

Printed in the United States of America

Dedicated to:

Eugene and Callista Anuforo, (Maryland, USA)
&
Members of Our Lady Queen of All Saints Church, Ville Platte (LA, USA)

"If you plan for a year, plant a seed.
If for ten years, plant a tree.
If for a hundred years, teach the people.
When you sow a seed once, you will reap a single harvest.
When you teach the people, you will reap a hundred harvests."

—K'uan-Tzu, 551-479 B.C.

Contents

Acknowledgment

This book was written over a period of three years during my travels and researches in Nigeria, Europe and America. And to this effect, I have had the hand of many people in its creation, from the beginning to its completion. I thank the authors whose materials I have used. There were enriching discussions with Denis Osuagwu and Fr. Randall Moreau (who were very generous with their time, library and resources in Louisiana, USA), and valuable suggestions from David Ihenacho (New York). Others who, at various times, critiqued my ideas included Cletus Obasi (Birmingham, UK), Stan Onyemere, Emmanuel Ede, Moses Dike, Kate Ekwe, Dimitrice Uche and Sylva Ashimole.

Mon. Bernard A. Prince (Rome) and Dr Matthew Nwoko (German) not only read earlier drafts of this work, but also gave me great insights. I am grateful to Dr C. N. Okezie (Alvan, Owerri) for reading some portion of this work. I thank Charlie and Immaculate Amanze (Michigan, USA), Eugene and Callista Anuforo (Maryland, USA), and Eddy and Christy King (Canada) for helping me financially. I sincerely appreciate Prof B. Eke and his wife Mrs J. Eke plus their children—Ijeoma, Adaku, Oluchi, Ikechukwu and Ugochukwu—(Maryland, USA) for their support. Fr. Robert Kane (Scotland, UK) offered me good atmosphere to organize my work. I am also grateful to John and Mina Courtney, Annie and Danny Mina, Ann and David Ryan, Ann and Bill McGregor, Mr and Mrs Eddie Sweeny, and all the members of St Edward's Church Airdrie, Scotland.

Genevieve and Jake Ardoin, Greg Ardoin and family, Neil Rozas, Andy and Amy Poche, Ed and Roberta McCurry, Rhett and Sally Young, Joe and Sue Fontenot, Cheri and David Fontenot, J. and Ray Lamke, Gwen and Kevin Reed, and all the members of Our Lady Queen of All Saints Church Ville Platte, Louisiana, and Earl and Joyce Guillory (Lawtell) afforded me the environment of love, generosity and quite to reflect.

Finally, I owe my gratitude to Scholastica Ahanaonye, who helped with the typesetting; Joseph, Peter, Paul, Joan, Eucharia, Paulina, Maama (Sylvia) and Onyedikachi for their encouragement in various ways. At the end of the day, however, I bear responsibility for the contents and errors in this book.

Preface

Development and African Philosophy is a very provocative venture. After reading the work, several thoughts come to mind. It is no longer sufficient to view Philosophy and philosophical thoughts outside the realm of pressing needs of society. Dr Njoku's careful trace of the role of the concept of development in the history of Philosophy and there from attempt to create a new understanding of the concept of development suitable to Africa and African situation are a genial loop.

Development, as discussed in Philosophy, if it has to be meaningful, must be the development of the entire person, not merely some aspects of a person's life. If it is the development of the whole person, it is then the development of humanity itself. The stretch, which Njoku gives the concept of development—History—Philosophy—Socio-Politics—Africa—Religion/Theology, confirms this point. The logic of development conceived from the point of dictation by Eurocentric influence on history undermines this philosophical concept of development. Development of humanity has to be the development motivated and directed by all cultures.

African culture must have its own contributions to human development instead of waiting to be developed. I think the most deadly wound Africa received from colonial devastation is the deadly sore impressed on the minds of most Africans that Africa **has to be helped to develop**. This encourages all forms of degrading paternalism that make many Africans become perpetual beggars and slaves. To believe that you cannot develop except someone intervenes is already self-defeat. The idea that you have to be helped by someone else in order to survive relegates you to be a subordinate or a perpetual slave. The imperative is very clear: you have to take the bull by the horns. You use what you have to develop yourself. Do you have resources to develop? Are the resources being stolen away? Development starts, in this case, with hindering exploitation and waste. Njoku emphasized the concept of development through participation. I think an important aspect of participation in development is legitimate confrontation of the exploiters *a radice.*

Has religion anything to do with development? This work systematically disabuses the mind of the belief that religion is there to tranquillize the impoverished. Through the work, Dr Njoku challenges theologians to re-examine their mission in the work of human development. Part of the duty of religion is the protection and support of the weak to come out of the dungeon of poverty. Njoku drives the message home in his own words: "Jesus does not legitimize poverty…. The impression has wrongly been given that Jesus canonizes poverty in the Lucan Beatitudes for he makes it a source of special values and graces. Jesus does neither create the conditions of poverty nor does he love the sight of the poor; however, he makes the poor the recipients of his Gospel and the Kingdom of God." The Church has the duty to free the poor from those who impoverish them. It is a disservice to Christianity if the Church sees the impoverishment of a people and keeps quiet about it or takes to Pontius Pilate's alibi.

Some philosophers saw the impoverishment of a part of humanity and kept quiet. They did not only profit from it, but justified and appraised the impoverishment of human beings. Njoku's confrontation of Hegel and Hume's appraisal of slavery is admirable. A philosophy that is racist is no longer a genuine Philosophy. The reason is obvious. Such a thought system excludes itself from the fundamental premise of Philosophy: **universality**.

Back to *Development and African Philosophy*: What are the best options for Africa? Genuine Philosophy in the history of humanity has always been a way-pointer towards nation-building. In the case of Africa, it may not be out of place that philosophers and theologians give people some sense of direction in nation-building. Njoku's 'concept of covenant as offering a basis for a philosophy of right' is a very creative venture. It is a juro-ethical midway that may check the excesses of legalism and moralism on the one hand, and subdue the hideous ambience of power utilitarianism, which has institutionalized itself in modern politics, on the other hand. People need, as rightly put by Njoku, "an environment of trust to exercise and give effect to their willingness to belong to a common family-hood…." This means that leadership based on **covenant** receives an extended authority beyond mere legal norms or vague moral injunctions. It is then based on a higher level of relationship that involves even onto-religious trust—the **covenanted authority**. Dr Njoku's covenanted leadership and authority model could perhaps become the breakthrough for new understanding of democracy in African politics. It will surely need the test of time for credibility.

Rev. Dr. Matthew I. Nwoko
(Beauftragter)
Social Science Department
Catholic University of Applied Science
Köln Germany.

Introduction

The crisis of sense, in most cases, leads to a distorted image of theoretical models and judgments about truth. When the senses, whether internal or external, are defective, the faculties do not take in correct information about facts, persons, events and the environment around us. Distorted information can also come about as a result of inattention on the part of the subject. In other words, the senses can be in perfect condition, yet misjudgment can ensue because of mismanagement of the information recorded or obtained. The inability to gather facts correctly, as a result of inattention on the part of the subject or defect of the senses, can lead to the inability to interpret properly the facts generally.

When facts are not interpreted correctly, it becomes difficult to articulate beliefs. Since beliefs issue in rules of action, the crisis of theory inevitably turns into a crisis of practice. The combination of the crises of theory and of practice bubbles up as a crisis of value. The inability to build on strong theoretical principles can continuously hamper attempts to construct a stable practical base for the conduct of persons and governance of society.

The present book examines the African socio-political face sought at the level of economic, political and human development. To understand what has taken place in this area, a better tool is needed to situate development in general and how its economic and social aspects shaped particular political spaces during the period of colonialism in Africa.

Development and African Philosophy is about development and a certain philosophy of right needed to comprehend African social, economic and political scene. The European developmental imperative for Africa is put into perspective, from colonial period till date. Before this is done, however, the modern intellectual disposition that laid down the philosophy of domination and control of nature and humans is brought under review, having summarized the major theories of development that dominate development studies.

While the United Nations Human Development Reports are highlighted, this book seeks to establish a better theoretical model under which development with a human and dignified face is to be grasped, departing from the African context. But a new intellectual compass is needed to re-assess and re-define African life and reality. After all, "our view of realty is like a map with which to negotiate the terrain of life. If the map is true and accurate, we will generally know where we are, and if we have decided where we want to go, we will generally know how to get there. If the map is false and inaccurate, we generally will be lost."[1]

The conceptual tool needed to propose a human-faced and holistic development in Africa is a philosophy of right. A right is a claim. An African philosophy of right is carved out of a certain socio-political reality called *covenant* or pact.

A covenant is an agreement between parties or persons established through a solemn promise. In other words, an African philosophy of right is situated within a certain aspect of African reality, that is, covenant, and the environment that understands life as communion. But covenant and communion themselves are comprehended within community and individual dialogue relationships and complementary signification.

The process of dialogue and complementary signification is a movement towards complementary awareness, understanding and self-and-community donation in the construction of socio-political reality. The construction of reality, through dialogue by covenanted wills, brings into being a certain ethics of encounter. Such ethics structures the rights and inter-personal relationships of covenanted subjects.

Rights, as *Development and African Philosophy* argues, truly emerge within the environment in which free wills bond together, while at the same time transcending isolated claims of each covenant subject. Thus, a philosophy of right is used here to criticize and deconstruct the age old view that Africans are very community-centered; it is also used to construct a better reading of African life that takes on board African past and present in the journey of its socio-political emancipation.

The philosophy of right proposed, therefore, offers a theoretical ground that puts in perspective the quest for leadership and authority. Since the lack of effective leadership has not only made African continent grope in the dark so long, it has suffocated the social, economic and political development and potential of its people. If economic and human developments are read from the perspective of covenant-derived philosophy of right, it will indeed wear at once a human and eco-systemic face. In this way, the book responds to the call repeatedly made to African philosophers to offer conceptual tools from within for the social and political reconstruction of African life.

---

1.   David L. Bender, ed., *Constructing A Life Philosophy: Opposing View Points* (San Diego, USA: Greenhaven Press, Inc., 1993), 18.

With a covenant-based interpretation of authority and leadership, it becomes very realistic to justify initiative-democracy where sovereign power is rightly rooted in, and remains, with the people as against the distortion of democracy in its so-called representative fashion. A covenant motivated understanding casts intelligent light on the reading of the political economy of development.

The present day Nigerian democracy seems to be a travesty of democracy. A bad and manipulated democracy is only propaganda, even if it passes for what the world wants to hear about the existence of absence of military rule. The absence of military rule where people are led into believing that they are in control through their representatives does not resolve the issue of a democratic authority. Thus, a philosophy of right, I believe, offers a better conceptual framework for deriving practice from theory, as a way forward for African socio-political economy; it instills an understanding that political power is a delegated power in the atmosphere of covenant; it should be used to create conditions where capital will be formed and security maintained so that people can truly flourish.

Francis O. C. Njoku, cmf
January 2004.

PART I

Economic and Human Development in Perspective

1

Understanding What Development Generally Means

What is meant by Development?

The root of the word 'development' comes from the French verb 'veloper' which means to wrap. In other words, to develop is "to cause to grow gradually, fuller, larger, stronger and better."[1] It is a progression towards maturity and better exemplification of the nature of the type in question. The concept of development embodies progress and growth as a goal. At the level of the individual, development, according to Walter Rodner, implies an "increased skill and capacity, greater freedom, creativity, self-discipline, responsibility and material well-being."[2] The major claim at the individual level is that development is the unfolding of potentials that help the individual to flourish fully.

Anselm Uba articulates the psychological overtone of the word 'development,' when he writes:

> The term development means the gradual and orderly unfolding of the characteristics of the successive stages of growth involving the emerging and expanding of capacities of the individual to provide greater facility in functioning. It means essentially progress toward a goal. It involves changes from simplicity to complexity and implies an increasingly progressive maturity of behavior as well as organization of personality and character.[3]

---

1. S. I. Udoidem, *Values and National Development* (Lagos: African Heritage Research and Publications, 1992), 110.
2. Walter Rodner, *How Europe Underdeveloped Africa* (Washington DC: Howard University Press, 1982), 9.
3. Anselm Uba, *Fundamental Psychology of Childhood and Adolescence* (Ibadan: Claverianum Press, 1980), iv.

Psychologists consider development, at the individual level, as human development. For them, 'human development' is "the scientific study of how people change and how they stay the same over time."[4] The change here can be quantitative and qualitative. A quantitative change is a change in number or amount of something. Such an alteration might bear on size, height and weight or number of something. A change in kind, structure or organization, for example, such as the nature of a person's intelligence, or the way the mind works, is a qualitative change.[5] A study in human development is interested in the factors that affect the growth and development of the human person in their internal and external dynamics. People are not passive sponges, soaking up influences. They actively shape their own environment, and respond to the environmental forces affecting them. Human development in its integrative aspect includes physical, intellectual, personal and social development, plus the environment and experiences that influence and shape development itself.

Social groups as well have a way of organizing their life-world and to this extent 'development' means the capacity to regulate both internal and external relationships. The whole issue of movement towards independence and greater maturity hover around the concept of development.

What Economics Is About

Economics is about economy. One's first impulse might be to think of economy as "a system for the production and distribution of the goods and services we use in everyday life."[6] As Thomas Sowell says, this understanding is correct to a certain extent, but it is not enough. The production and distribution of goods and services are situated in the context of scarcity. The need to economize is parasitic on the fact of scarce resources. If there is an abundance of resources, there will be no need to economize.

The word 'economics' comes from two Greek words, namely: 'oikos'—house and 'nemein'—to manage. Households, firms, and governments are to be understood in terms of houses. They constantly house or husband all available resources in order to manage them prudently, that is, to economize them. The fact of scarcity is that people want more than there is.

---

4.   Diane E. Papalia and Sally Wendkos Olds, *Human Development*, 5d., (New York: McGraw-Hill, Inc., 1992), 3.

5.   See *Ibid.*, 3.

6.   Thomas Sowell, *Basic Economics: A Citizen's Guide to the Economy* (New York: Basic Books, 2000), 1.

Economics is regarded as a social science that analyses the way available resources are used and allocated among competing needs and uses. Human beings have many wants or needs but the resources that face human needs are limited; that is, they cannot keep everyone satisfied at all times. Human histories show that resources have been scarce relative to human wants. It is in this regard that economics "is the study of the use of scarce resources which have alternative uses."

There is no doubt that science and technology have helped to relieve scarcity by creating new needs. For example, with the help of technology, synthetic rubber freed the world from dependence on natural rubber; rayon and nylon ended people's dependence on cotton. However, while technology relieves us from one end, it creates new needs or aggravates old ones. An example of this is: uranium became scarce when people learned how to use it to generate atomic energy. Whereas people enjoy the comfort of gasoline-powered automobiles, they seem to be losing the battle to have at the same time clean air in modern cities. Thus, economics has to deal with alternative uses:

> If each resource had only one use, economics would be much simpler. But water can be used to produce ice or steam by itself or innumerable other mixtures and compounds in combination with other things. A virtually limitless number of products can also be produced from wood or from petroleum, iron ore, etc. How much of each resource should be allocated to each of its many uses? Every economy has to answer that question, and each does, in one way or another, efficiently or inefficiently. Doing so efficiently is what economics is all about.[7]

The success or failure of people in terms of affluence or poverty depends on how well they allocate or manage their resources. A country may have abundant natural resources but still remain poor because it lacks the skills for efficiently turning its resources into abundant output. Nigeria, at present, is a classic example of a country that is potentially rich but actually poor because of mis-management of resources. Countries, on the contrary, with very small resources have turned in abundant output because of efficient allocation or management of their limited resources. Japan, Italy, Switzerland and many others are in the group that has created high standard of living for their people by making proper use of their limited resources.

---

7.   *Ibid.*, 1-2.

Development in Socio-economic Terms

Of late, the term 'development' has come to be conceived exclusively in economic terms, although it is measured against other social features. "A society," Walter writes, "develops economically as its members increase jointly their capacity for dealing with the environment."[8] In other words, development involves the pooling together of resources in order to organize environmental and social relations for the enhancement of the members of the society. If this enhancement of the human person is lacking extensively, such a development will not be an authentic human or economic development. No doubt Donal Dorr insists that all genuine human or economic development should be self-development—of the individual, the community or the nation. Development, he rightly criticizes, is not mere relief services nor is there really such a thing as development "for others."[9]

'Underdevelopment,' on the contrary, is not the absence of development; rather it is a comparative outlook towards the level of development in human social and economic configuration. Against this platform, the discovery that some people or nations have matured advanced and become wealthier than others, which are still immature, primitive, poor and backward makes this comparison obvious. However, 'underdevelopment' is employed in modern parlance to express a particular relationship of exploitation, namely, of one country by another. In this regard, "all of the countries named as underdeveloped in the world are exploited by others; and the underdevelopment with which the world is now pre-occupied is a product of a capitalist imperialist and colonialist exploitation."[10]

Professional economists, in a more articulate manner, speak of National Income Per Capita in comparing the levels of distribution of incomes in African and European countries. It is the gap between the income distribution levels in these countries measured in per capita income that allows one group to be classed as 'developed' and another as 'underdeveloped.' This gap has become so transparent and widened that some nations are becoming richer whereas the economies of others stagnate daily in a geometrical proportion. To some minds, of course, this is not a mere historical accident, but a strategy embedded in the western economic plan to keep the economy of African countries ever morbid and moribund in the context of the imperialist power politics.

---

8.   Walter Rodner, *How Europe Underdeveloped Africa.*, 10.
9.   See Donal Dorr, *Spirituality and Justice* (New York: Orbis Books, 1984), 206-207.
10.   *Ibid.*, 21.

2

Theories of Development in Perspective

Most authors on development studies trace the present discourse on development to the 1940s, giving the impression, albeit wrong, that the intellectual discourse about development within the socio-economic sphere began in the 20th century. Thus, one reads the following lines:

> Development is the process whereby other peoples are dominated and their destinies are shaped according to an essentially Western way of conceiving and perceiving the world. The development discourse is part of an imperial process whereby other peoples are appropriated and turned into objects. It is an essential part of the process whereby the 'developed' countries manage, control and even create the Third World economically, politically, sociologically and culturally. It is a process whereby the lives of some peoples, their plan, their hopes, their imaginations, are shaped by others who frequently share neither their lifestyles, nor their hopes nor their values. The real nature of this process is disguised by a discourse that portrays development as a necessary and desirable process, as human destiny itself.[1]

The passage just quoted portrays an understanding of development that dominated the imperial or colonial era. Tucker's points are quite taken but we have to go back pass the 20th century. Development understanding has not always been purely economic or clothed in socially manipulative forms. We can understand development theorizing under two broad perspectives, namely: the natural law and the mechanistic theories of development.

---

1. Vincent Tucker, 'The Myth of Development: A Critique of A Eurocentric Discourse,' in *Critical Development Theory* eds., Ronaldo and Denis O'Hearn (London: Zeb Books Limited, 1999), 1.

The Natural Law Theory of Development and the Metaphysics of Development

The refusal to trace development studies before the twentieth century implicitly denies that development is a natural process. We have stated that to develop implies a gradual growth towards a stronger and better status, a status that embodies a goal. Both at the levels of the individual and societies, development is an unfolding of potentials for the better flourishing of the individual, the entity or the society, since development is part of the maturing process—a goal. It is a natural process, contrary to Tucker's claim that "development is not a natural process."[2] The ancients had conceived development or progress in this light. The Aristotelian-Thomistic tradition, leaning on natural law platform, reflected on the metaphysics of development as a natural process. This tradition wanted to find the truth about development independent of ideological and utilitarian motives.

According to Aristotle, nature follows a course; animate and inanimate entities follow an order in their nature that corresponds to their purpose, which is so determined by their nature.[3] That which a being or an art or an inquiry aims at is identified as good.[4] The good is part of a structured whole that is rooted in the nature of the thing to which the process of development is a part. Aristotle's natural law is then rooted in the conviction that nature stands as a capacity for development inherent in particular things and aimed at a particular end or purpose both in respect to physical and moral phenomena.

In general, every art, being, substance tends towards something: aim/end/goal. This goal is rooted in the nature of the thing or being as an end product of a process, for Aristotle insists that nature does nothing in vain.[5] Thus, nature follows an order. That order, in the case of human beings, is rooted in humans' rational nature. Rationality is the distinguishing characteristics and judge of human development.

Aristotle believes that all causes, both proper and accident, may be spoken of either as potential or as actual; for instance: the cause of a house being built is either a house-builder or a house-builder building.[6] The point is that the final

---

2.   *Ibid.*, 2.
3.   Aristotle, *Generation of Animals*, 778b11-19.
4.   Idem, *Nichomachean Ethics*, 1094a1.
5.   See Idem, *Physics*, Bk., II, Ch., 8, 198b10-199b33.
6.   See Idem, *Physics*, 195b5.

cause (the end) imposes some necessity on the thing alongside that imposed by the material cause. One then grasps the concept of Aristotle's teleology that insists that things exist as products of nature or characteristics of each natural/separate kind; that is, they exist for the 'sake of':

> Everything then exists for a final cause, and all those things which are included in the definition of each animal, or which either are for the sake of some end or are ends in themselves, come into being both through this cause and the rest. But when we come to those things, which come into being without failing under the heads just mentioned, their cause must be sought in the movement or process of coming into formation of the animal. An eye, for instance, the animal must have of necessity (for an animal is supposed to be of such a sort), but it will have an eye of a particular kind of necessity in another sense, not the sense mentioned just above, because it is its nature to act or be acted on in this or that way.[7]

Nature has made everything for a purpose; thus, development processes have ends. And Aristotle conceives the final cause as that from which movement comes. For example, fishes will of necessity have fins; for, if their fins are destroyed, they will no longer swim because it is in the nature of fishes to swim. Animals and their parts, and plants and simple bodies are of the things that exist by nature. And the things constituted by nature have within themselves a principle of motion. And others that exist by other causes have a principle of stationariness. The point is that,

> things have a nature which have a principle of this kind. Each of them is a substance; for it is a subject, and nature is always a subject.
>   The terms 'according to nature' is applied to all these things and also to the attributes which belong to them in virtue of what they are, for instance the property of fire to be carried upwards—which is not a nature nor has a nature but is by nature or according to nature.[8]

The nature of humans is rooted in rationality; for humans to act according to their nature is to act rationally. Then Aristotle draws the connection between his treatment of substances and causes in his practical philosophy when he states, aware that nature does nothing without a purpose, that "every art and every inquiry, and similarly every action and choice, is thought to aim at some good,

---

7.   Idem, *Generation of Animals*, 778b11-19.
8.   Idem, *Physics*, Bk., II, 192b33-193a1.

and for this reason the good has rightly been declared to be that which all things aim."[9] The good is part of a structured whole that is rooted in the nature of the thing to which the process of development is a part. Aristotle's natural law doctrine is strongly rooted in the conviction that nature stands as a capacity for development inherent in particular things and aimed at a particular end or purpose both in respect to physical and moral phenomena.

Aristotle identifies the attainment of this state of goodness, for humans, as *eudaimonia* or happiness, to which both individuals and states aspire. He followed his master Plato to identify the end of the state with the ethical end of the individual, for the state is that which assures its citizens the best life. With habits as sets of dispositions, Plato and Aristotle argue, via natural progression towards fuller maturity, that both the state and individuals reach the end that is good. Development in the natural law tradition, therefore, is a natural, fuller and better growth with its appropriate perfection. To have developed or to develop is to reach a rational balance or equilibrium at the point of which the best in human, social and political spheres operates as an integrated whole, where people have the right natural dispositions and their operations in place.

The position that things tend to a purpose inherent in their nature posits a universal law that governs all things and development, which means: humans and entities have a true way of development that is inherent in their nature. It is the development that is proper to a thing or nature that can be described as good. In the case of humans, development is the development *per se* determined by the right reason of humans, not manipulated by selfish or utilitarian interests. At the level of social theory and human affairs, that is, at the level where people bring about changes in the world by their intentions and act for reasons, Cicero states that the true law is right reason, and it applies to all unconditionally,[10] and demands the inherent duty to respect its operations.

Human nature, in Aquinas' understanding, is conceived as a set of dispositional properties or inclinations,[11] dispositions that can influence a person's powers towards actualization. As John Finnis comments:

> One understands human nature by understanding human capacities, those capacities by understanding human acts, and those acts by understanding their

---

9.   Idem, *Nichomachean Ethics*, 1094a1.

10.   Tullius Cicero, *On the Commonwealth*, trans. George Holland Sabine and Stanley Barney Smith (New York: The Bobbs-Merrill Company, Inc. 1929), bk. iii, § xxii, 215-216.

11.   See Thomas Aquinas, *Summa Theologica* I-II, q. 26 a. 1c.

object. That is Aquinas' primary methodological or, if you like, epistemological principle for considering the nature of an active being…. But the objects of humanly chosen acts are precisely the basic purposes (fines), that is, goods (bona), with which Aquinas is concerned,…[12]

Aquinas examines human dispositions or inclinations at three levels: sensitive, animal and rational levels:

> Since, however, good has the nature of an end, and evil, the nature of a contrary, hence it is that all those things to which man has a natural inclination, are naturally apprehended by reason as being good, and consequently as objects of pursuit, and their contraries as evil, and objects of avoidance. Wherefore according to the order of natural inclinations, is the order of precepts of this natural law. Because in man there is first of all an inclination to good in accordance with the nature which he has in common with all substances: inasmuch as every substance seeks the preservation of its own being, according to its nature: and by reason of this inclination, whatever is a means of preserving human life, and of warding off its obstacles, belongs to the natural law. Secondly, there is in man an inclination to things that pertain to him more specifically, according to that nature which he has in common with other animals: and in virtue of this inclination, those things are said to belong to the natural law, *which nature has taught to all animals*, such as sexual intercourse, education of offspring and so forth. Thirdly, there is in man an inclination to good, according to the nature of his reason, which nature is proper to him: thus man has a natural inclination to know the truth about God, and to live in society: and in this respect, whatever pertains to this inclination belongs to the natural law; for instance, to shun ignorance, to avoid offending those among whom one has to live, and other such things regarding the above inclination.[13]

Thus, the sensitive level articulates what humans have in common with all substances—here the basic inclination is to preserve oneself in existence. In other words, human life is understood as a good because it is good to conserve oneself.[14] At the animal level, the basic inclination is the "mating of male and female," that is, procreation (marriage) and the education of children.[15] The inclinations that are typically human are appreciated by rationality. They include

---

12. John Finnis, *Aquinas: Moral, Political, and Legal Theory* (Oxford: Oxford University Press, 1998), 90.
13. Thomas Aquinas, *Summa Theologica*, I-II, q. 94, a2.
14. See *Ibid.*, II-II, q. 155 a. 2c.
15. See Idem, *Sententia* d. 26 q. 1a. 1c.

goods such as knowing the truth about God, companionship in society; acting according to reason (practical reasonableness); friendship; justice; love; and happiness (*beautitudo*) which is the fulfillment of all human goods.[16]

Martin Golding, like Finnis, assesses that the living dispositions are the basic requirements of human life in the sensitive level; at the animal level, the living dispositions are the basic requirements for the "furtherance of the human species"; at the rational level, they are the basic requirements for the "promotion of all human person's good as a rational and social being."[17] The fundamental human characteristics as indicated in the three levels, for Aquinas, are the necessary conditions for an adequate explication of the natural law theory and development studies.

Good is defined in terms of an end—the end here stands as completion of a developmental process, that is, the natural termination point. Therefore, the good or end is "built into the very process of development."[18] By conceiving the good in terms of an end, the formal cause (disposition, essence) is linked to the final cause—the end. This understanding of the metaphysics of finality unveils the crux of the natural law theory:

> The metaphysics of finality, on the other hand, argues that an end is to be attained, not because of a subjective desire or wish on the part of the agent, but because the end itself determines the well-functioning of the human person. The disposition has a part of its very nature, a tendency towards a specific end. This end, when realized, contributes to the well-being of the individual. This is the crux of natural law moral theory. Nature has 'determined,' as it were, the ends, which lead to the well-being of the individuals of the natural kind.[19]

As we have noted, the concept of an end is built into the very concept of disposition, hence Aquinas says that the good is an end. Against this backdrop, Lissaka writes: "If this end is what perfects the essence and if the perfection is what one means by 'well-being' or *eudaimonia*, then what does not lead to well-being hinders the development of the natural dispositions. The value is not derived

16.   Idem, *Summa Theologica* II-II q. 94 a. 2c. See Also John Finnis, *Aquinas: Moral, Political, and Legal Theory*, 81-82ff.

17.   See M. Golding 'Aquinas and Some Contemporary Natural Law Theories,' in *Proceedings of the American Catholic Philosophical Association* (1974), 242-243.

18.   Anthony J. Lisska, *Aquinas's Theory of Natural Law: An Analytic Reconstruction* (Oxford: Oxford University Press, 1996), 102.

19.   *Ibid.*, 107.

from the fact. The value is built into the fact as actualization is built into potency."[20] It is in this sense that reason determines the obligatory end or purpose of development. The obligatory end is part of what the development is. The obligatory end determines the nature and content of a human duty towards development. The theoretical reason determines the content of human nature; the end is what it is only because of the dispositions, and practical reason determines the obligation to undertake the actions, which lead to *eudaimonia* or human flourishing at all levels.

The theory of obligation, for Aristotle and Aquinas, depends upon human nature, whose essential property is *rationality*, and reason's function is to act rationally in both theoretical and practical spheres. To do the contrary is to act irrationally, since human ends make up the human essence. Human ends are determined by theoretical reason and pursued by practical reason. There are, in Aristotelian-Thomistic scheme, therefore, obligatory actions for human beings in their developmental process, and the society in which they live. In other words, laws, politics, economics and other programs of development cannot ignore the fact that certain obligatory actions, imposed by nature, will have to be followed to achieve the best development possible. But the mechanistic theory of reality throws overboard the purposive or teleological imprint natural law has left in the orders of existence.

The natural law theory of development insists that development is a human good, a value that is basic and forms part of the common good. One of the instruments of achieving the common good is law—a dictate of reason and a principle of human act.[21] The end of law is to realize the common good, and its effect is to make men good simply.[22] Furthermore, virtue is required on the part of all to realize the common good; hence, Aquinas writes, "the common good of the state cannot flourish, unless the citizens be virtuous, at least those whose business it is to govern."[23] It is Aquinas' belief that the precepts of the natural law are the first principles of human action (prima principia operum humanorum),[24] they determine the way development is to be conceived and nurtured; hence the specific goods in-built therein.

These goods are basic and can primarily motivate action, that is, human development in all its ramifications.

---

20. *Ibid.*, 108.
21. See Thomas Aquinas, *Summa Theologica* I-II, q. 90, a. 2
22. *Ibid.*, q. 92, a. 1.
23. *Ibid.*
24. *Ibid.*, q. 94, a1 ad 2.

The Mechanistic/Manipulative Theory of Development

The understanding of development, in mechanistic terms, is rooted in the 17th century worldview that believes that the laws of human progress are identical with the laws of physics. It contrasts with the ordered and purposive worldview of the Aristotelian-Thomistic tradition. As will be discussed in the next Chapter, the forerunners of the mechanistic reading of human affairs include Francis Bacon, Thomas Hobbes and Rene Descartes. All these derive practice from the theories of physics. No wonder Descartes says that he wants knowledge such that knowing the laws of physics; we can become lord of nature. The idea of progress of human society is that the laws of the physical sciences apply in the same way in the human sphere; thus from the domination of nature, humans can be dominated at all levels. In the mechanistic thinking, therefore, human development lies in the worldview of the experimental sciences. Using the apparatus of the physical sciences to dominate nature to our use, humans can also be subjected to the laws of progress and utility.

The problem with this development perspective is that it is mechanistic and utilitarian in its goal. Unfortunately, this is the understanding of development and treatment of humans that the 1940s till date took over. It took deep root in the 17th through the 19th and 20th centuries. It is good to know the background of the idea we are discussing, and our intellectual tools or theoretical pretensions. The element of power or manipulative knowledge in whatever form by one to dominate and manipulate the other has not left the world space of development studies. The mechanistic theory of development takes several forms in its historical processes or contacts. We shall discuss three major forms that have dominated development talks till date.

The Imperialist/Colonial Theory of Development

At the beginning of the imperial era, Europe had a superior power and knowledge of humans and nature. Colonialisation was conceived as a form of development, which interest was to meet the needs of the colonizer:

> The idea of progress with its attendant notions of perfectibility and inevitability gained pre-eminence in the period of the French and English revolutions. Armed with the confidence of having history if not nature on their side, the new economic and political revolutionaries of Britain and French set about

changing the world and the way in which it was perceived. With time, their worldview came to be intuitively self-evident and was believed to be universally valid. As such it provided a conceptual and moral basis for colonialism and imperialism.[25]

Imperialism implants itself through a medium of culture-contact or acculturation. In the process of acculturation, it is seen to be a reality that the values of the culture with stronger force dominate, even if the contact is simply a case of mutual cross-cultural pollination:

> Although, theoretically, acculturation could occur as a result of contact between two relatively simple but significantly different cultures, it soon became evident that most available examples of acculturation involved the impact of colonizing or industrializing societies upon smaller, less industrialized, or 'traditional' societies.[26]

Imperialism, as a means of acculturation, refers to a body of beliefs that presents itself as superior with the sole end of conquering and dominating other people. It later crystallized in the head of the colonizer that advanced people had the right to dominate and guide others, following the advanced person's cultural constructs. Colonialism was then development by imposition, achieved by the exercise of an alien political power over a conquered territory through all kinds of arbitrary measures designed for the economic exploitation and social degradation of the colonized people. Nicolo Machiavelli, as we shall see later, articulated the low political morality of colonialism.

The British Indirect Rule and the French's and the Portuguese's policies of assimilation were evolved to rule and exploit colonized territories for the interest of their home economies. The era of colonialism was the period of development of Europe on the shoulders of Africa and Asia, in which the colonized felt 'developed' or said to have been led to the possibility of the doors of development by simply coming into contact with Europe. In simple terms, colonialism was an idea that was not originated to develop Africa's vast potential; it was rather meant to expand Europe's grip on the colonized people.

---

25.   Vincent Tucker, 'The Myth of Development: A Critique of A Euro centric Discourse,' in *Critical Development Theory* eds., Ronaldo and Denis O'Hearn, 4.

26.   Ralph C. Beals et al, *An Introduction to Anthropology* 5d., (New York: Macmillan Publishing Co., Inc., 1977), 27.

Modernization theory of Development

Modernization is not synonymous with development, but some take it as a form of development. "Although, strictly speaking, *modernization* might properly be used to refer to any current changes in any society, it has often been used as synonymous with Westernization and Americanization. A more acceptable use of the term is in reference to current worldwide patterns in which local cultures and communities undergo rapid cultural change in response to a variety of overwhelming pressures generated by national cultures. "[27] Modernization is a metropolitan society which derives true benefits from colonization of a traditional society. It is acceptable to say that the modernization theory of development within the UN development thinking was brought to the center stage between 1940 and 1960. We have stated already that the origin of development thinking predates the period the UN or the world powers began to pay close attention to it.

At the end of World War II, the economy of the world was in bad shape. There was monetary instability and countries lacked credits and could not pay for their imports. This led to an adoption of protectionist policies by nations. Something needed to be done; hence the Bretton Woods conference held in New Hampshire:

> To this end the Bretton Woods conference gave rise to the International Monetary Fund (IMF) and the International Bank for Reconstruction and Development, which became known as the World Bank. In 1947, the Bretton Woods system, as it came to be known, was rounded out by the General Agreement on Tariffs and Trade (GATT). All were designed to create as stable and freely flowing an international trading environment as possible.[28]

The aim of the GATT, as a treaty organization, was to reduce, over time, tariffs, or taxes on imports, thereby lowering the barriers to trade among member states. The IMF, in its turn, was to provide short-term loans to governments facing balance-of-payments difficulties. Trade imbalance is the problem a government encounters when more money leaves its economy than it attracts or receives: more money leaves its economy through imports, capital flows, and

---

27. *Ibid.*
28. John Rapley, *Understanding Development: Theory and Practice in the Third* World (London: Lynne Rienner Publishers, 1996), 5.

spending abroad than enters it. In this regard, the IMF helped member states and governments in the First World come out of depression.

Later, the Third World countries were to join the IMF. They were advised to be patient, since it was envisaged that the benefits of development tracing from the First World would 'trickle down' to the Third World, while the Western countries worked out how to modernize the Third World. John Rapley points out thus:

> Modernization theory sought to identify the conditions that had given rise to development in the First World, and specify where and why these were lacking in the Third World. Modernization theorists, depending on their focus, reached varying conclusions: To some, the problem of the Third World was a mere shortage of capital; development required a rise in the savings rate. To others, it was a question of value system: Third World peoples lacked the cultural values, such as the profit motive, that would make them entrepreneurial. In this case development required Westernizing the elites, or some kind of education in capitalist values. Yet whether from a sociological, political, or economic standpoint, modernization theorists generally concurred on one important point: Underdevelopment was an initial state. The West had progressed beyond it, but other countries lagged behind. However, the West could help speed up the process of development in the Third World, for instance by sharing its capital and know-how, to bring these countries into the modern age of capitalism and liberal democracy.[29]

Thus, modernization rationalized within the 'trickle down' ideology came to be translated into massive importation of the goods and technology of the First World by Third World countries.

The goods of the First World flooded Third World markets. Both continued to buy from the same market. Capital imports from the West were paid by proceeds from agricultural products of the Third World countries. However, the more goods the Third World countries bought and paid for by their agricultural products, the more they emptied themselves and dropped lower into starvation. The more they exported, the more they drained themselves, and the more debts they incurred in the bid to keep up with Western interests.

The First World countries got richer; their citizens spent more money on finished goods, but "demand for primary goods varies less with income. No matter how rich they get, people will buy only so much coffee."[30] There was a problem

---

29. *Ibid.*, 16-17.
30. *Ibid.*, 14.

in the structure of relationship, since the "requirement of increased primary production would in turn gobble up a growing share of their nation's resources,
reducing what was left for development. There was only one way to break free of
this syndrome: alter the structure of the economy's production."[31] For wealth,
the Third World will have to rely more on industry and less on products of the
agriculture or primary sector.

The Third World countries were required to industrialize. Modernization the-
orist thought that the establishment of industries will help the Third World
countries re-appropriate their resources: for "independence will be illusory if the
colonial economic structure was not overthrown along with the colonial masters.
Looking to the First World, Third World leaders saw that industry was the key to
modernity and wealth. The ability to produce finished goods, and not rely on the
imports of the old masters, would signify the complete rupture of the ties that
had bound Third World economies so long."[32]

The slogan, 'industrialization as the way out,' echoed in the ears of many
Third World countries. But they did not have money to build industries. Claude
Ake writes:

> The first post-independence development plans in Africa—Nigeria's Develop-
> ment Plan, 1962-68; Kenya's First Development Plan, 1966-70; Tanzania's
> First Plan, 1964-69; Zambia's White Paper on Industrial Policy, 1964; Mali's
> Report sur le Plan Quinquennial de Developpement Economique et Social de
> la Republique du Mali, 1961-1965—all assumed capital, technological, mar-
> ket, and management dependence. The Nigerian plan projected 50 percent of
> capital requirements from external sources; Tanzania's plan projected 78 per-
> cent of development expenditure to be financed externally. Like most African
> countries, Tanzania carried its financial dependence into the postcolonial era.
> The apparent resignation of African countries to dependence was as much a
> reflection of objective necessities as of subjective contingencies. To begin with,
> the dependence of the economies left hardly any room for maneuver.[33]

The industrialization idea seemed as liberating as it sounded. Again, the Third
World countries have to look upon the West for guide and help in the bid to
industrialize, even with the added, although misguided, idea that industrialization or development was a burden someone was to bear for them.

---

31. *Ibid.*, 15.
32. *Ibid.*, 12.
33. Claude Ake, *Democracy and Development in Africa* (Ibadan: Spectrum Books Lim-
     ited, 1996), 66.

Thus, the industrial-modernization process under the guide of the West first sought the help of local elites, trained in western values to continue the First World agenda. The modernization process, as accentuated by the First World, did not make the process of development light and considerate for the Third World. Something was still wrong: the relationship at the level of industrialization was still unequal. Actually, instead of the situation helping matters, the structure of relationship creates all the more a culture of dependence, even when Third countries had taken directives from the First World and borrowed from international financial institutions.

The Dependency Theory

Dependency theory departs from the conviction that the interest of the bourgeoisie is at the center of capitalist society. Since the capitalist class is the dominant class in a capitalist society, inevitably the foreign policies of First World countries would primarily be concerned with the promotion and protection of capitalist interests. Capitalist interests are maintained in the Third World countries through the co-operation of their local elite:

> The capitalist states of the First World were able to thwart the development of the Third World by striking alliances with the dominant classes of the Third World, the dependent bourgeoisies. This later class was essentially a rural oligarchy, although it often had interests in the modern sector in trade and services. It benefited from its dependence by earning its revenue on the export market and spending its profit on imported luxury goods. A national industrialization strategy would threaten the well-being of the members of the dependent bourgeoisie, because it would entail heavy taxes on their income to fuel savings, and protective barriers that would block their access to cherished luxury goods. Keeping its country backward thus preserved the wealth and privilege position of a Third World ruling class.[34]

One can then understand the situation in Nigeria where efforts to change the status quo in which the local elite feasts on the shoulders of the poor are thwarted. Why cannot a nation such as Nigeria with huge deposited of natural resources feed her citizens? Why cannot the refineries be made to work? Why does the 6th greatest exporter of petroleum not provide enough fuel for her citizens? Why do Nigerian politicians and big oil merchants prefer to import oil

---

34. John Rapley, *Understanding Development: Theory and Practice in the Third* World, 18-19.

instead of repairing and maintaining the refineries in the country? It is because the local oligarchy is benefiting from the pathetic system; hence it sabotages the development of an economy that will fight its privileged interests. Thus, the present structure in the name of industrialization under the directive of the West is still: either that industries in the Third World are totally owned by the First World countries or they are staged-managed even when established in Third World territories. The Third World countries remain in a position of "classical dependence." Their industries are established with direct dependence on the First World—through their expatriates in Third World countries. In fact, industrialization in the Third World does not emerge from the Third World but from the First World:

> First World companies seeking access to protected Third World markets, or to their cheap labor, would export capital-intensive assembly plants, but none of their research and development capacity. Thus, Third World industry would be based on second-generation production technology and would be owned by foreigners who processed imported inputs and created few jobs or linkages to other producers in the economy. Capitalism would not spread far beyond these firms, and the need for imported inputs would drive up the country's bill.[35]

The dependency theory insists that the First World countries create conditions that generate incomes aimed at supporting their home economies. To counteract this state of affairs, dependency theorists argue that states of the Third World should intervene, to stop the exploitation of their resources, through welfare legislation, nationalization of private industries and immense public programs. Laws could be used to foster and protect emerging local industries and create new ones. Actually, states of the Third World have intervened to protect their markets and economies through import substitution industrialization, thereby protecting domestic markets.

However, the problem with the dependency theory is that it concentrated with fighting the traitor from without (the First World capitalist in the Third World) and forgot the traitor from within (the local elite or oligarchy):

> It was limited in that it restricted its attention almost exclusively to the economic and, to a lesser extent, the political mechanisms of domination and control. It challenged the ethnocentrism of a political economy derived exclusively from the experience of Europe and the United States and often general-

---

35. *Ibid.*, 19.

ized to the rest of the world. It provided a trenchant critique of the crusading imperialism of the modernization theorists and provided an alternative vision, which accorded more closely with the experience of the Third World countries. But dependency theory failed to address the cultural dimension of domination.[36]

Development, one believes, must seek a holistic face and take strong root from within; hence cultural and environmental factors will have to be taken seriously. Third World countries cannot deny their contact with Europe. Therefore, the non-Eurocentric perspective will have to dialogue with the Western hegemony, and negotiate as equals. Part of the aim of the present book is to present a certain development perspective and offer theoretical tools that can help broaden its understanding in the light of the African socio-cultural milieu. By creating a broader basis for the development-talk, I wish to offer a theoretical tool that will at once be cultural and trans-cultural, and help countries, especially African countries, negotiate their way in world development talks. In other to assess meaningfully contemporary discussions on development and its impacts, we must identify their intellectual roots or philosophical ancestors.

---

36. Vincent Tucker, 'The Myth of Development: A Critique of a Eurocentric Discourse,' in *Critical Development Theory* eds. Ronaldo Munck and Denis O'Hearn, 12.

3

Founding the Modern Project and the Western Logic of Development

The modern project was an intellectual and material orientation of the seventieth century designed to simply reduce nature, whether material or human, to utility. The philosophies of Galileo, Bacon, Hobbes, Descartes, Locke and Hume largely embodied the utilitarian, materialistic understanding of the world of nature. This understanding influenced the development of modern science and the subsequent power politics that dominated the age of British imperialism and colonialism.

The Platonic, Aristotelian and Thomistic traditions had posited a rational universe against which coherent principles of human and natural operations could be explained. These traditions maintain that things—physical and moral events—follow a certain law of nature; and to develop authentically both human and natural entities must conform to the law of nature.

The natural law of reason distinguishes humans from the rest of animals. However, the humans' pride of reason notwithstanding, humans stand in existential inter-dependability with other creatures and their environment. But the modern project was to sever this respected inter-dependability between humans and the world of nature, positing one as a subject who manipulates the world of nature and another as a object to be calculated, manipulated and controlled.

Galileo Galilei's Introduction of Mathematics into Physics

Galileo Galilei had insisted on knowledge of nature that was not based on guesswork. His concern for accurate measurement and experimentation intensified the role of mathematics into physics. Galileo contended that the truths of physics were not reducible to the truths of theology, so the two camps of knowledge should be kept in their right perspective. But he did not imply any severance between nature and the human spirit or their creator. All he insisted upon was that the truth of theology and science or philosophy belonged to different levels. His grounding principle was to measure and quantify. He rejected the Aristotelian presuppositions that every material body had a 'place' in the order of things and that motion was to be explained by the natural tendency of each body to seek its own place. In stead, he observed, weighed, measured and calculated in order to test his mathematical hypothesis. He was convinced that the order of mathematics revealed the structure and laws of the universe. In the *Assayer*, Galileo writes:

> Philosophy is written in this ground book, the universe, which stands continually open to our gaze. But the book cannot be understood unless one first learns to comprehend the language and read the letters in which it is composed. It is written in the language of mathematics, and its characters are triangles, circles and other geometric figures without which it is humanly impossible to understand a single word of it: without those, one wanders about in the dark labyrinth.[1]

The philosophical underpinning of Galileo's investigation was the presupposition that mathematics was the key to understanding the universe; hence his maxim, "measure what can be measured, and make measurable what can be measured."

Bacon's Transformative Knowledge through Observational Method

Francis Bacon, born in 1561, endorsed the Galilean passion for experiments. In his *Novum Organum*, he sought a new beginning for knowledge; he even gave account of methods by which knowledge might be acquired or increased, recorded and stored, and passed on. In a posthumous work, *New Atlantis*, Bacon stated a description of 'Solomon's House,' an elaborated institution of workshops, laboratories, and libraries, all dedicated to the systematic and collaborative pursuit of knowledge; for "the end of our foundation is the knowledge of causes,

---

1.   Galileo, *Assayer* (1623), 237-238.

and secret motions of things; and the enlarging of the bounds of human empire, to the effecting of all things possible."[2]

Human knowledge will be stored and processed for the benefit of humankind.[3] But the study should greatly be sought in the sciences, needing a good tool, according to Bacon. He writes, "the ignorance of the cause frustrates the effect; for nature is only subdued by submission, and that which in contemplative philosophy corresponds with the cause in practical science becomes the rule."[4]

There is still, according to Bacon, an evident lack of method in the comprehension of the sciences of his time; hence he claims, "our present sciences are nothing more than peculiar arrangements of matters already discovered, and not methods for discovery or plans for new operations."[5] It is Bacon's conviction that the present state of activities in the sciences does not offer intellectual and practical maps for new terrain because of lack of proper observation or experiment.[6] So Bacon wants a system, a method that will lead to a new and improved knowledge of nature that is at once certain and useful to humankind.

Bacon believes that one does not need religion and metaphysics to explain natural causes; hence his criticism of the Aristotelian orthodoxy of his time. He recognized the greatness of Aristotle but he thought that the Aristotelian way was unfruitful for Aristotle was "only strong for disputations and contentions, but barren of the production of works for the benefit of the life of man." Referring to the science of his time, Bacon writes:

> All which matters are unknown and unattempted by the sciences, in their present heavy and inactive state. For, since every natural act is brought about by the smallest efforts, or, at least, such as are too small to strike our senses, let no one hope that he will be able to direct or change nature unless he has properly comprehended and observed these efforts.[7]

For Bacon, the underlying structure of nature is quite simple. Nature consists of a basic set of *forms*. When we discover these forms, we are enabled to under-

---

2.   See Francis Bacon, *New Atlantis* in the *Great Books of the Western World* ed. Robert M. Hutchins (London: Encyclopaedia Britannica, Inc., 1952), vol. 30, 210.

3.   *Ibid.*, 214.

4.   Francis Bacon *Novum Organum* in the *Great Books of the Western World*, Bk. I, § 1, 107.

5.   *Ibid.*, § 8.

6.   See *Ibid.*, §§ 9-13.

7.   *Ibid.*, Bk. II, § 6, 139.

stand the multifarious complexity of the surface of the world as apprehended through the senses:

> To generate and superinduce a new nature or new natures, upon a given body, is the labor and aim of human power: whilst to discover the form or true difference of a given nature, or the nature to which such nature is owing, or source from which it emanates (for these terms approach nearest to an explanation of our meaning), is the labor and discovery of human knowledge; and subordinate to these primary labors are two others of a secondary nature and inferior stamp. Under the first must be ranked the transformation of concrete bodies from one to another, which is possible within certain limits; under the second, the discovery, in every species of generation and motion, of the latent and uninterrupted process from the manifest efficient and manifest subject matter up to the given form: and a like discovery of the latent conformation of bodies which are at rest instead of being in motion.[8]

The basic forms of nature help us to create and superimpose new nature. And this creation resides in the human power.

The Baconian forms are the forms of "simple natures." Simple natures may be shared by substances and are such things as hot, wet, cold, heavy and so on. They are like "an alphabet of nature" from which many things can be composed. Bacon refers to the forms as 'laws.' They are the determinants and elements of the fundamental structures of the world: "The form of a nature is such, that given the form the nature infallibly follows. Therefore it is always present when the nature is present...absent when the nature is absent." Bacon declares:

> For although nothing exists in nature except individual bodies, exhibiting clear individual effects according to particular laws, yet in each branch of learning, that very law, its investigation, discovery, and development, are the foundation both of theory and practice. This law, therefore, and its parallel in each science, is what we understand by the term form, adopting that word because it has grown into common use, and is of familiar occurrence.[9]

Bacon believes that he who has learnt the cause of something has only acquired an imperfect knowledge of the things. Knowledge of efficient and material causes can lead to new discovery in matters of similar nature, and prepared for the purpose. This knowledge is still deficient because it "does not stir the limits of things which are much more deeply rooted." The knowledge of the forms

---

8.   *Ibid.*, § 1, 137.
9.   *Ibid.*, § 2.

equips one with the comprehension of the unity of substances, generating new natures that will result in genuine knowledge and free practice.[10]

Man is no longer simply part of nature, but knowledge of man and the universe is power. The claim that knowledge is power, by Bacon, underlines the practical value of knowledge. Man is seriously intervening in nature and beginning to control it. Scientific knowledge of nature, initiated in the Renaissance, was good; but it had its side effects:

> The technical revolution that began in the Renaissance led to the spinning jenny and to unemployment, to medicines and new diseases, to the improved efficiency of agriculture and the impoverishment of the environment, to practical appliances such as the washing machine and the refrigerator and pollution and industrial waste. The serious threat to the environment we are facing today has made people see the technical revolution itself as a perilous maladjustment to natural conditions. It has been pointed out that we have started something we can longer control. More optimistic spirits think we are still living in the cradle of technology, and that although the scientific era has certainly had its teething troubles, we will gradually learn to control nature without at the same time threatening its very existence and thus our own.[11]

The desire to control nature continues. It appears rather that the more the human subject attempts to control nature recklessly, the more he turns out in the process as a piece of quantifiable matter in the universe.

Descartes' desire to become Lord of Nature

Rene Descartes came to the scene advocating the abandonment of traditional opinions and criterion for truth; he made himself—the inner ego—alienated from others—the only enduring first principle of philosophy; hence his *cogito ergo sum*: I think, therefore, I am.[12] The Cartesian philosophy separates the soul from the body, and claimed that both could exist independently, with the soul as the only clear and distinct idea. He proves the existence of body as an extended entity, which is to be dominated and appreciated in relation to its usefulness to

---

10. *See Ibid.*, § 3.
11. Jostein Gaarder, *Sophies World: A Novel about the History of Philosophy*, trans. Paulette Moller (London: Phoenix House, 1995), 169-170.
12. See René Descartes, *Discourse on Method and the Meditations* trans. John Veitch (New York: Prometheus Books, 1989), Part IV—'Discourse on the Method of Rightly Conducting the Reason, and Seeking Truth in the Sciences,' 30.

the *ego*. The existence of the soul and body is hooked to some kind of makeshift theological foundation, (which body and soul could do without), a benevolent God, whom Descartes says could not be a deceiver. Even if God becomes a deceiver, his first principle of philosophy stands. Descartes brings in the idea of God as the guarantor of certainty; that is, all clear and distinct ideas such as those of the soul and mathematics proceed from the perfect Being who exists and does not deceive.[13] But God's works, in the Cartesian worldview, do not necessarily need him for their continued existence; and God has no particular purpose attached to their existence. Since there is no teleology in nature, any discernible purpose should be man made. This could be achieved if we possess knowledge that will make us lords of nature. Descartes writes:

> I have never made much account of what has proceeded from my own mind; and so long as I gathered no other advantage from the method I employ beyond satisfying myself on some difficulties belonging to the speculative sciences or endeavoring to regulate my actions according to the principles it taught me, I never thought myself bound to publish anything respecting it.... But as soon as I had acquired some general notions respecting physics, and beginning to make trial of them in various particular difficulties, had observed how far they can carry us, and how they differ from the principles that have been employed up to the present time, I believed that I could not keep them concealed without sinning grievously against the law by which we are bound to promote, as far as in us lies, the general good of mankind. For by them, I perceived it to be possible to arrive at knowledge highly useful in life; and in room of the speculative philosophy usually taught in the schools, *to discover a practice, by means of which, knowing the force and action of fire, water, air, the stars, the heavens, and all the other bodies that surround us, as distinctly as we know the various crafts of our artisans, we might also apply them in the same way to the uses to which they are adapted, and thus render ourselves the lords and possessors of nature.*[14]

Descartes claims to have found a principle, derived from the principles of physics that will help us assess both the speculative sciences and morals or manners. At the end of part six of the *Discourse on Method,* Descartes summarizes his philosophy for the new science, and the development of the modern world:

> In conclusion, I am unwilling here to say anything very specific of the progress which I expect to make for the future in the sciences, or to bind myself to the

---

13. *Ibid.,* 34.
14. *Ibid.,* 47-48. (Italics mine).

public by any promise which I am not certain of being able to fulfill; but this only will I say, that I have resolved to devote what time I may still have to live to no other occupation than that of endeavoring to acquire some knowledge of Nature, which shall be of such a kind as to enable us therefrom to deduce rules in medicine of greater certainty than those at present in use; and that my inclination is so much opposed to all other pursuits, especially to such as cannot be useful to some without being hurtful to others, that if, by any circumstances, I had been constrained to engage in such, I do not believe that I should have been able to succeed.[15]

The Cartesian intuition presents the vision that the principles of physics hold the key to the modern world and the enjoyment of mankind. Thus, the technology envisaged by the modern project, in Cartesian terms, is founded on utility. The dualistic vision presented by Descartes had its sympathizers in opposite direction. Many moderns were quick to reduce all their inquiries to the realm of matter, given the possibility that God could not have created the world with any specific purpose. Thomas Hobbes took over the mechanistic implications of the new science and reduced everything to matter in motion.

Hobbes' View that we are Matter in Motion

Thomas Hobbes thinks that Galileo had grown something worthwhile from the seeds of natural reason. In his attempts to understand the paths taken by projectiles and falling bodies, Galileo had "opened to us the gate of natural philosophy, which is the knowledge of the nature of motion."

Hobbes' *Leviathan* is a classic account of man's move from a primitive state of nature, in which life is "solitary, poor, nasty, brutish, and short," into an organized society, with absolute power vested in the hands of the supreme authority.

Hobbes sees reason as a power of abstraction and the conceiving of consequences regarding things, numbers and relationships. He writes:

> Writers of politiques, adde together *pactions*, to find mens *duties*; and lawyers, *lawes*, and *facts*, to find what is *right* and wrong in the actions of private men. In summe, in what matter soever there is a place for *addition* and *subtraction*, there also is place for reason; and where these have no place, there *reason* has nothing at all to do.[16]

---

15. *Ibid.*, 57.

Hobbes defines reason as nothing but reckoning of the consequences of general names agreed upon, for the marking and signifying of our thoughts. Thus, in the power of reason is the capacity for adding and subtracting when we reckon. Hobbes believes however that while humans are capable of reason, right reason is denied them by nature; therefore, men should set right reason in their interactions "for want of a right reason constituted by nature."[17] Implicitly, reasons are passions of men agreed upon, he claims. There is no one mode of dealing with things set by nature; hence Hobbes denies that there is right reason or ordered end embedded in nature.[18] The order or purpose has to be imposed by humans given what use they want to put themselves and nature to.

For Hobbes, a clear beginning is necessary for knowledge. Commenting on Hobbes, Diané Collinson writes: "Hobbes saw that any enquiry that was to command respect must be conducted in such a way that its conclusions could be unequivocally recognized as knowledge: speculation, opinion and pronouncement would not do. And since the deductive reasoning of the kind used in geometry and Galilean physics produced conclusions that were logically incontrovertible, he resolved to reason deductively to arrive at a like knowledge concerning the organization of political society."[19]

Hobbes follows the geometrical method of Galileo. Geometrical reasoning proceeds from a 'given':—that is, it has basic premises or set of premises. From the basic premises it moves step by step to conclusions, which cannot be otherwise. Galileo used this method; for example, given the data about weights, distances and angles, he was able to deduce and so predict the movement of material bodies. In his *Autobiography*, Hobbes writes: "One thing only is real, but it forms the basis of things we falsely claim to be something, though they are only like the fugitive shapes of dreams or like the images I can multiply at will by mirrors; fantasies, creatures of our brains and nothing more, the only inner reality of which is motion."[20]

---

16. Thomas Hobbes, *Leviathan* ed. C. B. Macpherson (London: Penguin Books, 1968), Part II, Ch. 5, 110-111. (All spellings and punctuation are left as in the original text)..

17. *Ibid.*

18. *Ibid.*, 112.

19. Diané Collinson, *Fifty Major Philosophers: A Reference Guide* (Routledge: New York, 1987), 52.

20. Thomas Hobbes, *Autobiography* (The Rota, Exeter, Devon, 1979); See also Diané Collinson, *Ibid.*, 52.

One recalls that Bacon, against the background of an Ockhamite distinction between faith (or inspired divinity) and philosophical knowledge, divided philosophy into: natural divinity, knowledge of man, and natural philosophy (or knowledge of nature). Hobbes shares the Baconian distinction.

Hobbes distinguishes between *faith* and *knowledge proper*. Knowledge is in the horizon of philosophy. According to him, philosophy is divided into: i) natural philosophy (or physics), and ii) civil philosophy (that which is concerned with man). Civil philosophy is in turn divided into: a) ethics, and b) political philosophy. For Hobbes, politics is dependent on ethics, and ethics on natural philosophy or physics, and all of them come under his definition of philosophy. In Hobbes' judgment, both natural philosophy and civil philosophy as "such knowledge of effects or appearances, as we acquire by true ratiocination from the knowledge we have first of their causes and generations. And again, of such causes or generations as may be from knowing first their effects."

Thoughts of man, Hobbes argues, are considered as representations, that is, representations of some quality or other accident of the body, called object. The object could be of the eyes, ears, etcetera of any of the senses, "for there is no conception in a man's mind which hath not at first, totally, or by parts, been begotten upon the organs of sense."[21] External bodies or objects stimulate or cause our senses. The object presses an organ proper to each sense and through the mediation of nerves and membranes of the body continues inward to the brain, and heart. And the effect is fancy which men call sense:—eyes see light, ears hear sound, and so on:

> All which qualities called sensible, are in the object that causeth them, but so many several motions of the matter, by which it presseth our organs diversely. Neither in us that are pressed, are they anything else, but diverse emotions; (for motion produceth nothing but motion.) But their appearance to us is fancy, the same waking, that dream. And as pressing, rubbing, or striking the eye, makes us fancy a light; and pressing the eare, produceth a dinne; so do the bodies also we see, or hear, produce the same by their strong, though unobserved action.[22]

In short, an object causes an image or fancy; fancy is caused by pressure or motion of external things upon the eyes, ears and other organs.

---

21.   Thomas Hobbes, *Leviathan*, Pt. 1, Ch. 1, 85.
22.   *Ibid.*, Pt. 1, Ch. 2, 86.

Hobbes is most famous for his political ideas. His political ideas are however founded on his physics or natural philosophy. Hobbes states that causation is a matter of motion and philosophy is knowledge of effects acquired from knowledge of generative causes, or knowledge of causes acquired from knowledge of generative effects.[23] Convinced that everything is matter in motion, Hobbes argues that human beings are sensory creatures. Sensory creatures have sensory experience. According to him, "so many several motions of matter" cause sensory experience. Our thoughts or what Hobbes calls "conceptions of the mind" are also motions of matter. Thoughts or conceptions of the mind are products of organs of senses. In fact, Hobbes' intention, in the first five chapters of the *Leviathan*, is to show that human beings are part of motion. Having made this claim, he proceeds further yet.

In Chapter Six of the *Leviathan*, Hobbes moves on to give a description of human nature. The 'given' he finds in human nature is that human beings have "voluntary motions" or passions. Hobbes distinguishes between "voluntary motions" and "vital motions." Vital motions are products of such organs as the heart and lungs. They are motions, which are generated to maintain life, as it were on their own accord. Voluntary motions or passions are instigated or initiated by *endeavors*. Endeavors, according to Hobbes, are small movements of the brain. An endeavor, as a movement toward something, is an appetite or desire; it is an aversion when it is a refraining from something.[24] Desires and aversions translate into love and hate:

> That which men desire, they are also sayd to love: and to hate those things, for which they have aversion. So that desire, and love, are the same thing; save that by desire, we always signifie the absence of the object; by love, most commonly the presence of the same. So also by aversion, we signifie the absence; and by hate, the presence of the object.[25]

With his general reduction of everything to matter in motion, Hobbes will deduce the circumstances required for peaceful co-existence.

Hobbes' *Leviathan* has continued to be criticized for it regards human beings as bits of matter in motion; it offers a grim picture of human nature and of life in the natural condition. The modern project in Hobbes was to reduce everything to matter and quantifiable effects.

---

23. See R. S. Woolhouse, *The Empiricists* (Oxford: Oxford University Press, 1995), 32.
24. See Thomas Hobbes, *Leviathan*, Part 1, Ch. 6, 119.
25. *Ibid.*

Locke's Optimism that we have enough for our Uses

Locke believes that the search for truth should be limited to experience, aware of what human faculty is capable of. The sixteenth century saw the rediscovery of the ancient Greek skepticism. This attitude continued in the seventienth century. Against this background, Locke notices a kind of intellectual pessimism, a "despair of knowledge of anything," into which it is possible to fall after repeated failures in the search for knowledge. He argues that "men, extending their enquiries beyond their capacities, and letting their thoughts wander into those depths, where they can find no sure footing; 'tis no wonder, that they raise questions, and multiply disputes, which never coming to any clear resolution, are proper only to continue and increase their doubts, and to confirm them at last in perfect skepticism."[26] It is Locke's belief that the understanding is the most elevated faculty of the soul. The search for knowledge by the understanding is a fun. In the Epistle to the Reader, in the *Essay*, he writes that the quests for truth by the understanding "are a sort of hawking and hunting, wherein the very pursuit makes a great part of the pleasure. Every step the mind takes in its progress towards knowledge, makes some discovery, which is not only new, but the best too, for the time at least."[27]

In the face of doubts concerning knowledge, Locke does not despair. He follows Bacon and Hobbes whose forthright reactions are that what is really needed is simply the adoption of a correct method, paying attention to what the human faculty is capable of.[28] Locke insists that "when we know our *strength*, we shall the better know what to undertake with hopes of success: And when we have well surveyed the powers of our own minds, and made some estimate what we may expect from them, we shall not be inclined either to sit still, and not set our thoughts on work at all, in despair of knowing anything; nor on the other side question every thing, and disclaim all knowledge, because some things are not to be understood."[29]

Locke recognizes the limits of our intellectual activities, and again that truth can often outrun our ability to know it; but he does not accept that anything cannot be known. Thus, in the face of limits of knowledge, he does not advocate a

---

26. John Locke, *An Essay Concerning Human Understanding* ed. Peter H. Nidditch (Oxford: Oxford University Press, 1975), § 7, 47. (All punctuation and spellings are left as in the original text Henceforth to be cited as *Essay*).
27. *Ibid.*, 6.
28. *Ibid.*, Bk. I, Ch. 1, § 7, 46-47.
29. *Ibid.*, § 6, 46.

despairing skepticism. He concludes that, although there are indeed some things we cannot and would be immodest to hope to know, there are those that we can know. In Book II of the *Essay*, Locke declares:

> The infinite wise Contriver of us, and all things about us, hath fitted our senses, faculties, and organs, to the conveniences of life, and the business we have to do here. We are able, by our senses, to know, and distinguish things; and to examine them so far, as to apply them to our uses, and several ways to accommodate the exigencies of this life. We have insight enough into their admirable contrivances, and wonderful effects, to admire, and magnify the wisdom, power, and goodness of their Author. Such a knowledge as this, which is suited to our present condition, we want no faculties to attain. But it appears not, that God intended, we should have a perfect, clear, and adequate knowledge of them: that perhaps is not in the comprehension of any finite being. We are furnished with faculties (dull and weak they are) to discover enough in the creatures, to lead us to the knowledge of the Creator, and the knowledge of our duty; and we are fitted well enough with abilities, to provide for the conveniences of living: these are our business in this world.[30]

Therefore, although our capacities are limited, we are endowed with enough of them for our use: to live and do our duties to our Creator and to one another. Locke argues that perfect knowledge is not attainable by creatures of our kind. However, sufficient knowledge is available and attainable for the kind of life and work the Creator wants of us.

Locke holds that the objects of our thinking, accessible to the human mind, are Ideas. The sources of our ideas are sensation and reflection.[31] Whereas external, material things are the objects of sensation, the operations of our minds within are the objects of reflection; our ideas take their origin from sensation and reflection.[32]

Hume's loss of faith in Science and Nature

Since, according to Locke, what we have perceptions of are ideas and not the real object, David Hume concludes that the mind is only aware of its own ideas. Ideas are only copies of impressions, which mediate between the mind and the thing. And between objects and themselves there is nothing. Hume writes:

---

30.   *Ibid.*, Bk. II, Ch. 23, § 12, 302.
31.   See *Ibid.*, Bk. II, Ch. 1, §§. 1-3, 104-105.
32.   *Ibid.*, § 4, 105.

The authority of the will over its own faculties and ideas is not a whit more comprehensible: So that, upon the whole, there appears not, throughout all nature, any one instance of connexion, which is conceivable by us. All events seem entirely loose and separate. One event follows another; but we never can observe any tie between them. They seem *conjoined*, but never *connected*. And as we can have no idea of any thing which never appeared to our outward sense or inward sentiment, the necessary conclusion *seems* to be that we have no idea of connexion or power at all, and that these words are absolutely without any meaning, when employed either in philosophical reasonings or common life.[33]

Given these intuitions, Hume lands into skepticism, claiming that the so-called object of science is an illusion. We cannot know objects of the natural world. We only know impressions in our first contact with objects, which later leave faint copies[34] in the mind called, ideas.[35] And when the mind enters into itself, it stumbles on a variety of impressions replacing one another in a perpetual flux as bundles of impressions. Thus, we are made of webs of impression without any purpose in view.

Hume divides knowledge into ideas of relation and matters of facts. For him, knowledge really holds with regard to ideas of relation, which are ideas in the mind. All other alleged knowledge, such as matters of fact and existence, according to him, are but opinion or belief. Beyond the relation of ideas, the mind cannot legitimately go, otherwise the mind lands "by non-intellectual agency, viz. sympathy in the moral field, and belief, correspondingly conceived, in the cognitive field—agencies in regard to whose concluding causes, other than those of association, we are not in a position to speculate, much less to make scientific pronouncements."[36] In other words, Hume thinks that Locke's theory of idea supplies no sufficient ground for belief, and in the *Treatise* he accuses Locke of perverting the original meaning of the word *idea*; hence he sees part of his task as restoring the original meaning of the word 'idea.' Locke's inner sense or idea of reflection, therefore, has an opposite character in Hume. His ideas of reflection,

33. David Hume, *Enquiries Concerning Human Understanding and Concerning the Principles of Morals*, 3d., P. H. Nidditch (Oxford: Oxford University Press, 1975), sec. vii, pt. II, § 58, 74. Henceforth to be cited as *Enquiries*.

34. John Locke, *An Essay Concerning Human Understanding*, ed. Peter H. Nidditch, Bk. 2, Ch. 1, §§. 1-3, 104-105..

35. David Hume, *A Treatise of Human Nature* ed., P. H. Ndditch (Oxford: Clarendon Press, 1978). Bk. 1, pt. 1, sec. 1, 1. Henceforth to be cited as *Treatise*.

36. Kemp N. Smith, *The Philosophy of David Hume A Critical Study of its Origins and Central Doctrines* (London: MacMilliam & Co., Ltd., 1949), 63.

for Hume, are not ideas, thus they have no correspondent impressions. It is Hume's conviction that perceptions that are not obtained from sensation are traced to passions or feelings. Hume will carry this conclusion to his moral doctrine where moral distinctions are not based on reason but on feeling or sentiment. Thus, human adventure in science and morals is founded on feeling or sentiment, according to Hume.

The Morality of the Modern Scientific Project

The morality of the modern project has two arms, namely the Machiavellian principle and the principle of utility (hedonism and pleasure).

The running of the *polis*, according to Niccolo Machiavelli, is all about domination over men. He writes:

> All states and governments that have had, and have at present, dominion over men, have been and are either republics or principalities.... States thus acquired have been accustomed either to live under a prince, or to exist as free states; and they are acquired either by the arms of others, or by the conqueror's own, or by fortune or personal courage and talents.[37]

Machiavelli suggests to the Prince to go and conquer and acquire states; and to have a strong hold, for "one of the best and most efficient means is for the prince who has acquired them to go and reside there, which will make his possession more secure and durable."[38] He suggests the establishment of colonies, and the necessity of keeping large force of men-at-arms and infantry for the protection of the colony acquired by the prince. Any revolt from the colonies must be crushed, "and here we observe that men must either be cajoled or crushed; for they will revenge themselves for slight wrongs, while for grave ones they cannot. The injury therefore that you do to a man should be such that you need not fear his revenge."[39] The point is that Machiavelli is laying down ways for his contemporaries and those after him to annex and maintain, by the use of force and brutal practice, territories and peoples. Thus, he sees the desire for conquest as a natural one. While Bacon, Descartes and Hobbes were laying the foundation for the control of the natural world, Machiavelli draws the political curriculum for the mas-

---

37. Niccolo Machiavelli, *The Prince* trans. Christian E. Detmold (New York: Airmont Publishing Company, 1965), 13.
38. *Ibid.*, 17.
39. *Ibid.*, 18.

tery of peoples and territories of nature. Now everything that contributes to the designs of the prince or ruler is allowed. What matters is the design the prince wants to accomplish, which is good when successful. Machiavelli believes that to a large extent we can control fortune; thus, no pre-determined teleology is imprinted in the nature of things or states. The prince is simply concerned with what brings him praise or blame.

Machiavelli does not think that there is need for an ideal goodness to win the prince to the people; the reality, for him, is that "the manner in which men live is so different from the way in which they ought to live, that he who leaves the common course for that which he ought to follow will find that it leads him to ruin rather than to safety."[40] Thus, if a prince desires to maintain himself or hold strong to his conquest, he "must learn to be not always good, but to be so or not as necessity may require.... I say that all men when they are spoken of, and more especially princes, from being in a more conspicuous position, are noted for some quality that brings them either praise or censure."[41] Machiavelli thus recognizes that qualities such as liberality, generosity, mercy, faithfulness and sincerity are good qualities; they are contrasted with miserliness, cruelty, cunning, haughtiness and so many others; but he insists:

> I am well aware that it would be most praiseworthy for a prince to possess all of the above-mentioned qualities that are esteemed good; but as he cannot have them all, nor entirely observe them, because of his human nature which does not permit it, he should at least be prudent enough to know how to avoid the infamy of those vices that would rob him of his state; and if possible also to guard against such as are likely to endanger it. But if that be not possible, then he may with less hesitation follow his natural inclinations. Nor need he care about incurring censure for such vices, without which the preservation of his state may be difficult; For, all things considered, it will be found that some things that seem like virtue will lead you to ruin if you follow them; while others, that apparently are vices, will, if followed, result in your safety and well-being.[42]

In the Machiavellian picture, politics or state is about power to control; in this picture, human affairs have lost the ordered vision of the ancients and the Thomistic tradition's claim that things and state have their perfection that is part of their natural process. Thus humans and their organization come to be seen as

---

40. *Ibid.*, 76.
41. *Ibid.*, 76.
42. *Ibid.*, 77.

manipulable objects of nature or fortune tamable to one's needs or desires. Machiavelli summaries his modern project of might is right, and that nature is in our hands to be structured at will:

> I conclude, then, inasmuch as Fortune is changeable, that men who persist obstinately in their own ways will be successful only so long as those ways coincide with those of Fortune; and whenever these differ, they fall. But, on the whole, I judge impetuosity to be better than caution; for Fortune is a woman, and if you wish to master her, you must strike and beat her, and you will see that she allows herself to be more easily vanquished by the rash and the violent than by those who proceed more slowly and coldly. And therefore, as a woman, she ever favors youth more than age, for youth is less cautious and more energetic, and commands Fortune with greater audacity.[43]

With the confidence generated in the physical sciences rooted in the Baconian-Cartesian world views, ornamented by the proclamation by Machiavelli that force and vices are of greater advantage to maintain the control of nature and empire, the seeds of power politics and domination come to occupy the core of modern understanding of development in socio-economic spheres. No wonder in the introduction to the *Prince*, John J. Tobin comments:

> A scientific treatise with a hortatory conclusion, a work of detachment in its analysis of means, of passionate involvement as to its end, *The Prince*, apart from the ending, is written in a direct, unadorned, indeed apothegmatic style. The pithy judgments about fortune, initial impressions, virtue and vice, the aphorisms about war and cunning pleased an age which delighted in similar examples of compact wisdom from Erasmus through Bacon.

Machiavelli has painted the picture of the monopoly of things by the State: everything depends on the brute force of the State. In a way, the development of science furthered the economic and social interests of the bourgeoisie and the State. It is the accumulation of more wealth. This, in Britain, for example, led to the removal of the peasants from the means of subsistence. Man's labor came simply to be appropriated for the market rather than for immediate consumption. No wonder Hobbes could write "the value or worth of a man, is as of all other things, his price—that is to say, so much as would be given for the use of his power." Or Locke: "the universal consent of mankind gave to silver, on account of its qualities which made it suitable for money, an imaginary value." In

---

43. *Ibid.*, 122.

fact, the bourgeoisie of the time of Bacon, Hobbes and Locke were not involved or interested in revolutionizing technology; "they simply separated the workpeople from the means of subsistence so that their labor could be prolonged and the product placed on the market to render a profit. Nature and the workers who labored upon nature simply produced profit by the very act of conversion of their labor into value. 'Nature,' that is, the laboring people, gives up its value like water into a sponge. This view of value corresponded to the view of knowledge accumulated by simple receipt of sensations from Nature."

As we shall see later, development is to be sought at the pleasure and utility of the dominant powers. Machiavelli has already shown that there is nothing wrong to base politics, conquest and development on a low standard of morality, which he thinks the nature of humans permit. He claims to have painted, for the modern, the pictures of man, state and politics as they are.

According to Hobbes, human nature is locked in a constant war, a war of one against the other, and men as a whole are fundamentally selfish:

> That which men desire, they are also said to love: and to hate those things, for which they have aversion. So that desire, and love, are the same thing; save that by desire, we always signify the absence of the object; by love, most commonly the presence of the same. So also by aversion, we signify the absence; and by hate, the presence of the object.[44]

Moral judgment, Hobbes holds, is based on a person's feeling; hence, he arrives at this conclusion:

> But whatever is the object of any man's appetite or desire; that is it, which he for his part calleth good: And the object of his hate, and aversion, evill; And of his contempt, vile, and *Inconsiderable*. For these words of good, evill, and contemptible, are ever used with relation to the person that useth them: There being nothing simply and absolutely so; nor any common rule of good and evill, to be taken from the nature of the objects themselves; but from the person of the man...[45]

We have an aversion for those things that cause us pain, and derive pleasure from those things we love. Everyone acts to dominant everyone else. And the end of morality is to avoid pain and procure pleasure. That which procures pleasure, in this thinking, is necessarily right; and that which procures pain is necessarily

---

44.   Thomas Hobbes, *Leviathan*, Pt. 1, Ch.. 4, § 24, 119.
45.   *Ibid.*, 120.

evil. Thus, right and wrong are no longer categories inherent in the nature of things, but people's judgments of feelings in the light of utility to which they want to put nature and humans.

Locke, as we know, limits our source of knowledge to experience, within which he finds a place for God. Idea of relation furnishes us with the idea of God. But this idea is simply rationalistic and can easily open the way for a materialistic reduction. Locke has hit on the idea of God within experience. God has adapted our senses to their uses and mission. The importance of the senses in relation to us is their utility founded on the simple ideas of pleasure and pain. In any case, Locke corroborates the law morality of the modern scientific project. This is evident from the following lines:

> Things then are good or evil, only in reference to pleasure or pain. That we call *good*, which *is apt to cause or increase pleasure, or diminish pain in us; or else to procure, or preserve us the possession of any other good, or absence of any evil. And on the contrary we name that eveil, which is apt to produce or increase any pain, or diminish any pleasure in us; or else to procure us any evil, or deprive us of any good.* By pleasure and pain, I must be understood to mean of body or mind, as they are commonly distinguished; though in truth, they be only different constitutions of the mind, sometimes occasioned by disorder in the body, sometimes by thought of the mind.[46]

In Locke, the second division of human understanding is that which man himself ought to do, as a rational and voluntary agent, for the attainment of an end, especially happiness. This happiness, for Locke, is pleasure derived from utility embedded in experience. Thus ethics "is the seeking out those rules, and measures of human action, which lead to happiness, ands means to practice them. The end of this is not bare speculation, and the knowledge of truth; but right and conduct suitable to it."[47]

Locke reduces moral good or moral evil to conformity or disagreement of our voluntary action to some law, "whereby good or evil is drawn on us, from the will and power of the law-maker; which good and evil, pleasure or pain, attending our observance, or breach of the law, by the decree of the law-maker, is that we call reward or punishment."[48] Laws and morals are the same for Locke. They judge of the rectitude or privity of actions.

---

46.   John Locke, *Essay*, Book II, Ch. XX, § 2, 229.
47.   *Ibid.*, bk. 4, Ch.. 11, § 3, 720.
48.   *Ibid.*, § 5, 351.

In the line of Hobbes also, Hume does not find such words as hate, love, good, evil, virtue or vice, in the analysis of an object. He argues that they have reference only to the person using them, thereby arguing against a common rational rule in moral matters.

Reason, according to Hume, is not a species that causes or motivates action.[49] It can never prevent volition, and "is and only ought to be the slave of passions."[50] He insists, "morals excite passions, and produce or prevent actions. Reason of itself is utterly impotent in this particular. The rules of morality, therefore, are not conclusions of our reason."[51] Reason is "perfectly inert," according to him, and can never be the source of so active a principle as conscience or a sense of morals actions be true nor false, contrary or conformable to reason.[52] Virtue and vice are neither in the relations nor in matters of fact. They are not the objects of reason but of feeling or passion.[53] Thus, what serves a person's end or use is called virtue, and that which serves the contrary is vice. Moral good or moral evil belongs to the actions of the mind. It is derived from our situation with external objects; it lies between internal actions and external objects.

Hume is convinced that morality is determined by sentiments. He argues we regard what we approve of as virtuous; hence he defines virtue as *"whatever mental action or quality gives to a spectator the pleasing sentiment of approbation*; and vice the contrary."[54] Good and bad, justice and injustice, virtue and vice are not inherent qualities in the development and dispositional processes of natural kinds, "but perceptions in the mind." [55] When people make judgments like: honesty is a virtue, a good quality; dishonesty is bad; kindness is good; cruelty is bad, etc., they are drawing out words from a kind of social 'catalogue.' This catalogue expresses the content of our feelings, and from this content or general scheme emerges epithets with which we label actions. Thus, catalogues of virtues and vices are products of social conventions with reference to the utility of those who have set such catalogues.

In the 19th century England, Bentham gave a masterly exposition of the principle of utility in the social, legal and economic arena. He maintains that, although law differs from society to society, what it ought to be is in principle

---

49. See *Ibid.*, Bk. 2, Pt. 3, sec. iii, 413.
50. See *Ibid.*, 415.
51. *Ibid.*, Bk. 3, Pt. 1, sec., i, 457.
52. *Ibid.*, Bk. 3, Pt. 1, sec. i, 457, 458.
53. See *Ibid.*, 463-439.
54. D. Hume, *Enquiries*, §. 239.
55. D. Hume, *Treatise*, Bk. 3, Pt. 1, sec. i, 468-469.

everywhere the same, namely, legislation, which passes the utilitarian test. Three aspects of this advocacy can be distinguished. First, since men only desire happiness, they must approve a principle, which affirms that they ought to have what they want. Secondly, if one accepts the principle of utility, then all disputes about right and wrong will be reduced to disagreements about future matters of fact, and hence morals and legislation become scientific. Thirdly, since men are only motivated by pain and pleasure, properly drafted legislation can produce a coincidence between the interests of the individual and the interests of the community.[56] Bentham endorses the principle of utility as the moral principle that jurisprudence should adopt. He commends the principle of utility as a moral principle, which he thinks, any reader will find preferable to any other, given the truth of his assertions of human nature. Given appropriate rewards and punishments laid down by law, we can achieve a fortunate state of affairs in which a man will draw the same conclusions about the rightness of any proposed action of his, whether he calculates the effect only upon his own happiness or upon that of the community.

In his *An Introduction to the Principles of Morals and Legislation*, Bentham writes: "By the principle of utility is meant that principle which approves or disapproves of every action whatsoever, according to the tendency which it appears to have to augment or diminish the happiness of the party whose interest is in question: or, what is the same thing in other words, to promote or oppose that happiness."[57] The happiness of an individual will be augmented if there is an addition to the sum total of his pleasures, which is greater than any addition to the sum total of his pains. The interest of the community is composed in like manner.

The point that is put forward in this part of the essay is that the development inspired by the moderns' (Renaissance and the Baroque) spirit was conceived in terms of domination of nature and humans as measurable and quantifiable materials entities. This way of understanding humans and nature has not ceased since then.

The modern notion of development and technology began with low morality. It is our conviction that human progress is not to be judged solely in terms of tapping the energies in nature, but progress should be seen as "the ascent of conscience and where the ascent of conscience is linked to a superior level of

---

56. See *Ibid.*, 96, 104.
57. Jeremy Bentham, *Principles of Morals and Legislation* (New York: Prometheus Books, 1988), Ch. 1, § 2, 2.

organization."[58] A coercive unification that is not intended to impact on the progress of moral conscience through the development of relationships of justice, love and friendship is a pseudo-unity or agenda; hence J. Maritain declares:

> Science bears witness to the fact that 'coercive unification only gives rise to a surface pseudo-unity. It can assemble a piece of machinery, but it cannot bring about any basic synthesis; and, as a result, it does not engender any growth of conscience. It materializes, in fact, instead of spiritualizing.' Coercion will always have its part to play in human societies; but it is not therein that we must seek the law of progress. Unification by internal forces alone 'is biological.' 'It alone produces that wonder, the bringing of increased personality out of the forces of collectivity. It alone represents the true extension of the Psycho-genesis' at the close of which Man appeared, and which continues under new forms in the collective evolution of mankind. Finally, it is 'in the common attraction' exerted by a transcendent center, which is Spirit and Person, and in which men can truly love one another, that the development of humanity, thus animated and uplifted within the very order or temporal history, finds its supreme law.[59]

In moving humanity forward, then, attention must be paid by the many scientific endeavors to the world of values. Any attempt that simply materializes humans without considering their spiritual destiny will only end up in making humans monsters and agents of their own destruction. The journey of science alone loses the grip on true human progress.

---

58. Jacques Maritain, *The Rights of Man and Natural Law* (London: Geoffery Bles 1958), 20.
59. *Ibid.*, 21.

4

European Economic Concerns

Development and the Imperialist Politics of Power

However historians might judge European activities, especially British activities in Africa, one point is very clear that the imperialist era was a period of power politics masked as a project of development. Philip Darby argues, "it may be that the question of how far Britain's concerns were political rather than economic or moral/ideological admits no general answer, because different sectors within the society were influenced by different considerations and to some degree operated on different fronts."[1] But he acknowledges that the role of power offers the foundation for interpreting the politics of that imperialist era, as may be the case today. The fundamentals of power politics may have changed greatly in the last hundred years or so; "the interest of British policy-makers in power and strategy outside Europe was necessarily related to the perceived intentions and policies of the European powers."[2] The dominance of power may not have been fundamentally conceived at the earliest stages; however, "from the 1880s the play of power politics in Africa and Asia was at least in part a consequence of the diplomatic maneuvering in Europe."[3] In the quest for power translated into economic and social prestige, European powers were giving Africa over to themselves on a chessboard.

The pursuit of power among the powers does not need to be characterized by lack of complete order or accepted patterns of behavior, conventions, rules and international accords among the states. It was, first, against the need for an accepted pattern of behavior among them that the powers began to make room for 'moral considerations' in international politics. Morality was invoked here by

---

1.   Philip Darby, *Three Faces of Imperialism: British and American Approaches to Asia and Africa (1870-1970)* (London: Yale University 1987), 8.

2.   *Ibid.*, 9.

3.   *Ibid.*

the powers among themselves to safeguard their commonality of interest. The first impulse of morality had no consideration initially about the humanity or welfare of the colonized:

> To characterize states as players presupposes some commonality of interest and the acceptance of agreed procedures or codes of conduct—for example in relation to treaty-making and diplomatic representation. Account must also be taken of the techniques and contrivances—such as alliances and buffer states—which are developed and accepted as aids in the management of power. The persistence of such devices attests to the concern of European states to regulate the course of power politics.[4]

Up till the 1880s, attention was not paid to the colonized people's own point of view in the manipulation of power. The pursuit of power in international affairs was conditioned by the exigencies of the domestic politics of the colonial powers. Before the 1880s, the European diplomatic scene in Africa was just sectarian, every country trying to grab and secure as much as it could. No doubt one author has defined power in international relations or world politics as "the ability of an actor in the international stage to use tangible and intangible resources and assets in such a way as to influence the actions of international events to its own satisfaction."[5] Power is a means and all the abilities and resources or the totality of what is within the actor to dominate or colonize. The manipulation of power in the colonized territories was to satisfy the colonial masters.

European powers allowed themselves the latitude of externalizing and diverting their aggression to colonized lands. British economic interest, for example, had three broad tentacles that provided basis for the thinking that guided colonial policies: the British economy, that is, the needs of the home economy; an uncertain world order in which competition was fiercely pursued among European states; and the economic potential of Africa, for the market economic basis needed the development of Africa's potential to be sustained.[6]

---

4.   *Ibid.*, 12.
5.   Walter S. Jones, *The Logic of International Relations*, 7d., (New York: HarperCollins Publishers Inc., 1991), 241.
6.   Philip Darby, *Three Faces of Imperialism: British and American Approaches to Asia and Africa (1870-1970)*, 55-67.

The Beginning of the Western Economic Interest In Africa

By the 15th century, African continent had already had trade and diplomatic relations with Europe. The purported discovery of the West Indies by Christopher Columbus in 1492 was to give a new dimension to trade, for it was this discovery that motivated the trans-Atlantic Slave Trade. Historians such as Ikenga Ozigbo and others have made scholarly studies in this area, and they agree that developments in the West Indies, Brazil and Central America brought a new twist to trade during the 16th century. It was a period when African slaves were deployed at the various plantations to produce black labor for the exploitation of 'King cotton,' as Emma Ikoku calls it.[7] By the 18th century, this trade had definitively won the seal of British policy.[8] Eric Williams rightly concludes that the reason for the origin of Negro slavery was "economic, not racial; it had to do not with the color of the laborer, but the cheapness of labor."[9] Negro slavery provided the cheap labor that sustained European locally based industries.

The anti-slavery rhetoric in Britain was at once humanitarian and economic but largely exploitative in the final analysis. Some people of the humanitarian camps called on the British government for a better knowledge of the African geography and for a new form of economic exploitation of the "black continent." Whether they belonged to economic or humanitarian camp, they could all be termed 'situation opportunists," and they enthroned one uniform slogan that "the Bible and the Plough must regenerate Africa." With the 'dual mandate' as the British mode of economic and profit-oriented strategy which Lord Lugard gave a master's exposition in Nigeria, Europe was poised to go into the so-called development of Africa's vast natural resources. The trouble then began. European economic satellite stationed Africa into focus. The point is that "ideas about power and strategy did not stand on their own as a series of well-ordered theoretical constructs which constituted a blueprint for diplomatic action. Nor was power politics as a system of thought as self-contained as is often depicted. To argue that statesmen operated mainly in terms of power does not dispose of the significance of underlying economic concerns or broader cultural influences."[10]

---

7.   See Emma Ikoku, *Self-Reliance: Africa's Survival (Enugu: Fourth Dimension Publishers, 1980)*, 304.
8.   Eric Williams, "The Origin of Negro Slavery," in *African Philosophy: An Anthology* ed. E. C. Eze (Oxford: Blackwell Publishers, 1998), 386-387.
9.   *Ibid.*, 389.

Therefore, power politics had an economic dimension, and it must be maintained that "access to and control of resources was often part and parcel of the strategic imperative, as was denying them to a rival power. The ledger might be assessed in political terms but it was understood that some of the entries were economic."[11]

Birth of Idea of Colonialisation and Development From 1700s to 1950s

Economists' manuals show that the idea of colonialisation arose first not as a sincere effort to develop Africa's vast potentials as the quest by European exploiters to find primary products for European based industries. When around 1760 the steam engine was invented, the raw materials for the cotton industry was displaced and new needs for different industrial materials, like palm oil and metal bearing ores, dominated the scene. To guarantee this need of European-based industries, European powers sought new encounters; hence the idea of colonialism was born.

Colonialism is "the exercise of alien political power over a conquered territory." It is a systematic contact of Africa with Western rule, culture and technology, and a period of installation in Africa of alien rule and institutions, the plantation of Western economic measures, exploitation and rudimentary political socialization.[12] As E. Chukwudi Eze aptly captures, Colonialism is that:

> Indescribable crisis disproportionately suffered and endured by the African peoples in their tragic encounter with the European world, from the beginning of the fifteenth century through the end of the nineteenth into the first half of the twentieth. This was a period marked by the horror and violence of the transatlantic slave trade, the imperial occupation of most parts of Africa and the forced administrations of its people, and the resilient and enduring ideologies and practices of European cultural superiority (ethnocentrism) and 'racial' supremacy (racism).[13]

---

10.   Philip Darby, *Three Faces of Imperialism: British and American Approaches to Asia and Africa (1870-1970)*, 19.

11.   *Ibid.*

12.   N. S. S. Iwe, *Christianity, Culture and Colonialisation in Africa* (Port Harcourt: R. S. N. C.), 193.

13.   E. Chukwudi Eze, 'Modern Western Philosophy and African Colonialism', in *African Philosophy: An Anthology* ed. Emmanuel Chukwudi Eze, 213.

The decisive effect of colonialism is the fact that one's power of self-determination was taken away by the other, and by that lost one society is forced into underdevelopment.[14]

Political control ensures economic control; in this regard, imperialism, as the operation of alien finance capital in a territory, was installed alongside political and economic control.

European expeditions to Africa (especially Africa south of the Sahara) were therefore motivated by the will to exploit. I have called attention to this earlier. A closer study of the British Indirect rule or the French and Portuguese's policies of Assimilation convinces us of one thing: Europe, as a whole, never had the remotest intention of raising Africans to the Western level of sharing with them the instruments of physical, political or economic power. It was precisely their intention, their necessity to keep the people they ruled in a state of cultural anarchy, that is, simply in a barbaric state. Colonialism remains a deliberately constructed strategy for a systematic denial of economic and political right, and imposition of foreign domination in all spheres of the colonial economy. It was a modern program of development designed to under-develop the colonized area.

The Berlin Conference of November 1884 to February 1885 gave a hallmark to European economic expansionism. Between 1885 and 1906, four European powers: France, Britain, Germany and Portugal formally occupied and colonized West Africa. For example, the first act of the colonialisation process in the territory today known as Nigeria was formally achieved in 1861 with the annexation of Lagos. By 1886, other parts of Nigeria had been conquered and were administered separately under two protectorates, namely Northern and Southern. Whereas the Northern Protectorate had its capital at Zungeru, Calabar was the capital of the Southern Protectorate. In 1906, however, the two protectorates plus Lagos were unified.[15]

Between 1885 and 1886, the coastal regions of Nigeria were already in the hands of the British government. The British government handed over the Central Niger districts to George Pashwood Taubman Goldie's Chartered Trading Company—the Royal Niger Company. Everywhere in the conquered land, the program of education, legal institutions and corporations, civil and military services and other developmental projects were ordered to the interest of the occupying power. Roads and railway networks were built to carry cocoa, oil, and

---

14. Walter Rodney, How Europe Underdeveloped Africa, 224.
15. Chris N. D. Anyanwu, *The Law Matters: Federal Republic of Nigeria 1999-2003* 3d (Nigeria: Craft International 1999), 1.

groundnuts and so on to the shore *en route* European lands. The imperatives of the colonialists were predominantly economic, alien rule was imposed; and the level of development measured at the time was antithetical to human rights; development was simply an activity at the pleasure of the occupying powers.

For the most part, political and economic rights in the colonial administration were abused either by curtailment or total denial. In some areas, people were simply reduced to the status of hewers of wood and drawers of water in their own fatherland. Because their political destiny was not in their hands, they lacked self-determination in political matters; because they did not own what they produced, they had no economic control over their products or market economy. I have alluded to this fact of machinery for impoverishment of people elsewhere in an earlier writing.[16] About the colonial economy, Osita Eze concurs that it "was primarily intended to serve colonial interests. No serious foundations were laid for national development. The basis was already laid for dependent underdevelopment of the post colonial era, a condition inherited and sustained by and large by the post-colonial ruling class."[17] In his *Ahiara Declaration*, Chukwuemeka Odumegwu Ojikwu—General of the People's Army vividly articulates the bad and hidden agenda of European colonial masters, when he writes:

> Ever since the 15th century, the European world has treated the African continent as a field for exploitation. Their policies in Africa have for so long been determined to a very great extent by their greed for economic gain. For over three and half centuries, it suited them to transport and transplant millions of the flower of our manhood for the purpose of exploiting the Americas and the West Indies. They did so with no uneasiness of conscience. They justified their trade in men by reference to biblical passages violently torn out of context.
>
> When it became no longer profitable to them to continue with the depopulation and uncontrolled spoliation of Negro Africa, their need of the moment became to exploit the natural resources of the continent, using Negro labor. In response to this need they evolved their informal empire of the 19th century under which they controlled and exploited Negro Africa through their missionaries and monopolist mercantile companies. As time went on, they discarded the empire of informal sway as unsatisfactory and established the

---

16. See Francis Njoku, 'Machines that Manufacture the Marginalized' in *The Insight Magazine* 7 (no.1 June-December, 1990).

17. Osita Eze, 'Nigeria and Human Rights—Prospects and Problems' *Bulletin of Ecumenical Theology* 4 (Numbers 1-2, 1991), 11. See also Osita Eze, *Human Rights in Africa: Some Selected Problems* (Lagos: Nigerian Institute of International Affairs, 1984).

direct empire as a most effective means of exploiting our homeland. It was at this stage that with cynical imperturability they carved up the African continent, and boxed up the native populations in artificial states designed purely to minister to white economic interests.[18]

Somewhere along the line, some foresighted Africans began to complain and campaign against colonial abuses, and manifested their determined effort to reject the indefinite rule or control of Africa. This group of men rejected legal adoption and cultural assimilation by Europe; and in this, the colonial masters saw an intent to overthrow their rule.

The militant populists posited an uncompromising request for self-rule, economic and political independence as a way of compensating Africans for saving the British and Europe from the hands of the Germans during two World wars. In this regard, African men of rank and file during World War II joined the anti-colonialist elite to campaign against alien rule. They were impatient, rowdy, aggressive and violent; they found some leaders like Kwame Nkrumah, Leopold Sedar Senghor, Julius Nyerere and others to adopt their cause. They opted to use any means possible to accomplish their demands. But this group failed because it had not much in its control. Its death occasioned the triumph of colonial strategy by using another crop of men—the African petite bourgeoisie as pawns in the hands of Europe, even at the time of European absence on African soil.

It was in the 1880s that Africa came to occupy a place in European thinking about international politics. European powers did not want their isolated individual claims and struggles of the European powers endanger stability or spill over to Europe. Thus, in the 1880s, African questions became issues of national, not sectarian significance. Moreover, the political scene on the ground in Africa was changing: aggressive nationalism was springing up here and there, as monarchical solidarity had collapsed. One recalls Nkrumah saying that Africans have the right to govern or misgovern themselves. Thus, "in these circumstances European statesmen came to see Africa and Asia in a new light. Increasingly confronted with colonial issues from which it was no longer possible to stand aside, and pre-occupied, as they now are with calculations of national power, diplomatic advantage and military strategy, territorial claims and counter-claims overseas became instruments in the power struggle of Europe."[19] Against this background, the

---

18. Chukwuemeka Odumegwu Ojukwu, *Ahiara Declaration: The Principles of the Biafran Revolution (June, 1, 1969)* with the Declaration of Independence, speech before exile, the Cessation Declaration, call from Exile, and The Biafran National Anthem ed. Obi Harrison Ekwonna (Maryland USA: Rising Star Publishers, 2003),

great powers settled for making alliances to checkmate one another. The maintenance of power had become very complex, and it could no longer be confined to
Europe. Circumstances had forced the powers to extend the chessboard of European diplomacy from Europe to Africa. Primacy could no longer be given to
imperial considerations without administrative re-evaluation and paying attention to conflicts in colonized lands.

By the 1950s, although Europe had cleared anti-colonists and extremists, it
was obvious to her that her continued physical presence in Africa was being
received with contempt. Aware of this, the need for decolonization became a reality. However, the point remains that development at this period basically meant,
the "mobilization of the people to create pressure for the achievement of political
independence."[20]

To pursue the decolonization policy, an alliance was conceived between
Europe and the African petite bourgeoisie, that is, the middle class elite—people
who were interested in colonial rule because they benefited. In this alliance, they
were to act as "local foremen and gendarmerie for the European bourgeoisie,"
says Chinweizu. They were to undergo a period of political grooming and be very
colonized in their mentality after which they qualify to man the government. In
the case of Nigeria, Nnamdi Azikwe, in his *Political Blueprint* (1944), advocated
a period of 15 years after which a Nigerian elite will take over government.
Obafemi Awolowo, in his *Path to Nigerian Freedom* (1946), tolerated the period
suggested by Azikwe as a necessary evil at the end of which British trusteeship
would end and a truly westernized Nigeria would have emerged to take up control. Europe then made the timetable to save it for a rainy day. Chinweizu has an
interesting outline of the European decolonisation strategy, using the "middle
class solution." The timetable was to be as follows:

> Promote a loyalist, westernizing petite bourgeoisie and give them local power
> over each colony;
> Constrain their actions by way of an intense fetishism about international
> legality;
> Fasten moral and ideological blindfolds on their minds and manipulate them
> by flattery and censure;

---

19. Philip Darby, *Three Faces of Imperialism: British and American Approaches to Asia and
     Africa (1870-1970)*, 14.
20. Obiora F. Ike and Ndidi Nnoli Edozien, *Development Is About People: Business Is
     About Ethics* (Enugu: Catholic Institute for Development, Justice and Peace
     (CIDJAP), 2003), 9.

Fill the political and administrative machinery of the new style colonies with
strategically placed spies and pro-imperialist counselor;
Corrupt the petite-bourgeoisie leadership; bias the elite with commercial
bribes, subsidies to their budgets and colonial development aid, and ultimately
by economic controls as well as colonial exploitation of their land and people,
tie them down to a loyal and self-serving partnership with European imperialism.[21]

Furthermore, there were other economic preparations that were to take root
before European exit. European and American based companies quickly took
their stand in the European conditioned African trade and economic fare. Chase
Manhatan Bank of America, Gulf Oil, Texaco, Phillips, British Petroleum (BP),
Regnolds, UAC and many others landed as wolves in sheep's clothing by using
economic aid and stimulation. In the name of aid, Europe and America sent
droves of spies and experts to advise and mis-advise the African petite bourgeoisie
on imperialist policies. Their female secretaries, police and military technical
advisers were a bunch of economic mis-planners and legally constituted cheats.
At the end of it all, the mind of the African petite bourgeoisie was consciously,
systematically and devastatingly won to the advantage of Europe. Consequently,
Europe religiously handed over to their 'products' as trustworthy sons! Thus,
everywhere it was celebrated that Africa, South of Sahara, got her independence
on a platter of gold!

We can understand why African leaders who still have, directly or indirectly,
the colonial blood cannot think of a better alternative in leading their people.
Aimé Cesaire captures vividly the economically de-personalized and politically
alienated image of the African elite, when he writes:

Wherever colonization is a fact the indigenous culture begins to rot. And,
among these ruins, something begins to be born which is not a culture but a
kind of sub-culture, a subculture which is condemned to exist on the margin
allowed it by European culture. This then becomes the province of a few men,
the elite, who find themselves placed in the most artificial conditions, deprived
of any revivifying contact with the masses of the people.[22]

When in the 1960s agricultural growth was witnessed in the colonial territories, development became the buying cheaply of African agricultural products to
pay for the importation of modern technology and military weapon by African

---

21. See Chinweizu, *The West and the Rest of Us*, 161-162.
22. See James Baldwin, *Nobody Knows My Name* (London: Corgi Books, 1973), 39.

leaders. This did not bridge the gap between poor and rich nations. The point is that the political and economic development initiated in Africa, starting with the arbitrary partition of Africa at the Berlin Conference, as indicated by Bénézet Bujo, was wrongly conceived:

> While generally in Europe the nation preceded the state, it was the reverse in Africa where the State preceded the nation. Indeed different ethnic communities with different languages were clustered together without being asked if they had any desire to unite. The colonial powers did not have human interests in mind since they were more concerned with territories that were often full of resources. That is why today people belonging to one ethnic community are citizens of different countries. For example, the ethnic community of the Ewe can be found in Ghana, Togo and Benin. Yoruba unity was destroyed by the border between Benin and Nigeria. The Sara live in Chad as well as in the Central African Republic and in Cameroon. The Bakongo can be found in Congo-Kinshasa, Angola and Congo-Brazzaville. Sudan, Uganda, D. R. Congo, Rwanda, Burundi and Tanzania are in part populated by the same ethnic groups.... But one thing is certain: due to this arbitrary partition based on biased interests, the identity of many ethnic communities in Africa was partially destroyed. They were forced to join other nationalities and thus became estranged to one another. Visas became obligatory so that family members could no longer meet freely as in former times. Borders began to play an important role: they could no longer be crossed even if this had to (do) with essential things as grazing pastures, water, fishing, and so on.[23]

In the atmosphere of political independence oiled by forced economic interests, therefore, an African economic independence, as chorused by the West, will continue to remain a propaganda. One understands then why many blame Europe, even till date, for being responsible for the political and economic crises in the African continent. Later in the book, however, we will see whether African leaders themselves are totally exonerated from Africa's continued problems.

Imperialism Conceived as a Moral Responsibility

Before I go on to examine post-colonial economy it is important to point out some body of beliefs that under-girded European imperative in Africa.

---

23.   Bénézet Bujo, *The Ethical Dimension of Community: The African Model and the Dialogue Between North and South* (Nairobi: Paulines Publications Africa, 1998), 171-172.

As I have indicated earlier, the first impulse of moral considerations in the imperialist body of conduct exemplifying some accepted standards was put forward for mutual respect among the powers. However, back in Britain some really considered colonialism or imperialism as a moral responsibility on the following counts:

First, some believed that alongside the concern to secure diplomatic advantage and the desire for economic benefit,

> stood a body of thought and belief that advanced peoples had obligations to those less advanced. Societies which had traveled ahead, it was held, had some duty to offer guidance, instruction, even to rule. The signposts along the way were marked by concepts drawn from politics and economics—trusteeship, colonial development, modernization. Such guides to action were not simply theoretical constructs; they expressed something of the temper of the metropolitan society, or at least sections of it. Imperialism, according to this conception, was primarily a set of moral attitudes.[24]

This group thought that Britain had a moral responsibility to develop the underdeveloped, especially Africa and Asia, for its own use.

Second, there were those who thought on humanitarian grounds that Britain needed to pick up the pieces in colonized lands. Since imperialism had enthroned brutality, exploitation and cultural distortion, then a certain elevated sense of mission came to remain "in part a counterpoise to a very different record on the ground." It was against this background, in contrasting the great imperial aspiration with contempt and achievement, that Winston Churchill said: "The gap between conquest and dominion becomes filled with the figures of the greedy trader, the inopportune missionary, the ambitious soldier, and the lying speculator, who disquiet the minds of the conquered and excite the sordid appetites of the conquerors."[25] Moralists of this camp believed that it was not a very pretty thing to be very proud of stealing from those who happened to be of different complexion from Europeans. However, one may say that where humanitarian and religious considerations were smuggled in, they were not decisive in their own account or provided independent reasons why the colonized people should not be manipulated.

---

24. Philip Darby, *Three Faces of Imperialism: British and American Approaches to Asia and Africa (1870-1970)*, 31.
25. Winston Churchill, *The River War* (London: Eyre and Spottiswoode, 1951), 10.

The third group conceived colonialism as an ethico-religious affair. To sustain the imperialist sentiment at home and abroad, imperialism has to be presented as a faith. European officials, intellectuals and their people needed to sustain imperialism on strong faith as a moral impetus. In his speech presented in Birmingham in 1908, Viscount Curzon could be said to have articulated the imperialist manifesto, when he stated:

> I speak of Empire...because I am a convinced and unconquered imperialist, who by the accident of events has been called upon to spend the whole of his working manhood in the study or service of Empire, and to whom it has come to be a secular religion, embodying the most sacred duty of the present, and the brightest hope for the future...
>
> In Empire we have found not merely the key to glory and wealth, but the call to duty, and the means of service to mankind. Empire can only be achieved with satisfaction, or maintained with advantage, provided it has a moral basis. Let us no more forswear Empire than we would abjure our own souls...
>
> To the people of the mother state it must be a discipline, an inspiration and a faith. To the people of circumference, it must be more than a flag or a name, it must give them what they cannot otherwise or elsewhere enjoy; not merely justice or order, or material prosperity, but the sense of partnership in a great idea, the consecrating influence of a lofty purpose.[26]

In other words, British power or economic impulse was realized to a religious one where Empire came to be seen as an instrument of God's purpose in history. Darby articulates this very well:

> A consciousness of power was intrinsic to Britain's conception of her mission in Africa and Asia. The idealism of imperialism was not something which stemmed from selfishness or other-worldliness. It grew out of Britain's self-perception and the possession of the means to control. The assignment of role, and the implications which were attached to it, bear this out. Imperialists were the actors and initiators. They possessed the attributes of vigor and energy, and shaped the course of events. By comparison, Africans and Asians were essentially objects. Inarticulate, plastic, mostly passive, they were a material from which something could be made. Those who resisted tended to be left out of account because they did not fit the schema. The focus was primarily on those who acted, and the understanding of the imperial process was such

---

26. Viscount Curzo, 'The True Imperialism' in *Nineteenth Century and After* LXIII (Jan. 1908), 151-165 at 151, 158 and 165.

that the supposed beneficiaries were in the first instance drained of life and independent purpose.[27]

The colonized are piece of matter, malleable according to the interest of the colonizer.

There is a forth group that considered the colonizer as a true diplomat. A diplomat already in the conquered territory needed to exhibit "certain qualities inherent in the individual leader," which can be "described in the language of moral maxim even though fixed rules and laws of human conduct may lie beyond analysis."[28] The intention for this moral maxim is not that the colonizer believes that certain ways of treating the colonized are not inherently right, but he wants to maintain a relative peaceful atmosphere in the colonized territory so that he does not create more adversaries.

The so-called morality built on moral-maxims of power is not an end in itself but a means; it does not resolve the issue of morality in politics. The colonized and the colonizer are not working at the same moral platform or convergence. The point is that "there would be no moral problem in politics or foreign policy if the actors involved perceived one another's interests and goals in the same way. There would be no moral problems in foreign policy if the nations of the world had more or less convergent interests. Or, stated broadly, there could be no moral problem in foreign policy or politics, or in individual life for that matter, if everyone were pursuing one goal or interest, and only one."[29]

The colonialist, from his own side, thought he was performing a moral duty; he believed that through exploitation and control of the disadvantaged people, the colonized people could be raised to some kind of standard, which the colonialist would confer. At least, that was the way he understood his duty. However, whether or not the imperialists had moral principles behind their policies and actions, their particular ethics or morality was utilitarian and opportunistic. It was sustained by political and economic greed without much attention to the welfare of the people they were colonized.

---

27.   Philip Darby, *Three Faces of Imperialism: British and American Approaches to Asia and Africa (1870-1970)*, 38.

28.   Kenneth W. Thompson, *Morality and Foreign Policy* (Baton Roudge: Louisiana State University Press, 1980), 14.

29.   *Ibid.*, 15-16.

UN First Decade of Economic Development (The 1960s)

Right from its inception, the UN is committed to the idea of creating conditions necessary for peace and stability among nations. This idea is expressed in article 55 (a) of its Charter, to promote "higher standards of living, full employment, and conditions of economic and social progress and development.' In the light of this pledge, the UN has supported the development efforts of poorer nations. In fact, in 1960, "the General Assembly proclaimed three successive United Nations Development Decade in order to focus international action on concrete programs to aid development."[30] The declarations backing the proclamation of these decades were directed towards strengthening international co-operation for development. The First Decade was to run from 1960 to 1970, the Second, 1970 to 1980, and the Third, 1980 to 1990.

The UN economic and social development emphasis in the 1960s was on the need for a unified approach to economic and social planning in order to promote balanced and sound development. There was a declaration on social progress and development, adopted by the General Assembly in 1969. There were to be subsequent General Assembly resolutions calling for a unified approach to development analysis and planning adopted in 1983 and 1986:

> Before the end of the First United Nations Development Decade (1961-1970), the need for a world plan of action or 'strategy' for development became evident, and the General Assembly therefore adopted, in 1970, an International Development Strategy for the Second United Nations Development Decade (1971-1980), which set targets for progress and measures for achieving specific goals. The unanimous adoption of the International Development Strategy for the Second Development Decade was an important step in the promotion of international economic co-operation on a just and equitable basis.[31]

The UN first decade of development was a period of planning and setting specific goals, while at the same time seeking international co-operation among its members.

---

30. *Basic Facts About the United Nations* (New York: United Nations Publication, 1989), 93.
31. *Ibid.*, 94.

The Post-Colonial Economy and the Reality of Development

The post-colonial era in Africa is a period of stocktaking in all its ramifications. Tsenay Serequeberhan writes:

> For us, contemporary Africans, the condition that has resulted from the colonial obliteration of the 'standards and practices of our fathers,' to use Plato's words, and the consequent neo-colonial inertness of our contemporary situation is the necessary point of departure for any worthwhile or meaningful philosophical engagement. Thus, the closing years of the twentieth century are bound to be for Africa and Africans a time of prolonged, deep reflection and self-examination. Having achieved political 'independence,' for the most part, we now need to take stock of the victories, defeats, and compromises that constitute and inform our enigmatic present.[32]

The balance sheet of post-colonial economy so far has shown an economy at once confused and bankrupt. The colonialist knew that the nation-state framework institution in Africa was not generally suited to local realities. He ill-adapted the nation-state framework and organized an economy in response to external needs run by Western models, which will continue to oscillate between stagnation and decline. The post-colonial economy is "largely dependent" on public aid with an overall exploitation of its mineral wealth."[33] There is still lacking in the African leaders a sound political and economic imagination.

The leaders, as outlined in the celebrated timetable, were trained to help corrupt and raid their country, create hunger and trade deficit and to sustain the colonialist strategy, in which the elite were co-opted to maintain, so that Africa must look up to Europe for aid. Africa was and is still distorted in such a form that, for long, the relationship of industrialized goods and that of African agricultural potentials and crude oil will remain dominated by an unequal exchange. Both socialist and capitalist strategists are blamed for this. African leaders and countries have not found their feet yet in international affairs. The balance sheet of history has so far convinced us to look with suspicion on the concept of development posited to us by the West. This is not to deny that any good comes from the biblical Nazareth; however the cumulative effect of the African experience of

---

32. Tsenay Serequeberhan, 'Philosophy and Post-Colonial Africa,' in *African Philosophy: An Anthology* ed. E. C. Eze, (Oxford: Blackwell Publishers, 1998), 9.
33. Gérard Chaliand, *The Struggle for Africa: Conflict of the Great Powers* (1980), 8.

international economic co-operation with the West teaches us not to trivialize one basic reality. Our intelligent awareness gains more confirmation everyday on the old saying about the monkey—the higher it climbs the more one sees of its backside. It is felt that the Western concept of development, with reference to the less developed and underdeveloped nations, has become a conscious quest for self-interest, for which the context of forces, ideologies, means and stratagems are a mere battlefield. There is need for a better understanding of economic and human development.

Economic Development in a Better Perspective

A central issue in development as highlighted by the *World Development Report 1991* is the interaction between governments and markets:

> This is not a question of intervention versus laisser-faire—a popular dichotomy, but a false one. Competitive markets are the best way yet found for efficiently organizing the production and distribution of goods and services. Domestic and external competition provides the incentives that unleash entrepreneurship and technological progress. But markets cannot operate in a vacuum—they require a legal and regulatory framework that only government can provide. And, at many other tasks, markets sometimes prove inadequate or fail altogether. That is why governments must, for example, invest in infrastructure and provide essential services to the poor. It is not a question of state or market: each has a large and irreplaceable role.[34]

Much as this report recognizes the role of the market and governments in fostering development, the market is still dominated by those who have power at the international level. Actually, the UN 1991 Report defines development to include the increase of the economic, political, and civil rights of all genders, ethnic groups, religions, races, regions and countries. In this regard, economic development is regarded as "a sustainable increase in living standards that encompass material consumption, education, health, and environmental protection."[35] Development covers equal opportunity, political freedoms, and civil liberties. Thus, the economic is realized in the midst of all other socially and politically related factors. The economic is not simply to be calculated in that traditional sense of an increase in per capita income. This kind of consideration of income

34. *World Development Report 1991: The Challenge of Development* (Oxford: Oxford University Press, 1991), 1.
35. *Ibid.*, 31.

growth as indicator of economic development does not bring out real changes in welfare for large parts of the poor population, which defy statistical quantification: "Improvements in meeting the basic needs for food, education, health care, equality of opportunity, civil liberties, and environmental protection are not captured by statistics on income growth."[36] So, development encompasses rapid growth in income. A record of rapid income growth does not necessarily remove the inequalities that may exist alongside statistical economic increase.

Pope Pius XI indicated long ago that "immense power and despotic economic domination is concentrated in the hands of a few, and that those few are frequently not the owners, but only the trustees and directors of invested funds, who administer them at their good pleasure."[37] There is a lot of inequalities at the ground of exchange. And it was against this background that the Vatican Council for Justice and Peace of December 1986 noted:

> The debt of the developing countries must be placed in a broader context of economic, political and technological relations which point to the increased interdependence between countries, as well as to the need for international collaboration in pursuing the objectives of the common good. In order to be just, this interdependence should give rise to new and broader expressions of solidarity, which respect the equal dignity of all peoples, rather than lead to domination by the strongest, to national egoism, to inequalities and injustices. The monetary and financial issue therefore commands attention today in an urgent and new way.

The tendency for interdependence to create new waves of domination and inequalities needs to be addressed with a new ethics. Those who use the earth's resources will have to pay attention to social justice, a realization that resources are destined for the use of all in the human community. There is need to internalize a new ethics and adopt a humanist requirement, that is, the priority of labor over capital, as John Paul II insists.[38] The economic should be at the service of man, and not man be employed and manipulated at the service of the productive process. The Pontifical Council for Justice and Peace writes:

> It is however far from being 'an evident truth' for economists. Labor and capital are classically seen as the two necessary factors of production, which the firms should use in their most efficient proportions in order to be competitive.

---

36. *Ibid*
37. Pius XI, *Quadragesimo Anno* (1931), 105.
38. See John Paul II, *Laborem Excerms*, no. 12.1.

It follows, therefore, that there is no certain or universal absolute hierarchy between capital and labor. Indeed, there are recent examples of successful firms, which have emphasized either labor or capital. It would be easy to highlight contradictions between a financial approach and a human resources approach to the firm's development. In practice, successful firms seek a balanced combination by drawing on both approaches.

But the Church is not seeking to bring forward an alternative economic analysis. She is seeking to make a point about the underlying values. The priority of labor over capital is thus an appeal not to be content simply with a classical economic optimum (which is the legitimate role of the economist to highlight) but to situate economic efficiency in the context of its ultimate objective: the development of mankind. In this context, work, which is the central feature of human development, has a moral value, whose dignity has no equivalent. In view of the priority of labor over capital, company managers should not, therefore, refrain from using capital and labor as efficiently as possible in the production process, otherwise they might face bankruptcy. But they must not overlook the fact that human labor is more than a production factor.[39]

The point of this teaching is that human labor should not be solely considered according to its economic purpose. One observes that markets, which pace is set by the dominant powers, dominate the international arena. Markets and other prescriptions of technical economics determine economic activities. At the same time, one has to recognize that there are also "the norms, values and interests of the social and political systems in which economic activities are embedded."[40] There is the danger that political systems are increasingly dominated by those who have economic powers; thus everything comes to be read from the pace set by economics, and human labor comes to be neglected at all fronts. In the circumstances, an error of *economism* arises. To avoid *economism*, one must opt for a development with a human face.

---

39. Antonie De Salins and Francois Villeroy De Galhau eds., *The Modern Development of Financial Activities in the Light of the Ethical Demands of Christianity* (Vatican City: Liberia Editrice Vaticana), 20.

40. Robert Gilpin, *Global Political Economy: Understanding the International Economic Order* (Princeton: Princeton University Press, 2001), 12.

5

Towards A Human-Centered Development

"If you plan for a year, plant a seed.
If for ten years, plant a tree.
If for a hundred years, teach the people.
When you sow a seed once, you will reap a single harvest.
When you teach the people, you will reap a hundred harvests."

—K'uan-Tzu, 551-479 B.C.

The Call for A New International Order (The 1970s)

At the end of the World War II, the world economy wore a dilapidated look. The war aggravated the rate of exploitation of the less developed nations, which also needed to be modernized and developed. Third World countries needed development badly. In fact, from the early years of the independence in the Third World till the end of First Decade of UN Development Plan in 1970, development was seen as a process of civilization; and this civilization was conceived as a process of westernization, which "involved following the yellow brick road painted by Western societies towards an Oz of industrialization and consumerism. All countries should be striving for a society of skyscrapers, with televisions in every home, cars in every garage and combine harvesters in the fields, with everyone working in humming factories and carpeted offices."[1] By 1944, the International Monetary Fund (IMF) has already been founded to take care of the imbalance of trade between rich countries. But when the less developed countries were admitted, its rules became a means of exploitation against them. As Robert Gilpin writes:

---

1. Paul Harrison, *The Third World Tomorrow: A Report from the Battlefront in the War against Poverty* (Middlesex: Penguin Books Limited, 1980), 23.

> The World Bank, the International Monetary Fund, and regimes governing the world economy were established primarily to serve the interests of the dominant powers. Although industrialized countries have subsequently provided technical and financial assistance and given trade preferences, they have continued to resist LDC (less developed countries) demands for a development regime.[2]

Experience along the years has shown that African countries in this system have time without number fallen victim to the manipulations of the international capitalist system. The growth and stagnation of their economies were determined primarily by fluctuations in the needs and interests of the dominant nations.

African countries desperately needed modernization and development after the war. This development-modernization was theoretically conceived thus: the economic development racing from the West will 'trickle down' to the masses of the underdeveloped people. The trickle down was evident in the obsession with transfer-technology and the aid packages sent to African countries. However, the mass importation, and building of skyscrapers did not bring the needed relief from poverty:

> Despite the massive national and international development effort, poverty and inequality were actually increasing in many if not most developing countries. It was this conjuncture that formed the background to the new approach to thinking about development, which began in the early seventies and became almost a new orthodoxy towards the end of that decade.[3]

Aware of the trouble the Third World countries were in, at the end of World War II, the United Nations Organization signed a charter, which launched the aim at establishing "a new international order." Having come to witness the gap between poor nations and rich counties, the United Nations proclaimed the 1970s as the decade of economic progress that was to usher in a just distribution of wealth the world over.

---

2.   Robert Gilpin, *Global Political Economy: Understanding the International Economic Order* (Princeton: Princeton University Press, 2001), 305.

3.   Paul Harrison, *The Third World Tomorrow: A Report from the Battlefront in the War against Poverty*, 25.

Second United Nations Development Decade (1971-1980)

Thirty years after signing of the UN Charter (c. 1974), the less developed people, having tested so far the European and Western concept of development and modernization, began to react against it. Between March 18 and 24, 1974, a North-South Dialogue on World Development was held in Belmont USA with participants from across the globe. The Belmont statement was on self-reliance and international reform. The leaders of developing countries called for a change in economic relationships, insisting that "a new fundamentally different approach is required at the international level to complement the efforts of many poor countries to increase the participation of their entire population in the process of development and to ensure the more equitable distribution of its benefits."[4] The leaders argued that their test confirmed that the patterns of international economic co-operation were dominated by developed nations. There is no doubt that since World War II trade barriers have declined, deregulation and privatization have opened further national economies to imports, technology has brought a lot of advantages, more and more businesses have participated in international markets; however, in spite of all these developments, "most trade takes place among the three advanced industrialized economies—the United States, Western Europe, and Japan, plus a few emerging markets in East Asia, Latin America, and elsewhere. Most of the less developed world is excluded, except as exporters of food and raw materials."[5] It was against this backdrop that the leaders of the less developed countries wanted a change in the face of the new realism their countries had come to witness. And this "new realism" shelved the first United Nations' Development decade. And member states urgently called for the "establishment of a new international economic order based on equity, sovereignty, interdependence, common interest and co-operation among states, irrespective of their economic and social systems":

> The approach to development of all main agencies and aid donors underwent a sea of change during the Second UN Development Decade. One after another the United Nations Conference on Trade and Development, the International Labor Office, The World Bank, UNICEF, the World Health Organization, the United Nations Environment Program and UNESCO came out with their own brand new blueprints for the millennium. The mul-

---

4.   Emma Ikoku, *Self-Reliance: Africa's Survival*, 93-94.
5.   Robert Gilpin, *Global Economy: Understanding the International Economic Order*, 6.

tiplication of models, the plethora of new slogans, was bewildering: the New International Economic Order, growth with redistribution, basic needs, basic services, participation, eco-development, endogenous development. Each had a slightly different emphasis, but all had a common ground of values based on the idea that growth, pursued regardless of who benefited from it, was making little impact on the poverty of nations and of people.[6]

Following the end of the first United Nations development decade, one specifically recalls the International Symposium on 'Patterns of Resource Use, Environment and Development Strategies,' which produced the Cocoyoc Declaration. At the time, it called for the adoption of the pending UNO's Charter on Economic Rights and Duties of States. It made a personal statement on development that won the approval of experts from developing and developed countries alike. Part of the Cocoyoc Declaration reads:

> Thirty years have passed since the signing of the United Nations Charter, which launched the effort to establish a new international order. Today, that order has reached a critical turning point. Its hope of creating a better life for the whole human family has been largely frustrated. It has proved impossible to meet the 'inner limits' of satisfying fundamental human needs. On the contrary, more people are hungry, sick, shelterless and illiterate today than when the United Nations was first set up.

The "new international economic order," after the "new international order" launched in 1945, will be aimed at correcting inequalities and redressing existing injustices and the gap that has come to stay between developing and developed countries; it will be a move that will ensure peace and justice for future generations. As a further step to promote the establishment of a new economic order, the UN General Assembly adopted, in December 1974, the Charter of Economic Rights and Duties of States, stipulating that every state has sovereign control over its wealth and natural resources." It can "regulate foreign investments within its national jurisdiction, and nationalize, expropriate or transfer the ownership of foreign property." But this stipulation did not always met with concrete action; hence "measures to implement both the new international economic order and the Charter of Economic Rights and Duties of States have not enjoyed the same relative consensus as did their original adoption. Efforts to establish follow-up mechanisms for each have not yielded significant progress in recent years."[7]

---

6.   Paul Harrison, *The Third World Tomorrow: A Report from the Battlefront in the War against Poverty*, 25-26.

The Cocoyoc meeting criticized the whole Western concept of development and condemned its emphasis on *thing* rather on *person*. It argued that human beings had basic needs: food, shelter, clothing, health, education; and any process of growth that did not lead to their fulfillment or even worse, disrupted them, was a travesty of the idea of development. Thus, the economic development envisaged by African countries through the 'almighty' trickle down proved illusory. Development is not only economic, for it has to go with the guarantee of other human freedoms.

The Third United Nations Development Decade (1981-1990)

There was a call in 1979, by the General Assembly, for the launching, in 1980, of global and sustained negotiations on international and economic co-operation for development. The 1980 launching ushered in the Third UN Development Decade. However, subsequent negotiations did not yield fruit as envisaged at a special session held in September 1980; but at the Assembly's regular session in the same year, an International Development Strategy for the Third United Nations Development Decade (1981-1990) was, through a consensus, adopted. The International Development Strategy for the Third United Nations Development Decade adopted on 5 December 1980, states that "in an interdependent world economy, problems such as high inflation and unemployment, prolonged monetary instability and intensified protectionist pressures cannot be solved without resolving the particular problems facing the developing countries, and that the accelerated development of developing countries is of vital importance for the steady growth of the world economy, and essential for world peace and stability."[8] These were the specific goals set for the third decade (1981-1990). The goals were to be met by various policy measures covering food, international trade, international monetary and financial issues, industrialization, science and technology, energy, transport, environment, human settlements, disaster relief and social development and many others.

In 1985, the UN General Assembly met and recommitted itself to the strategy it set for the Third United Nations Development Decade; however, it set a committee to review and appraise the implementation of the goals set for the third decade. Accordingly, "the review document contained broad guidelines for future

---

7. *Basic Facts About the United Nations,* 94-95.
8. *Ibid.,* 96-97.

action and singled out trade, the international monetary system, international debt and access to financial resources as areas demanding special attention. The Committee reported modest progress in some areas but noted that key targets had not been met."[9] There is still not a better handle on world's economic problems. Thus, at the 1988 session, the General Assembly decided to prepare an international development strategy for the Fourth United Nations Development Decade (1991-2000). The UN General Assembly had a meeting in March 1989. In this meeting, it decided to convene a special session in 1990 to be devoted to international economic co-operation, and the revitalization of economic growth and development particularly in developing countries. The 1990 special session is to "review problems facing the world economy, to consider pressing priority issues in international economic relations, and to address those issues taking into account their interrelationships."[10]

Emphasizing Human Development

It has to be recalled that before the call for a new international order by less developed countries, in 1974, Pope Paul VI had already, in his *Populorum Progressio* (On the Development of Peoples) 1964, counseled that economic and technological growth had no meaning if it was devoid of the welfare of people. The Pope wrote: "Development cannot be limited to mere economic growth. In order to be authentic, it must be complete: integral, that is, it has to promote the good of every man and of the whole man."[11] Pope John Paul II, in his *Sollicitudo Rei Socialis* (On Social Concern) of December 1987 updates and extends the theme of development of peoples of *Populorum Progressio*. The Pope surveys the contemporary world. In spite of the enthusiasm ushered in by the UN past three decades of development, the optimistic hope of development was still far from realization. There was no doubt that certain results were achieved, but the gap between the poor and rich nations, the North and the South, continued to widen.[12] John Paul II insists thus:

> Responsibility for the deterioration from bad to worse in so many underdeveloped regions rests on both the developing nations, especially on those holding economic and political power, and on the more developed nations, which

9.   *Ibid.*, 96.
10.   *Ibid.*, 95.
11.   Pope Paul VI, *Populorum Progressio* 1964, no. 14.
12.   See John Paul II, Solicitudo Rei Socialis, no. 14.

have not made a sufficiently great effort. One must denounce the economic, financial, and social structures that are manipulated by the rich and powerful for their own benefit at the expense of the poor.[13]

The Pope calls for the corporation of all in an interdependent world for the realization of true development. To achieve this, all must be aware of the indicators of true underdevelopment: homelessness, unemployment and international debt.[14] The world delayed in eradicating these problems mostly because of ideological divisions into blocs between the world powers and arms race.[15]

It was against the backdrop of a relationship of exploitation between developed and underdeveloped countries that the Belmont Conference and the Cocoyoc Declaration called on the UN for a "New International Economic Order," for healthy trade, economic relationship and co-operation between the less developed or developing and developed countries. Development will have to carry with it political, human and economic liberations.

Thinking African leaders saw the call for a new international economic world order as a call to end the right to be exploited which the present economic relations gives them: a situation of economic inequality. Julius Nyerere's Arusha Declaration puts the situation of exploitation through trade by the West in the following words: "Today, the only right the economic order gives us is the right to sell cheap and buy dear."

In Nigeria in 1980, President Shehu Shagari told the UN General Assembly that the 'new emphasis' being demanded by less developed nations was urgent. It was to be pursued with vigor. "Political independence," said the president, "would have to be followed by economic independence." What Nyerere demanded in the 1960s, Shagari asked for in the 1980s, when he said: "We must refuse to subsidize the economies of the rich by continuing to sell cheaply our raw materials and labor to them (the industrialized nations) in return for their exorbitantly priced manufactured goods."[16] Shagari thought of fortifying this 'new emphasis' at the continental level; hence, Nigeria hosted the special OAU Summit Conference in Lagos in 1980, which exclusively devoted itself to the consideration of economic issues. The outcome of this meeting was an adoption of the

---

13. *Ibid.*, 16.
14. See *Ibid.*, 17-19.
15. *Ibid.*, 21-24.
16. Shehu Shagari, 'Address to Nigerian Institute of International Affairs' in *Third World Diplomacy Press*, Winter vol. 1, 3d., 1982), 20.

Lagos Plan of Action aimed at operationalising the concepts of development and co-operation in the economic front.[17]

The basic talk about human development is that it is a process of "enlarging the range of people's choices—increasing their opportunities for education, health care, income and employment, and covering the full range of human choices from a sound physical environment to economic and political freedom."[18] Human development is concerned at once with developing human capacities and with using them productively. In other words, it requires investing in people and that people contribute to GNP growth and employment. People can only contribute to this if they have employment opportunities and do indeed work. Human development is not concerned with a certain section: for example, economy or education or health. No. It is holistic:

> Development *of* people is certainly vital, but it is only one part of the picture. Human development also means development *for* people, including the creation of economic opportunities for all. And it means development by people, requiring participatory approaches. Human development comprises all three aspects, not just one.[19]

One needs then to develop all the potentials of the people; such potentials need the requisite environment for their flourishing, and that people indeed make their development a reality by participation.

Since 'development' in general is a process, no society can say that it has attained a total human development. In this regard, human development is not only restricted to poorest societies with the primary goal of satisfying basic needs. Granted that the basic needs are to be generally satisfied, in fact, the goals of human development "can range from the most basic ones of human survival to the most advanced human agenda of modern science and technology. People's choices take center stage, but the choices differ at different stages of development."[20] Furthermore, the 1992 Report states:

> Human development is thus a broad and comprehensive concept. It covers all human choices in all societies at all stages of development. It broadens the

---

17. See Siddique Mohammad and Tony Edoh eds., *Nigeria: A Republic in Ruins* (1986), 293.
18. *Human Development Report 1992* (Oxford: Oxford University Press, 1992), 2.
19. *Ibid.*
20. *Ibid.*

development dialogue from a discussion of mere *means* (GNP growth) to a discussion of the ultimate *ends*. It is as concerned with the generation of economic growth as with its distribution, as concerned with the basic needs as with the entire spectrum of human aspirations, as concerned with the human dilemmas of the North as with the human deprivation in the South. The concept of human development does not start with any predetermined model. It draws its inspiration from the long-term goals of a society. It weaves development around people, not people around development.[21]

It has to be recalled that the 1990 Human Development Report indicated three major points for human development index, namely: life expectancy, educational attainment and income indicators. These give a composite measure of human development. Following this, the Human Development Report of 1992 reviews human development in a global context and arrives at five major conclusions:

i) "Economic growth does not automatically improve people's lives, either within nations or internationally," for in the most of economic and technological advancement, the poor might still have limited access to credits and capitals.

ii) The competition between rich and poor countries in the global market is conducted on an unequal basis, for "developing countries have very weak bargaining power in international markets."

ii) "Global markets do not operate freely" because of restrictions placed by advantaged competitors:

> The restrictions are most evident for goods and for labor. Tariff and non-tariff barriers keep out many manufacturers from developing countries, and immigration restrictions prevent workers from migrating in search of higher returns for their labor.
>
> Trade barriers in industrial countries protect national markers from imports from a whole range of countries—rich and poor. Non-tariff measures, for example, are imposed mostly on products in which developing countries are more competitive—on intensive-intensive exports such as textiles, clothing and footwear. And tariff levels, for a wide range of goods, increase with the level of processing. This is true for spices, jute and vegetable oils as well as for tropical fruits, vegetables and beverages. Such increases discourage developing countries from processing their primary commodities—from making chocolate out of cocoa or carpet-backing out of jute.[22]

---

21. *Ibid.*
22. *Human Development Report 1992*, 5-6.

iv) "The free working of markets often tend to increase the disparities between rich and poor." Thus, the world community needs policies in place to provide a social safety net for poor nations and poor people. The result will be that global efficiency will be combined with global equity.

v) "Industrial and developing countries have the opportunity to design a new global compact—and to ensure sustainable human development for all in a peaceful world." Looking back at history, all will learn from past failures; past failures will be sources of instruction and not sources of political paralysis or inaction.[23]

Any economic development that does not pay attention to human development will be a sheer propaganda. Human development is person-and-community-centered. A human's full potential is developed in the community of persons. In this way, community becomes a reflection of the persons whose development it embodies; hence S. I. Udoidem states:

> A community is developed when the full human potentials are harnessed for the purpose of promoting mutual welfare, growth, creativity and meaning in striving for good over bad and wrong. It is only in a humane community that the culture of maintenance and concernfulness will be cultivated so that the rural roads will be maintained, drugs and doctors will be found in hospitals. For the community to be developed the schools must be properly equipped and staffed so that the best can be brought out of the community children. We have a community only when the conscience of our public persons are tailored toward caring for the common good as against their private interest.[24]

The common good secured by community and person-centered development is a horizon of self-enhancing values. The various projects (rural electrification, roads, and pipe-borne water) undertaken by many African communities, unassisted by their various governments, are indicative of the realization that they have to champion their own development in the midst of irresponsible governments. Robin Broad et al are correct to call such initiatives, in Asia, Africa and Latin America, "people power," resulting from the failure of governments in the development of their peoples.[25]

---

23. See *Ibid.*, 8.
24. S. I. Udoidem, *Values and National Development*, 30.
25. See Robin Broad et al, 'Development: The Market Is Not Enough,' in *International Political Economy: Perspectives on Global Power and Wealth* eds. Jeffry A. Frieden and David A. Lake (New York: St Martin's Press, 1995), 440.

The Academic Staff Union of Universities (ASUU) in Nigeria ended a seven-month strike action in July 2003. What were the universities striking for? They were striking for better teaching infrastructure so that Nigerian children could be well trained. The *ASUU* members were asking the civilian government of President Olusegun Obasanjo, that allocated only 1% of the budget to education, (a rate far below the United Nations' recommendation of 26%), to pay attention to the provision of adequate infrastructure for the education of Nigerian young people. Ike and Edozien corroborate the UN Human Development Reports in noting six principles, which underline the need and necessity of involving people in development.

Development is to be defined in terms of pro-life; it is pro-people since people are the basic source of development; development pays attention to priorities chosen by the people themselves with which they identify; development has a democratic sustainability for people are masters of their own destiny in their own governance and development; development is brought about by "conscientisation and awareness education," that is, people can be brought to the consciousness of their role in development—an enlightenment that comes through education; development has to be relevant and gradual as it is rooted in the people's circumstances and environment of occurrence.[26] In contrast to these principles that necessarily guide development perspectives, the following hinder people's participation in development.

Elitism or expertism hinders development. Elitism is the view that development has to be solved by experts or some groups with solutions to underdevelopment "made 'abroad' or 'at the continental level' simply to be implemented in the localities of their own choice, with imported experts and in the style of their own choice."[27] Other factors that hinder people's participation in development are emphasis on externalism and quick results; bureaucratic methods of work; under-estimation of people and lack of trust; dislike for public accountability; marginalizing development education; and ignoring the cultural factor in development.[28]

The point is that development is people centered, that is, people are to be put first before profit. In other words, there is a priority of the human person over capital or faceless economics.

One immediately notices the problems faced in Nigeria and many developing economies. There is non accessibility of capital and resources for the disadvan-

---

26. Obiora F. Ike and Ndidi Nnoli Edozien, *Development Is About People Business Is About Ethics*, 12-15.

27. *Ibid.*, 15.

28. See *Ibid.*, 15-17.

taged; lack of funds to undertake projects for self-reliance and self-help; the affordable training capacities are hijacked by a few as their birthright; there is "poor infrastructure and inadequate provisions by government for roads and tele-communications, thus reducing access to markets for community based enterprises"; the middle class is evidently wiped away due to mass poverty; women and youth are grossly marginalized for the family and children are not taken care of because of absence of finance—this hampers investment for the future of the children; there are poor institutional infrastructure of indigenous enterprises and micro-finance intermediaries; and there is lack of proper integration of the various aspects of the social, economic and political spheres in bringing about a participatory atmosphere of co-ordination of the various groups in the society.[29]

Summary of UN Human Development Reports (1990 to 2004)

The United Nations Human 1990 Development Report is titled 'Concept and Measurement of Human Development.' Its chief concern is "the question of how economic growth translates—or fails to translate—into human development. The focus is on people and on how development enlarges their choices. The Report discusses the meaning and measurement of human development, proposing a new composite index. However, its overall orientation is practical and pragmatic."

The 1991 Report, 'Financing Human Development' examines political contribution in human development, and concludes "lack of political commitment rather than financial resources is often the real cause of human development."

'Global Dimension of Human Development' is the title of the 1992 UN Human Development Report. In spite of increase in wealth, the gap between the poor and rich populations continues to widen. The Report points out that "the richest 20% of the population now receives 150 times the income of the poorest 20%." It "suggests that a two-pronged strategy to break away from this situation. First, making massive investments in their people and strengthening national technological capacity can enable some developing countries to acquire a strong competitive edge in international markets (witness the East Asian industrializing tigers). Second, there should be basic international reforms, including restructuring the Bretton Woods institutions and setting up a Development Security Council within the United Nations."

---

29. See *Ibid.*, 25-26.

The UN captioned the 1993 Human Development Report, 'People's Participation.' An authentic human development will have to involve the people. This Report concerns itself with people's participation in the events and processes that shape their lives. It underlined "people-friendly markets, decentralized governance, and community organizations" (especially NGOs—Non Governmental Organizations) as the three major means of people's participation. In any case, the Report states that something has to be done about the problem of increasing unemployment plaguing many countries.

The 1994 UN Report, captioned 'New Dimensions of Human Security,' introduces "a new concept of human security which equates security with people rather than territories, with development rather than arms." People are at the center of security, not things that are external to them.

'Gender and Human Development' was the caption of the 1995 UN Human Development Report. According to this Report, gender analysis should cease to be ideological. The work of women should be included, and gender opportunities enhanced.

The 1996 UN Human Development Report focused on 'Economic Growth and Human Development.' Economic growth is not always good news, the Report says. If it is not managed well, it can create "jobless, voiceless, ruthless, rootless and futureless state of affairs in the face of human development. Thus, human development does not endorse any kind of growth. Its vision of growth is qualitative instead of quantitative. Only qualitative development is a truly sustainable development.

'Human Development to Eradicate Poverty' is the title of the 1997 UN Human Development Report. Its message is that "eradicating poverty everywhere is more than a moral imperative—it is a practical possibility.... The world has the resources and the knowledge to create a poverty-free world in less than a generation."

The 1998 Report, 'Consumption for Human Development,' insists that consumption and production, which are made available to people, should ginger leaders to seek to achieve more equitable and more human advance in the 21st century.

In 1999, the emphasis of the UN Human Development Report was on 'Globalization with a Human Face.' The Report claims that a network of global solidarity in terms of markets, technology, and ideas is needed to enrich the lives of people everywhere. Thus, "the challenge is to ensure that the benefits are shared equitably and that this increasing interdependence works for people—not just profits."

The year 2000 saw the UN Human Development Report concentrating on 'Human Rights and Human Development.' The 2000 Report insists that human rights are intrinsic to development. In fact, to develop is to realize human rights, and human rights "bring principles of accountability, and social justice to the process of human development."

'Making new Technologies work for Human Development' is the caption of the 2001 UN Human Development Report. Technological networks have to be weaved into the map of human development. This will help transform people, and widen their options and horizons.

The 2002 UN Human Development Report, 'Deepening Democracy in a Fragmented World,' emphasizes the idea that politics is as important to successful development as economics. It is difficult to achieve the desired human development where people are poor and have no political power; thus, building democratic governance at all levels of society is a step in the right direction. Better democratic regimes, it is hoped, will reduce poverty. Moreover, the international political environment is changing: "Instead of facing one superpower with thousands of nuclear weapons, we confront the threats of terrorism; proliferating nuclear, chemical, and biological weapons; information warfare; and international drug trade and organized crime."[30]

The UN Human Development Report of 2003 is titled 'Millennium Development Goals: A Compact Among Nations to End Human Poverty.' It recognizes that human development in the world is still vast but uneven. In the midst of "astounding progress," some areas wallow in stagnation and decline. The Report is aware that "balance and stability" in the world will require "the commitment of all nations, rich and poor alike, and a global development compact to extend the wealth of possibilities to all people."

The UN Human Development Report 2004 is titled 'Cultural Liberty in Today's Diverse World.' The Report recognizes human development occurs in many diverse ways, in spite of the fact that there are many sources of affliction of human development such as lack of health care and poor education. However, the underlying motivation of human development in the diverse areas it appeals to is "to search for ways of enhancing people's lives and the freedom they can enjoy. Denial of cultural liberty can generate significant deprivation; impoverishing human lives and excluding people from the cultural connections they have

---

30. Lee H. Hamilton, 'The Making of U.S. Foreign Policy: The Roles of the President and Congress over Four Decades,' in *Rivals of Power: Presidential-Congressional Relations*, James A. Thurber, ed., (Oxford: Rowman & Littlefield Publishers, Inc., 2002), 211.

reason to seek. So the human development perspective can be extended to accommodate the importance of cultural liberty."[31]

There is a connection, the Report insists, between cultural deprivation and economic poverty; hence culture establishes an important relation between relative incomes and absolute human capabilities; but at the same time, deprivation in the local community can lead to absolute deprivation.[32] Deprivation at all levels hampers people's freedom. The Report boldly states:

> The building of humane and just societies demands adequate recognition of the importance of freedoms in general, which include cultural liberty. This calls for securing and constructively expanding the opportunities that people have to choose how they would live and to consider alternative lifestyles. Cultural considerations can figure prominently in these choices. Emphasizing cultural liberty is not exactly the same as going all out for cultural diversity. It is certainly true that allowing diversity in cultural practices can be extremely important, since the exercise of cultural diversity depends on it. This, however, is not the same as championing cultural diversity for its own sake.[33]

Thus, cultural diversity needs to be fostered through an attitude of cooperation and positive participation. An awareness of cultural diversity opens the way for tolerance of others. In this era of economic globalization, people want to participate and be part of the decision-making process regarding the kind of society they want to live in.[34]

So alongside cultural tolerance stands political tolerance. And globalization can incorporate multiple interactions or identities. Cultural diversity should not be seen as a threat to national cultures. One, at the same time, must realize that integration follows a gradual process of understanding that does not happen overnight.[35] We live in a "globally interdependent world" that needs broader bases for citizenship and incorporating the fundamental principles of human rights "into a multicultural strategy for advancing human development—a strategy that benefit everyone."[36] A realization that people live in diverse society calls for sacrifices and tolerance on the side of every member of the society; hence the 2004 Report states:

---

31. *Human Development Report 2004*, 1.
32. *Ibid.*, 1-2.
33. *Ibid.*, 10.
34. *Ibid.*, 8.
35. See *Ibid.*, 115.
36. *Ibid.*, 119.

Democracy and equitable growth are important in fostering cultural inclusion. But they are not enough. Multicultural policies for cultural inclusion—recognizing difference, supporting diversity and mitigating asymmetries of power—are also needed. Individuals have to shed rigid identities if they are to become part of a diverse society. International institutions have to respect other cultural traditions and create enabling conditions for developing local cultural resources. Poor countries and marginalized communities have to be given a greater voice in negotiations involving their cultures and rights and fair compensation for the use of their resources. Only under these circumstances will multiple and complementary identities evolve across national boundaries. Only then will identity and freedom flourish in a culturally diverse world.[37]

In other words, talks about cultural diversity and liberty that close their eyes to the yearning for equality and justice will be mere propagandas.

The bid to eradicate poverty was continued in the World Development Report of 2004 titled 'Making Services Work for Poor People.' The Report insists that the lack of basic services makes poor people suffer severely. Since people are at the center of service provision, the way to achieve effective reform is to give them strong voice in policy making. Thus, service providers will have to learn effective ways of delivering the basic services.

As will be shown in the subsequent parts of this work, I will attempt to indicate the foundations of a philosophy that will take on board a broadly human-centered development that is realizable within a political state of affairs. Such a political state of affairs will be a product of people's compact or covenanted will.

Sustainable Human Development

The shift from thing-centered development to person-centered development is intended to state that, although development involves growth, not every kind of growth enhances persons. Notwithstanding that developmental process and growth will have to be imperative, "the issue is not only *how much* economic growth, but *what kind* of growth. The growth models of developing and industrial countries must become models of sustainable human development."[38]

Sustainable human development is integral and pays attention to the various facets of human life. But one of the things that undermines the global talk about human development or human life is the fact that as more and more people join

---

37. *Ibid.*
38. *Human Development Report 1992*, 2.

the race of economic development more and more people are equally impoverished. In the midst of the joy and comfort that economic development brings,
much poverty still abides for so many in our shared world. The Fathers of the
Vatican II are aware of the fact of mass poverty, when they write:

> Ours is a new age of history with critical and swift upheavals spreading gradu-
> ally to all corners of the earth. They are the products of man's intelligence and
> creative activity, but they recoil upon him, upon his judgments and desires,
> both individual and collective, upon his ways of thinking and acting in regard
> to people and things. We are entitled then to speak of a real social and cultural
> transformation whose repercussions are felt too on the religious level.
>
> In no other age has mankind enjoyed such an abundance of wealth,
> resources and economic well-being; and yet a huge proportion of the people of
> the world is plagued by hunger and extreme need while countless numbers are
> totally illiterate. At no time have men had such a keen sense of freedom, only
> to be faced by new forms of slavery in living and thinking.[39]

The Fathers further point out that alongside the experience of the sense of
unity is also the reality of bitterness that exists between opposing camps; whereas
men and women could boast of a free exchange of ideas, they are still divided as
to what the concepts of their public intercourse mean, deep-rooted in a world
that seems to have lost a sense of spiritual anchor. The modern person emerges
impoverished in his material, economic, social, environmental and spiritual bearing in the face of the so-called scientific and technological progress.

The development of the human person has to be integral and sustainable in all
its aspects. As Valentine Udoh James writes, sustainability is realized when people's abilities are projected beyond external assistance, when leadership from
within is enhanced and adopted to impact on desired goals; and when capacity
from within grows with confidence from knowledge and experience to function
independently and effectively in the on going process of technology, institutional
innovation and change.[40]

---

39. *Vatican II, Pastoral Constitution on the Church in the Modern World* (Gaudium et
    Spes), 7 December 1965, no 4.
40. See Julius S. Prince et al, 'Sustainability of Danfa Ghana Group of Health Projects:
    A 26-year Overview,' in *Sustainable Development in Third World Countries: Applied
    and Theoretical Perspectives* edited by Valentine Udoh James (London: Praeger Pub-
    lishers, 1996), 105.

Development and Environmental Sustainability

The Earth Summit in Rio de Janeiro in 1992 recognized that integrity of people and their environment should be taken together in the search for a sustainable development which should become the creed of everyone: individuals, groups, governments and the governed. In Rio, the United Nations Conference on Environment and Development reaffirmed the United Nations Conference on Human Environment adopted on 16 June 1972 at Stockholm. In the awareness that inter-dependence exists between humans and the environment (the Earth, which is the home of all), the following proclamations were made:

1. Human beings are at the center of concerns for sustainable development. They are entitled to healthy and productive life in harmony with nature.

2. States have, in accordance with the Charter of the United Nations and the principles of international law, the sovereign right to exploit their own resources pursuant to their own environmental and developmental policies, and the responsibility to ensure that activities with their jurisdiction or control do not cause damage to the environment of other States or areas beyond the limits of national jurisdiction.

3. The right to development must be fulfilled so as to equitably meet developmental and environmental needs of present and future generations.

4. In order to achieve sustainable development, environmental protection shall constitute an integral part of the development process...

5. All States and all people shall cooperate in the essential task of eradicating poverty as an indispensable requirement for sustainable development, in order to decrease the disparities in standards of living and better meet the needs of the majority of the people of the world.

6. The special situation and needs of developing countries, particularly the least developed and those most environmentally vulnerable, shall be given special priority. International actions in the field of environment and development should also address the interests and needs of all countries.

7. States shall co-operate in a spirit of global partnership to conserve, protect and restore the health and integrity of the Earth's ecosystem.... States have common but differentiated responsibilities. The developed countries acknowledge the responsibility that they bear in the international pursuit of sustainable development in view of the pressures their

societies place on the global environment and of the technologies and financial resources they command.

8. To achieve sustainable development and a higher quality of life for all people, States should reduce and eliminate unsustainable patterns of production and consumption and promote appropriate demographical policies.

9. States should cooperate to strengthen endogenous capacity building for sustainable development...through exchanges of scientific and technological knowledge, and by enhancing the development, adaptation, diffusion and transfer of technologies.

10. Environmental issues are best handled with the participation of all concerned citizens, at the relevant level. At the national level, each individual shall have appropriate access to information concerning the environment that is held by public authorities...and the opportunity to participate in decision-making processes. States shall facilitate and encourage public awareness and participation by making information widely available. Effective access to judicial and administrative proceedings, including redress and remedy, shall be provided.

11. States shall enact effective environmental legislation. Environmental standards, management objectives and priorities should reflect the environmental and developmental context to which they apply. Standards applied by some countries may be inappropriate and unwanted economic and social cost to other countries, in particular developing countries.

12. States shall cooperate to promote a supportive and open international economic system...Trade policy measures for environmental purposes should not constitute a means of arbitrary or unjustifiable discrimination or a disguised restriction on international trade. Unilateral actions to deal with environmental challenges outside the jurisdiction of the importing country should be avoided. Environmental measures addressing transboundary or global environmental problems should, as far as possible, be based on an international consensus.

13. States shall develop national laws regarding liability and compensation for the victims of pollution and other environmental damage. States shall also cooperate in an expeditious and more determined manner to develop further international law regarding liability and compensation for adverse effects of environmental damage caused by activities within their jurisdiction or control to areas beyond their jurisdiction.

14. States should effectively cooperate to discourage or prevent the relocation and transfer to other States of any activities and substances that cause

severe environmental degradation or are found to be harmful to human health.

15. ....the precautionary approach shall be widely applied by States according to their capabilities. Where there are threats of serious or irreversible damage, lack of full scientific certainty shall not be used as a reason for postponing cost-effective measures to prevent environmental degradation.

16. National authorities should endeavor to promote the internalization of environmental costs and the use of economic instruments, taking into account the approach that the polluter should, in principle, bear the cost of pollution, with due regard to the public interest and without distorting international trade and investment.

17. Environmental impact assessment, as a national instrument, shall be undertaken for proposed activities that are likely to have a significant adverse impact on the environment and are subject to a decision of a competent national authority.

18. States shall immediately notify other States of any disasters or other emergencies that are likely to produce sudden harmful effects on the environment of those States. Every effort shall be made by the international community to help States so afflicted.

19. States shall provide prior and timely notification and relevant information to potentially affected States on activities that may have a significant adverse trans-boundary environmental effect and shall consult with those States at an early stage and in good faith.

20. Women have a vital role in environmental management and development. Their full participation is therefore essential to achieve sustainable development.

21. The creativity, ideals and courage of the youth of the world should be mobilized to forge a global partnership in order to achieve sustainable development and ensure a better future for all.

22. Indigenous people and their communities, and other local communities, have a vital role in environmental management and development...States should recognize and duly support their identity, culture and interests and enable their effective participation...

23. The environment and natural resources of people under oppression, domination and occupation shall be protected.

24. Warfare is inherently destructive of sustainable development. States shall therefore respect international law providing protection for the environment in times of armed conflict and co-operate…

25. Peace, development and environmental protection are interdependent and indivisible.

26. States shall resolve all their environment disputes peacefully and by appropriate means in accordance with the Charter of the United Nations.

27. States shall cooperate in good faith and in a spirit of partnership in the fulfillment of the principles embodied in this Declaration and in the further development of international law in the field of sustainable development.[41]

It is the responsibility of all—citizens and governments alike—to make the earth retain its dignity and be safe for all.

Of all factors that mock integral human development, poverty is the greatest: "Global poverty is one of the greatest threats to the sustainability of the physical environment and to the sustainability of human life. Most of the poor live in the most ecologically vulnerable areas—80% of the poor in Latin America, 60% in Asia and 50% in Africa. They overuse their marginal lands for fuel wood and for subsistence and cash crop production, further endangering their physical environment, their health and the lives of their children. In developing countries, it is not the quality of life that is at risk—it is life itself."[42] It is not enough to identify places where the greatest number of the world's poor live; it is important to bend down and see the poor within the social, economic and political structures in which they exist. I am afraid that governments in particular and human communities in general may be knowingly or unknowingly building structures that manufacture the poor. Some of these structures will have to be exposed to help shade light on the brand of development that will lay the theoretical foundations for better economic and human development.

---

41. Michael Grubb et al eds., *The 'Earth Summit' Agreements; A Guide and Assessment: An Analysis of the Rio '92 UN Conference on Environment and Development* (London: Earthscan Publications Ltd., 1993), 87-89.

42. *Human Development Report 1992*, 2.

6

Machines and Structures that Manufacture the Poor

Our world is a machine that manufactures the poor. Our structures are the facilities that hatch the eggs of poverty. Our land is a maintenance machine that services the structures that generate the poor.

The fact of sin, injustice and poverty and other moral evils tends to suggest to some minds that the first human beings were not created perfect. Sin or poverty, in this regard, is a natural imperfection. Since society has been evolving from nomadic to sedentary life, from polygamy to monogamy, some think that human society will out-grow slavery, poverty and political colonialism. This is an evolutionist view about the reality of sin, injustice, poverty and moral evil. But this argument is flouted and flawed by the fact that moral evil, injustice and poverty seem to be on the increase.

The injustice and poverty that affect the lives of many people assume alarming rate even in the midst of affluence. There are the attitudes, policies, economic sanctions, religious reasons, scientific and technological advancements that build structures in the human environment. These support the maintenance of poverty and injustice: oppression of the people, fraud at high places, lack of funding in educational, medical and social spheres.

In the conceptual schemes of the "man come of age," the words, 'the poor,' 'poverty,' 'the oppressed,' 'oppression' and 'injustice' have become of the same social genre. Commenting on the Lucan beatitudes, Segundo Galilea articulates: "the 'poor,' the 'hungry,' and 'those who weep' for their affliction are all the same category of people."[1] The theology of liberation of Latin America defines the poor against the background of inhuman situations within the socio-economic

---

1. Segundo Galilea, *The Beatitudes: To Evangelize as Jesus Did* (New York: Orbis Books Maryknoll, 1984), 2.

set-up. But the poor will include, in addition, those who are discriminated against in terms of their culture and religion. In this regard, the socially degraded, the politically alienated, the materially disadvantaged, the economically insolvent, the anthropologically impoverished and the religiously alienated are our poor in this book.

What Is Done About the Poor?

A lot of sympathy is expressed about the poor. Jesus talks about the poor, and even called our attention to their presence in our midst; Jesus announced that the primary beneficiaries of the Good news are the poor (Luke 4:18).

Injustice done to the poor is widely condemned by many people. Aid and services are sent to the poor and poor countries. In July 2003, President George W. Bush of US announced that ten billion US dollars are to be spent on fighting AIDS in Africa. Books upon books are written about the poor and the need for a just world. And so the giving of 'handouts' to the poor and oppressed has become as charitable as it is legitimized. One only needs to be relevant and good according to the spirit of the age in responding to the needs of the poor in practical terms, by proclaiming one's gift to the poor openly. The gifts are given as if prayerfully: "O God, here is my gift for the poor. I love the poor and detest poverty!"

We are charitable indeed! But I am afraid we have got the whole thing wrongly. Even in our calculated effort to be charitable, pretend-lovers of the poor, to excuse ourselves and shift the blames of our actions, we have remained carriers of injustice. Our world, our action is rather a machine that manufactures the poor. Before I develop this further, it is good to say a few words about God and the poor.

God And The Poor

It is not a good thing to be poor. The Old Testament sees poverty as a curse, an evil. God himself is not poor for it will at once be disastrous and terrible for us if we have a poor God. The Psalmist praised the richness of God, which swells like a river in heaven, brimming over and thus providing for the earth (Ps. 64). Since man is not God, and poverty is a curse, yet it is not very easy to exercise the required control over riches without turning one's face against God. Thus, the wisdom writer prays for the grace in-between two extremes.

> Two things I beg you, (Lord) do not grudge me them before I die: Keep false-hood and lies far from me, give me neither poverty nor riches, grant me only my share of bread to eat, for fear that surrounded by plenty, I should fall away and say, Yahweh who is Yahweh? Or else, in destitution, take to stealing and profane the name of God. (Proverb 30:7-9).

Jesus does not legitimize poverty. Although much has erroneously been preached to suggest the contrary under the cloak that Jesus was born at Bethlehem in a poor manger for he was of poor parents, who belonged to the low class comparatively. Granted that his parents were not of a high financial class of the Jews (at least status-wise), they were not however beggars. Joseph, the foster father of Jesus, had a profession (carpentry). And the Gospel text, "while they were there the time came for her to have her child and she gave birth to a son, her first born. She wrapped him in swaddling clothes, and laid him in a manger because there was no room for them at the inn," (Luke 2: 6) does not suggest that Joseph did not procure a place in the inn because he was materially poor, that is, because he could not afford the bills. However variable the interpretations of scholars and exegetes might be, the thrust of the Lucan text is the absence of a vacant room in the inn, not discrimination or the inability to provide money.

The impression has wrongly been given that Jesus canonizes poverty in the Lucan Beatitudes for he makes it a source of special values and graces. Jesus does neither create the conditions for poverty nor love the sight of the poor; however, he makes the poor the best recipients of his Gospel and kingdom of God. Segundo has reflected on this point, when he writes: "The Kingdom is for the poor not because they are good or because they are better than others…but simply because they are poor and needy."[2] Along this line, Albert Nolan, in his article, 'The Option for the Poor in South Africa' highlights what attracted the company around Jesus. Jesus' company included sinners and tax collectors, people who were hungry and thirsty and begging in the streets. Jesus was moved to identify with them not because of their piety but because of their suffering or affliction.

Scholars are yet to find the most fitting interpretation to what Jesus meant, when he said: "you have the poor with you always…." (Matthew 26:10). It does not either imply that Jesus is contradicting the New Testament tradition that emphasized the obligation to provide for the poor. It suggests that Jesus will not immediately give his blessing to any kind of action, packed with self-glory, claimed to mitigate the suffering of the poor. Judas Iscariot did not bring the poor into the discussion because he loved them; his was a pretext for love of

---

2.   *Ibid.*, 14.

money. Jesus does not in turn canonize poverty as pointed out above, but a quick handout given just to avoid them does not solve the problem. Developed countries can build walls to protect themselves, and give handouts to developing countries to keep them stationed in their own environment.

The poor in human standards are accursed, disadvantaged and abandoned. But for God, their state, created by human exigencies, is in turn a fertile ground for hatching the values of the Gospel. And to them is likened the recipients of the kingdom of God on earth, for "the kingdom is to be anticipated here in history, and that this anticipation will lead to love, justice, freedom peace, and a community of brothers and sisters—then the Gospel of the kingdom must already be at work today, changing unjust situations into just ones, oppressive ones into liberating ones, divisive ones into communitarian ones."[3] So oppression, poverty-forsakenness and injustice are antithetical to the Gospel standards; love, justice, freedom peace and fraternity are at once divine and human values that are realizable only with the co-penetration of the divine spirit and human structures.

God is involved in the affairs of the poor as a compassionate being and a co-sufferer in Jesus. He raises the poor from ash heaps against the expectation of world powers (Luke 1: 39). This is one of the important points process theology rightly insists upon. God models his action on service and care, not on power or domination. Denis Carol comments on this way of God:

> Rather than stand over and against creation, God enters it, is part of it, draws it upwards and forwards. All things have their inner (cognitive) and their outer (quantitative) aspects. They retain their freedom and their purposiveness even in their relation to God. God is the persuasive lure of their inner life. In this view, God feels with the universe in its pain, in its failure, in its joy. Not only does God give life and love, God is responsive to that life and love.[4]

God, in Jesus, has specially got involved in creation and human affairs; in the same way, He bridges the gap between the poor and the rich, the 'haves' and 'have-nots,' by the Gospel of *kenosis*—self-emptying. God, affected by human suffering, empties himself in Jesus (Phil. 2:6-11) in solidarity with men and women in their weakness. In Christ, God is involved in ordering things aright; uprooting human structures that take the advantage of the weakness of the poor (Luke 4:18-19). In saying, "Blessed are you who are poor for yours is the king-

---

3.   *Ibid.*, 15.
4.   Denis Carroll, *Towards A Story of the Earth* (Dublin 1: Dominicans Publications, 1987), 168.

dom of God" (Luke 6:20), Luke indicates the priority of the envoy of God to restore wholeness and justice to the poor.[5] In contrast, then, it is our thesis that our world has rather remained an agent of planting structures that maintain poverty. If we do not opt for people, over dry economics, we may be consciously or unconsciously building structures that maintain rather than remove poverty.

At the International level: Machines that Manufacture the Poor

The dominant powers have not ceased their battles in their extremes. They fight and the grass (the poor) suffers. The poverty that is very evident in the world in the midst of plenty humiliates the international community. Most of the world's economic and political programs end up voting out the poor. Funny enough mankind has gone back to the thesis it set out to disprove that conflict is not the order of nature, that might is not right.

In retrospect, Machiavelli had argued that a ruler of the human world should possess the aggressivity of the lion and the cunning of the fox. Human history, thought Hobbes, had shown man as wolf to man. In Hobbesian style, Hegel concluded that might was right. Friedrich Nietzsche opted for the shattering of the "old law tables" that put sanity in man and in its replacement enthroned his superman who would be beyond good and evil; he would be his own moral law and stand as an incarnation of domination. This attitude pumped the whole air of Europe. The world was set for a war of aggression.

The First imperialist war broke out (between August 1, 1914 and Nov. 11.1918) and lasted for 4 years, 3 months and 10 days, and 38 states were involved. What interests us here is to note:

> The war brought incalculable suffering to the peoples. The total number of causalities reached 10 million killed, as many as had been killed in all earlier European wars over one thousand years, and 20 million wounded, 3.5 million of which were crippled. During the First World War Poisonous gases were used for the first time killing a total of one million people. The war with all its concomitant sufferings and privations, hunger and devastation placed mankind on the edge of a precipice.[6]

---

5.   See John Fuellenbach, *The Kingdom of God: The Message of Jesus Today* (New York: Orbis Books, 1995), 127.

6.   Soviet Monthly Digest August 1989, 104.

At the end of World War I, the Predatory Treaty of Versailles was signed and the world re-divided between capitalist states. But this did not suppress the urge to dominate; hence the foundation was laid for new contradictions. World War II broke out, drew into its vortex 61 states and about 80% of the World population and lasted for 6 years. The struggle for power among the big horns brought incalculable suffering, poverty and privation to the people of the world. Going through this historic and sad memory, one must not fail to assert:

> The Second World War was the greatest test faced by mankind in the twentieth Century and, arguably, in the whole history of human civilization. Nazis tried not only to subjugate the whole world but to establish a global 'new order,' to trample with jackboots the centuries old cultural values of the world, to violate the moral norms of humanity, and to make hatred of man, racial and ethnic intolerance a universal moral law.[7]

Mankind had to sacrifice tens of thousands of lives on the altar of the Great Victory to stop the enslavement of the world by Adolfus Hitler.

The last decade of the 20th century saw the Allied Forces bombardment of the Iraq of Saddam Hussein to prevent the repeat of the pursuit of ambitions of the type of Hitler. Terrorist organizations are being dismantled because of the inhuman tragedy of September 11, 2001 attack at the World Trade Center in New York. The 21st century, in its third year, again started with a war against Saddam Hussein in which innocent civilians were killed and many coalition soldiers lost their lives to free Iraq. By 7th of September 2004, 1000 American soldiers had lost their lives since the announcement, by President George W. Bush, of the end of major combats two and a half years ago. And so our world has been impoverished by the tragedies of two world wars and numerous terrorist attacks in which many lives have been lost. They are yet to make a comprehensive list of the number of Iraqis killed in the war to overthrow Saddam Hussein and fight terrorism.

Poverty, at the world level, has become, in addition to oppression, synonymous with human despair for an end to life, victims of nuclear war, third world, those who live perpetually under the threat of war. With nuclear bombs and biological weapons, the world is set on a keg of gunpowder. Even worse, nuclear bombs are tested in the territories of poor countries and the world's industrial waste shipped to them.[8] When poor countries ask for money to promote human

---

7. *International Affairs A monthly Journal of Political Analysis* (Moscow: All-Union Znaniye Society, Moscow, 1985),70.

8. See S. I. Udoidem, *Values and National Development*, 36-50.

dignity and agriculture they are given war weapons for self-annihilation at an attractive rate. Expressing concern over this calculated evil-doing, a Nigerian top military officer and also a one time ambassador to one of the neighboring states expressed his shock over the fact that a loan from one of the overseas banks for agricultural development was refused Nigeria whilst she got without delay millions of US dollars on loan for manufacture and maintenance of ammunition, while many lose the battle against hunger in the same country.

The question persists: is the world getting better in the face of scientific and technological advancement? This is certainly an issue where opinions will greatly differ. Tribal wars and ethnic cleansing in East Africa and other parts of the world continue.

The West have learnt the evils of war; hence, they do everything to avert wars within their territories while the Third World countries battle in the quarrels engineered by the super powers to make them viable customers for their products (war weapons); hence Julius Nyerere warned African states before hand. He condemned the first scramble for Africa but pointed out a more serious one that would be destructive of the African personality in no less measure. It is one in which Africans themselves act as means in the hands of outsiders to fight themselves. On this note, then, people talk of African unity not for the purpose of uniting Africa, but for the purpose of dividing it. It is no longer the case of Africa alone. The evils of bombs and terrorist attacks put every country on the front line; everyone is a potential target. Human creations of weapons of mass destruction and their use have made our common world a war zone.

There is the anthropological impoverishment of the black man all over the globe. He is toyed with, cruelly treated, labeled anything and classified anyhow, accused of everything wrong and manipulated to infinite variables. Their so-called Western experts in biology and racial classification have assigned a place to the African that he cannot easily get over. Thus, the *status quo* is then that an African is (one who is) poor. Since I am an African, I am poor. I am supposed to be poor. Bassie Head once wrote: "Poverty has a home in Africa—like a second skin. It may be the only place on earth where it is worn with an unconscious dignity."[9] There seems to be then a calculated maintenance of poverty in the Third World and Africa in particular. Like all other groups, the matriculated union of the Third Worlds, Africa for them, represents a reality in which the memory of the crudest cultural past of mankind is conserved. James Baldwin drives this point home when he writes "Europeans never had the remotest intention of rais-

---

9.   Bassie Head, *Tales of Tenderness and Power* (Johannesburg: A.D. Douker, 1989), 41.

ing Africans to the Western level, of sharing with them the instruments of physical, political, or economic power. It was precisely their intention, their necessity, to keep the people they ruled in a state of cultural anarchy, that is, simply in a barbaric state."[10]

After the scramble for Africa, the age of colonialism, a structural type of destabilization has been articulated in the concept of *anthropological Poverty*. This is meant, in Donal Dorr's own words, "the disruption of the traditional life of African peoples, the destruction of the social fabric of their societies, and the loss of their values, cultures, and religious beliefs. It is a form of impoverishment caused by colonialism and, more recently by economic and cultural neo-colonialism."[11]

African peoples are walking on a platform eroded by colonialism; surely wherever colonialism is a fact, the indigenous culture begins to rot, a subculture emerges, condemned to exist on the margin allowed it by European culture. "This then," writes Baldwin, "becomes the province of a few men, the elite, who find themselves placed in the most artificial conditions, deprived of any revivifying contract with the masses of the people. Under such conditions this sub-culture has no chance of growing into an active living culture."[12] It requires a Herculean effort to work against this *status quo* inherited by Africans; and the bid to eradicate poverty from African soil would be likened to the effort of one who mistakenly fights the flame instead of the base of the fire.

It is because of this cunning attitude that we think that colonialism, at the onset, was meant to impoverish Africa, even with the invocation of the Bible alongside the colonial expedition. James Marcus lamented that when the Christian arrived in Africa, he had the Bible and the African had the land, but before long, the African had the Bible and the Christian (Missionary) had the land. Colonialisation does not objectively enrich a people; it makes them poor and incapable. Here the Bible is bound up with Western colonialism and some Africans think it is continuing the work of colonialism, underdevelopment and oppression in the way it had been introduced by the West.

The brand of poverty, which the Africans are battling against, is not just that they are poor but that someone is dictating to them the way their economy is to be run. African leaders do not want to care, but are willing to co-operate for their own selfish interests. How can Africa survive if her political destiny is not in her hands, when she is manipulated directly or indirectly from outside? Aimé Cesaire

---

10.   James Baldwin, *Nobody Knows My Name* (London: Corgi Books, 1973), 38.

11.   Donald Dorr, *Spiritual and Justice* (New York: Orbis Books Maryknoll, 1984), 167.

12.   James Baldwin, *Nobody Knows My Name*, 39.

sums it up when he says that any political and social regime, which destroys the self-determination of a people also destroys the creative power of that people. Thus, the more African countries borrow from international monetary institutions, the more bankrupt they become! International politics and market economy are manipulated against African countries. Foreigners determine the price of their resources. These are the principalities and powers that militate against the upliftment of the African or the black person.

On the Nigerian Level

Our laws, decrees, attitudes and institutions are party to machines that manufacture the poor.

Economy: Each regime inherits the debts of the other. No country that spends itself in paying debts is solvent enough to survive. The Nigerian economy could be a perpetual receptor of forces and instructions that work against it. We consult the West on how our economy is to be run. We invest and carry our money to store with them, yet they find it insecure to invest with us. It is said that one Nigerian fugitive of the third republic had a huge sum of money overseas capable of paying 1/3 of the debts of African nations. As long as money is only controlled by a few, we remain poor as a whole. This attitude of the selfish emptying of the nations purse is encouraged by our own brand of running our economy, a state built on kleptocracy. This creates structural poverty objectified and institutionalized in our trade and politics. The right the present so-called democracy gives the ordinary citizen is the right to be exploited by greedy and reckless politicians. In this regard, Africa's underdevelopment, especially Nigeria, is as a result of the combined work of colonizers (Europeans) and Africans in government.[13]

There is the so-called distribution business obtainable in government owned firms, the unmerited profit of the boss simply because he is a top government official, and the businessman who has card for the actual distribution, fixing his own price and in turn is paid by the poor fellow who must buy such commodities. Generally, the market situation tells much about the poor who buy at the same price as the rich. Yet the government is poised to improve the lot of the poor!

Even a call for the privatization of firms or businesses does not solve the problem. When the call is made, only the rich come forward to buy them. Then the

---

13. See Richard Sandbrook, The Politics of Africa's Economic Recovery (Cambridge: Cambridge University Press, 1993), 21.

exploitation here is even doubled. In whichever case, no one can claim in the open that he or she is interested in helping the poor. The Nigerian economy is planned to benefit the rich, to take from the poor and give to the rich, the politically greedy. The present political economy has largely succeeded in creating greed and affluent politicians and a listless, scarred public. In fact, the myth that communalism is a way of African life has to be abandoned. Our experience so far is that the government, the politician is the greatest armed robber, victimizer or oppressor in Nigeria.

Education: It is clear that the self-acclaimed bid by the Nigerian government to banish illiteracy has not yielded any practical results. By 1990, there was propaganda to banish illiteracy by the year 2000. Today, it is 2004; the structures to realize such a dream have collapsed and the dream itself has vanished. Nigeria began the year 2003 with the ASUU strike; it was in its seventh month in July 2003. The government was not bothered and was not prepared to fulfill any agreement. The executive and the legislature were distracted with their election campaigns, while Nigerian university students were increasingly getting bored at home.

Universities and public secondary schools have collapsed. Only private schools are effectively in operation. The private schools are very expensive and outside of the reach of the poor. The children of the poor will have to wait to go back to ill-equipped schools with dilapidated structures, where they pass out as sons and daughters of their fathers, who must look up to the rich as a slave looks up to his master for his daily bread.

This tragedy can play out in a different form. The present government's interest in education does not lie beyond primary education. Now the best available for each citizen is basic primary education. As for the development of manpower and talents that comes at the secondary and university levels, there is the calculated intention to destroy higher education in Nigeria so that when the need arises, Nigeria will fall back to the expatriates who would flood the Nigerian market with their technical expertise and food. Another form of intellectual colonialisation is on the way. As always, however, a good number of Nigerian elite will benefit through the back door!

The Church

The Nigerian Church has shown much enthusiasm in helping and speaking for the poor by practices and through series of documents such as Pastoral Letters,

Conference Communiqués, Exhortations and other writings. Thus, under the umbrella of the Catholic Bishops Conference of Nigeria, Obiora Ike writes:

> The task for the Nigerian Church today must be first and foremost that of a fundamental option for the poor, the marginalized—God's children who have been brutalized and dehumanized by an insensitive, alienated and unconcerned elite. Dealing with poverty, therefore, must be an imperative of the highest order in the Nigerian context.[14]

The Nigerian hierarchy is indeed ministering to the poor. The clergy are experts in Church matters, thus they give direction to the poor to follow suit. All the same, the Pharisees of Jesus time were also experts in religious laws. In fact, they articulated in their tradition about 613 commandments or prohibitions of the Torah or the *Halakah*, which must be meticulously observed. In these prescriptions, however, Jesus saw a force for oppression that blocked communion with God. So the hierarchy that speaks for the poor, for peace and justice in the name of Christ can be a force unknowingly or knowingly for oppression and poverty. There is, therefore, need for a new hermeneutics of language and services. What do we mean by the poor? Who is serving who? Who are the oppressors? The oppression to which the Pharisees contributed was borne out of an in-built attitude and rule within the ecclesiastical framework until Jesus psychoanalyzed the structures.

The Co-operation of all in Oppression!

In the final analysis, the state and its institutions, the Church and individuals, either by omission or commission, are the machines and structures that manufacture the poor. Everyone at whatever level is caught up in this whole issue of keeping the flag flying for the generation of poverty. There is need then for a proper psychoanalysis in order to usher in a model that can transform our operational base.

It is not enough to give money to the poor, especially when one pretends to give them in alms what we own together with them. Attracted by the suffering of the poor, not their virtues, we are called to uproot structures that keep the poor in chains. These structures could be material, institutional or spiritual. Whichever one, one thing is clear: God does not ordain poverty; poverty is contingent,

---

14. *Justice: The Foundation For Peace, Catholic Bishops of Nigeria Speak*, iv.

things could be otherwise. Commitment and option for the poor should go beyond theoretical statements. Dorr has counseled:

> to make an option for the poor is not to opt for poverty but to opt for people. It is to commit oneself to acting and living in a way that respects people, especially those who are not treated with respect in our society. It is to proclaim by one's action that people are more important than the systems that deprive them their basic rights—the right to eat, the right to work, the right to participate in decision-making....[15]

Even, having sought the help of Dorr to buttress my point, I am quite sure we are yet to find a counter-mechanism that will destroy the global and structural machines that manufacture the poor. It is still an object of mediation that we live in a world where affluence co-exists side by side with massive poverty. And our presupposition can affect the way we look at things: "Political practices and religious teachings cannot be understood except in terms of their root presuppositions. The practical running of a state makes sense only in the light of the assumptions of the people. Revolutions happen not only because policies are unjust but also because radical philosophies differ. Policies flow out of premises. The same is true of religion."[16]

How do we explain human development in a century so rich, so poor? We need a new conceptual tool to re-interpret society and found political associations. The next section will attempt to offer a conceptual tool, in that direction, against the backdrop of African philosophy.

---

15. D. Dorr, *Spirituality and Justice*, 77.
16. Thomas Dubay, *Happy Are You Poor: The Simple Life and Spiritual Freedom* 2d., (San Francisco: Ignatius Press, 2003), 39.

PART II

Development and Philosophical Considerations

7

Philosophical Development in the light of Nation-Building

What Is Philosophical Development?

There have been many philosophies in the past. People have philosophies of life. Everyone has one kind of philosophy or another. Along this line, we can outline, under three headings, attitudes towards philosophy, namely: philosophy as an existential tendency of people; philosophy as a personal cherished way of life; and philosophy as an intellectual discipline.

To the first category, it is defensible that every group of people has a philosophy consciously or unconsciously, at least, as a guiding principle that conditions their collective line of valuation as a people. T. Uzodinma Nwala has put it that "philosophy may mean a world-view (weltanschaung), that is, the basic beliefs which people have...about the origin, nature and end of the universe, life or existence whether the ideas are explicitly stated or implied in action."[1] When people adopt a particular attitude as culturally unique and invaluable to them, we can call it their philosophy.

When the man on the street (representing the second category) prefers a certain line of action to another, he acclaims it his motto, his 'philosophy.' Shall we deny the title of philosophy to it? No. This same man when he hears philosophy talked about in a way that transcends his knowledge looks to it as, "a possession of wisdom that equips its possessor to interpret life situations." Furthermore, when one gives a well-sustained argument on a given topic, one may be referred to as a 'philosopher.' Philosophy, in this regard, Izu Marcel Onyeocha says, is "a very complicated abstract intellectual activity meant for only an advanced breed of men. Thus philosophers are regarded as lone rangers as they are useless theoreticians."

---

1.   T. Uzodinma Nwala, *Igbo Philosophy* (Nigeria: Latern Books, 1985), 2.

Certainly, philosophy as understood by philosophers (the third category) is not just any kind of thing. Etymologically, the word *philosophy* comes from two Greek words, namely: *philia* and *sophia*, that is, love/friend and wisdom respectively, which literally translates as love of/with wisdom. Philosophy is a science understood not as a mere statement of facts of knowledge but as an organized body of knowledge. As a scientific discipline, it is a critical examination of views and an evaluative tool for testing the pretensions of beliefs. Although there is no universally accepted definition of philosophy in the intellectual arena, this does not mean that it has no range. Its range is a comprehensive and systematic view of reality. To unravel this, philosophers voice out from different points of view.

For Plato, philosophy is the science that is the science of itself and of others, that is, the most excellent of arts that equips its possessor with wisdom. It is simply a "science of being as being," for Aristotle. John Dewey affirms that philosophy "is the criticism of criticisms." Dewey believes that the chief functions of philosophy are to free men's minds from bias and prejudice, and enlarge their perception of the world about them. Ludwig Wittgenstein defines philosophy from a linguistic point of view when he says that it is "the logical clarification of thoughts, and its function is the uncovering of one another of plain nonsense and of bumps that the understanding has got by running its head up, the limits of language." It is William James' belief that philosophy is "a collective name for questions which have not been answered to the satisfaction of all that asked them."[2] One will have to state, however, that all these definitions put forward by philosophers are complementary rather than contradictory.

Development, as we have said, is a gradual process of growth. But how do we describe philosophical development? Bernard J. F. Lonergan highlights that "if one attends to the circle of development itself and to the structure of what can be known of proportionate being, the development is philosophic."[3] Thus, a development that is proportionate to a human being could be referred to as philosophical. By philosophical development in general is meant a process in which the person engages in actualizing himself or herself, that is, a search for self-fulfillment of the person in a relational world backed by wisdom. Socrates tells us that an unexamined life is not worth living. Plato insists on getting philosophers to tutor politicians, for the health of the body politic when he opts for philosopher-kings.[4] Philosophical development will answer how far wisdom or practical rea-

---

2.   See *The Encyclopedia of Philosophy* s. v. 'Philosophy' by John Passmore, vols. 5 & 6.

3.   Bernard J. F. Lonergan, *Insight: A Study of Human Understanding* (London: Longmans, 1957), 458.

4.   Plato, *Letters: VII* 326a-6.

sonableness has been employed in the progress of persons and their societies in the quest for meaning, relevance and human flourishing. It is in this light that we can re-examine the growth of the African nations in their march towards liberation and self-fulfillment, wading through the waters of colonialism and imperialism.

The Search for An African Nation in Development (Nigeria)

In the search for socio-political stability, Nigeria has been many things both to herself and to others. Sometimes she exaggerates her worth, at other times she under-estimates her capacity in cases where she ought not. In many occasions, she has blown herself out of proportion and ended up a victim of insolent pride. All these culminate in the quest for an authentic identity. However, she does not seem to have realized that "the path that every human community must walk in its quest to ascertain deeper meaning of its existence is the path of truth about man in his totality."⁵ Under the reign of the military dictator—Sani Abacha—Nigerian soldiers were restoring democracy to Liberia, and Nigeria was importing fuel. Then Nigeria came to be described as a nation that exported what it had not but imported what it had!

With this kind of image in the present in which we live, for the problems with which we struggle from year to year, to consult history primarily in order to refresh and strengthen our awareness in this regard will be enlightening. Just as John Paul II has put it, "if you want to understand the situation in Africa, its past and its picture, we must start from the truth of the African person—the truth of every African in his or her concrete and historical setting."⁶ Therefore, Nigeria's case is not an exception. To adjust comfortably in the right direction in the present for a better future, we will evaluate the past briefly to see the quality of existence that has accrued so far.

At one time or another, every country has struggled with poverty, power, self-affirmation, self-sufficiency, war and peace: call these economic, social, political and cultural crises. Some countries have solved some or most of them. Since some countries have succeeded in solving some of these problems, it means that these problems are essentially surmountable. Thus, they cannot be accepted as permanent ways of life; they can be otherwise if the right attitude is adopted. Edmund

---

5.   John Paul II, *Africa, Apostolic Pilgrimage* (USA: St Paul Editions, 1980), 200.
6.   *Ibid.*

Husserl has reminded us that a particular attitude, (that is, phenomenological epoche), is needed to ensure a fair meeting between the subject and the object. With it, "the experienced world is kept exactly with the contents which actually belong to it."[7] In this spirit, a closer scrutiny is needed for the political, economic and social sectors on the Nigerian polity.

The political realm has not given good guidance for the healthy establishment of an organized political economy. Many African countries such as Nigeria continue to struggle to keep stable economy. These "African countries have from time to time fallen victim to the manipulations of the international capitalist system. The growth or stagnation of their economies is determined primarily by fluctuations in the needs and interests of the dominant nations."[8] As a reaction against this, most African nations such as Nigeria have therein intensified their call and move towards self-sufficiency, with the basic aim to build or pursue a good program for economic development; however, so far, both the ideal and the means have run the risk of lopsided development. At one time, emphasis is placed on industry; at another it is on agriculture, and so on. The overall outcome is not coherent; it is only a product of truncated and contradictory policies and ideologies. Nigerian leaders lack economic wisdom in managing the nation's vast resources. Nigeria is at present a pathetic country that struggles to survive in the midst of affluence.

The Nigerian political scene has allured many writers precisely because it assumes the role of a light in the dark for all other sectors of the nation. Thus, the political reality remains the talk of the day, a nation immersed in kleptocracy: government robbery and looting of public funds by greedy and reckless politicians. When Chinua Achebe vividly states that "the trouble with Nigeria is simply and squarely a failure of leadership,"[9] he is not mincing words. The cause of the failure of Nigeria as a nation in seemingly all spheres of life is "the seminal absence of intellectual rigor in the political thought of our founding fathers—a tendency to pious materialistic wooliness and self-centered pedestrianism."[10]

There is no doubt that the founding Fathers worked tirelessly for Nigeria's independence. However, part of the wisdom that was at the foundation of their

---

7.   See Alfred Schutz, 'Phenomenology and Social Sciences' in *Phenomenology and Sociology* ed. Thomas Luckmann (New York: Penguin Books, 1978), 276.
8.   Yolamu Barongo 'Alternative Approaches to African Politics' in *Political Science in Africa: A Critical Review*, Yolamu Barongo ed., (London: Zeb Press, 1983), 148.
9.   Chinua Achebe, *The Trouble With Nigeria* (Nigeria: 4th Dimension Publishers, 1983), 1.
10.   *Ibid.*, 11.

aspiration for an ideal Nigerian society could be seen in the following pledges. Nnamdi Azikwe pledged: "Henceforth I shall utilize my earned income to secure my enjoyment of a high standard of living and also to give a helping hand to the needy." In his turn, Obafemi Awolowo said: "I was going to make myself formidable intellectually and morally invulnerable, to make all the money that is possible for a man with my brain and brawn to make in Nigeria."[11] With this kind of intellectual and moral motivation, one wonders whether the outcome of the bid to build a just nation would have been different. Wole Soyinka must be right when he states: "Any faith that places the conscious quest for inner self as goal for which the context of forces are mere battle aid is ultimately destructive of the social potential of that self...Suspect all conscious search for the self's authentic being, this is favorite fodder for the enervating tragic muse."[12] It is not surprising then that, with the frame of mind of the Azikwes and Awolowos, we have had leaders of various dispositions competing, trying to steer the course of the country wherever it suits their interests. Leaders, both civilian and military, replace each other in the reckless scramble for the so-called 'national cake,' Nigerians' name for the common good! What a misnomer!

One is aware that international politics is largely manipulated to suit the taste of developed nations, and that countries have had foreign rule or domination forced on them. Alioune Diop, in the opening address presented on the occasion of Conference of Negro-African Writers and Artists on Wednesday September 19, 1956 in Sorbonnes Amphitheatre Descartes in Paris rightly stated: "A people deprived of political sovereignty finds it very nearly impossible to re-create, for itself, the image of its past, this perpetual re-creation being an absolute necessity for, if not indeed, the definition of a living culture."[13] Tafawa Balewa once observed: "It must be obvious that no Nigerian can be contented so long as any major sector of the economy is controlled by foreigners."[14] However, no one convinces anybody in Nigeria now that the cause of lack of effective co-ordination for the attainment of common good in Nigeria, since it attained self-rule, is due to the experience of colonialism. Colonialism can no longer be taken as the cause of inadequate and ineffective provision of food, light and basic infrastructure to

11. James Booth, *Writers and Politics in Nigeria* (London: Hodder and Stoughton, 1981), 49. See also Chinua Achebe, *The Trouble with Nigeria,* 11.

12. Wole Soyinka, *The Man Died* (Prison Notes) (England: Penguin Boos, 1972), 88-89.

13. James Baldwin, Nobody Knows My Name (London: Corgi Books, 1965, 25.

14. James O. Ojiako, *13 Years of Military Rule 1966-79* (Lagos: Daily Times Publication), 1.

the Nigerian people; it is not a reason to neglect education and loot the nation's treasuries.

Although Nigeria professed to be united in spite of whatever differences (tribe or tongue), daily experience in Nigeria betrays this pledge. One's place of origin, tribe, and tongue continue to determine what one gets. In short, statism in Nigeria is a discriminative tool, and should be scrapped. Why? The present state-structure is conducted along ethnic lines. There is a lot of discrimination on account of tribe, religion and tongue, as we have said. In pointing out some of the reasons for the rejection of evils of Nigerianism that occasioned the Biafran revolution, Ojukwu states:

> Nigeria persecuted and slaughtered her minorities; Nigerian justice was a farce; her elections, her census, her politics—her everything—was corrupt. Qualification, merit and experience were discontinued in public service. In one area of Nigeria, for instance, they preferred to turn a nurse who had worked for five years into a doctor rather than employ a qualified doctor from another part of Nigeria; barely literate clerks were made Permanent Secretaries; a university Vice-Chancellor was sacked because he belonged to the wrong tribe.[15]

The evils pointed out in the early years of the Nigerian independence have continued to plague Nigeria still.

When Chinua Achebe states that the problem with Nigeria is that of leadership, he is not making an overstatement. What we have had so far is the logical conclusion of our founding motivation in coming together as an aggregate: to appropriate all the money to ourselves individually in a federally engineered, dramatic deception. The class that controls the instrument of power mostly represents this canker worm. The Nigerian leadership so far is an instrument of individualist appropriation of the so-called national cake at the expense of the masses. It is a tool for the abuse of power that seeks perpetual legitimization of its creed and ego. One recalls the words of Shakespeare, mocking earthly power:

> ...man, proud man;
> Drest in a little of authority,
> Most ignorant of what he is most assured.

---

15.   Chukwuemeka Odumegwu Ojukwu, *Ahiara Declaration: The Principles of the Biafran Revolution (June, 1, 1969)* with the Declaration of Independence, speech before exile, the Cessation Declaration, call from Exile, and The Biafran National Anthem ed. Obi Harrison Ekwonna (Maryland USA: Rising Star Publishers, 2003), 21.

His glassy essence, like an angry ape,
Plays such fantastic tricks before high heaven.
As make the angel weep; who, with our spleens,
Would all themselves laugh mortals.[16]

Both the military and civilian administration are not only continuously haunted by the same ghost but have always remained guilty of the same offence. There seems to be no difference in the way in which either of the groups runs the economy at present. What Nigerians are trying to fix is the degree at which each rips off, raids and rapes the country. In fact, the events of the 2003 elections seem to make others think to prefer a military form of government! We have a system that sponsors individual, group and government fraud, and violence and intimidation by those in power. The 2003 Nigerian elections were regrettably a show of public fraud pontificated over by the president and his group of matriculated rogues, wearing the baptismal name of a party—Peoples Democratic Party (PDP).

The spirit of building a cohesive nation has been betrayed by the leaders' lack of vision, and a perpetually misdirected emphasis. A way forward is to re-think our point of departure. One agrees with Gustav Emil Muller when he declares: "Man discovers himself as essentially or as Husserl says a transcendental subject, when he knows himself constituted by all that which he essentially intends, knows, sees, loves, pursues, hopes, imagines, believes. To know myself through my knowing my essential intentions is self-knowledge."[17] This is philosophy, and the way to think at once philosophically and humanly.

It is accepted that "the historically predominant life experience of man has taken the place within the more or less well defined limits of small countries. The tribes, the clan, the village, the small town represented kinds of small worlds within which all of man's living was done."[18] Our temporal and spatial commitment has been, to a greater extent, in Nigeria with an intention of building a united nation where peace and justice shall reign. At least, this has remained our ideal. However, it must be pointed out that our social life or character simply does not portray this so-called ideal.

---

16. Quoted from Piete Geyle, *Encounters in History* (London: Collins & Sons Co., 1963), 19.
17. Gustav Emil Muller, *Origins and Dimensions of Philosophy: Some Correlatives* (New York: Pageant Inc., 1965), 88.
18. Benita Luckmann, 'Small Life-world of Modern Man' in *Phenomenology and Sociology* ed. Thomas Luckmann, 276.

There is no reward for hard work and excellence. Talents are not only ignored and underdeveloped, but living in the country as a whole is at each person's risk. The present state of affairs has enthroned a culture of mediocrity, and many prefer to leave the country than risk their destiny, yet with the nostalgia to be associated with the vindication of the Nigerian dream. The Nigerian, like a typical African, has become a displaced, dejected and distressed personality, an experience that Luckmann says of modern man in general: "Instead of being a full-time member of one 'total and whole' society, modern man is a part-time citizen in a variety of part-time societies. Instead of living within one meaningful world system to which he owes complete loyalty he now lives in many differently structured 'worlds' to each of which he owes only partial allegiance."[19] The Nigerian leadership so far has only succeeded in draining the intellectual and material resources of the nation. It is a leadership with dwarf vision and mediocre intelligence. It is miserable for one's government or society to have antipathy for excellence, education and hard work.

The phenomenon of tribalism cannot be ignored in Nigeria. It promotes tribe consciousness at the expense of national consciousness. There is the fact of social injustices of all forms: lack of payment of workers' salaries; reckless mis-management of public funds, the systematic destruction of learning in schools at all levels in Nigeria—the constant strike actions of teachers, workers and students of higher learning because of the governments nonchalance in education; the perpetual gap in wage differences between the leaders and the led; the denial of merits or the mingling of governmental policies with sectarian preferences; the issue of the hopelessness of youths who live in a country that creates so many debilitating conditions in the way of their growth—the production of a delinquent generation in a delinquent country for a delinquent future. The Claretian Missionary Fathers in their 19th General Chapter are correct to observe: "The integration of youth into this world of mass production represents a serious problem to which society has offered no convincing solutions, as anyone can see from extremes of protest and apathy that generally characterize today's young people."[20] Nigeria's

---

19. Benita Luckmann, 'Small Life-world of Modern Man' in *Phenomenology and Sociology* ed. Thomas Luckmann., 282.

20. *The Mission of the Claretians Today: Document of the 19th General Chapter* in *The Claretian Mission of the Claretians Today and the Claretian in Process of Congregational Renewal: Documents of the 19th and 20th General Chapters of the Congregation of Claretian Missionaries*, trans. Joseph Daries (Philippines: Claretian Publications), par. 14, 11-12.

young people are miserable. They will have a faceless and hopeless future, if things continue the way they are.

I once encountered two Nigerian professionals, a doctor and a judge. Whereas the doctor said that if the present generation of Nigerian doctors was the caliber to take care of him in his old age then he was in real trouble, the judge wondered about the future of a country where the average young lawyer could not present a case in court. It is not that Nigerian children are not intelligent; it is simply that the country and its institutions are antithetical to their development: the government sabotages family values, ruins educational institutions by lack of funding and manipulation of students, rigs elections openly to insist that politics is about dishonesty, and that honesty does not pay. Nigeria makes its citizens miserable and delinquent, and makes its higher institutions a camp for mediocrity and a den of robbers.

There is a lot of social or environmental contradictions. For example, everyone is asked to keep his or her environment clean without places to dump refuse and provision of amenities that will reduce environmental pollution; teachers are asked to go back to the classrooms without salaries; the government talks about education but sabotages its progress in action.

Towards A Realistic Quest: Dropping the Rhetoric of Colonialism

We really have a difficult task of living together in Nigeria, a country with much imbalance in the distribution of wealth and social amenities. No nation will live meaningfully and justly with deep-seated tribalism, social indignity, injustice and poverty of the mind and body. Nigerians have been called names; but all the evils in the world cannot be predicated on them alone. It is accidental that Nigerians have to experience them; but Nigerians cannot settle with them as a way of life. We must reject them because they do not promote the dignity of the person and the reality of a united nation. The question posited to mankind as a whole by Lewis Mumford can plunge us into thinking in a new way: "What are the possibilities of mankind's acquiring a fresh grip on reality and shedding the compulsive fantasies that are pushing us to destruction?"[21] This question can only be answered with a clear and distinct intention and realistic commitment towards achieving our ideal as a nation. As Mumford indicates once again, "the test of

---

21.   Lewis Mumford, 'How War Began' in *Adventures of the Mind* ed. Richard Thruelsen and John Kobler (London: Victor Gollancz Limited, 1960), 187.

maturity, for nations as for individuals, is not the increase of power, but the increase of self-understanding, self-control, self-direction and self-transcendence. For in a mature society, man himself, not his machines or organization, is the chief work of art."[22] A reckless disregard for value, unless what accords with one's egoistic desires, cannot help nations build a community where everyone will realize himself or herself.

A new orientation or attitude of mind needs to be re-kindled in our people, instead of brooding over the past and shifting blames. African nations need to face the problems created by their indigenous sons and elite. The present problem is not so much the effect of colonialism as the enthronement of greed by those who presently occupy the positions of power once held by colonizers. Large numbers of the continent's sons are her traitors. There is no denial that the world of international exchange is still manipulated by the developed nations and multi-million corporations; it is also evident that one does not need the service of a lawyer to reach the understanding that people need the basic necessities of life in a country rich in abundant natural resources, in which there is a freely elected government in place. The colonizers have been blamed enough in the little and evident things we can do for ourselves, but which we culpably neglect or disregard. A new hermeneutics is needed at two levels for a way forward.

At the international level, words such as liberation, development, liberal market, democracy and aid should be understood as not neutral. Developed nations continue to develop at the expense of under-developed nations. The policies that the developed nations suggest to the Third World seem to suit in disguise the economies of the developed world. So, there are no presuppositionless economic political grounds at the international level.

There is need for a change of attitude too, at the national level. Politics, governance and economics are about the right attitude in dealing with people and managing resources in such a way that everyone flourishes fully. One then understands why Julius Nyerere calls for an *ujamaa*, an attitudinal change in a people's mind. The enemy is not only the colonizer—traitor from without. No. The enemy is the traitor from within, that is, Nigeria: its leaders and citizens. The need to re-direct our vision from within is based on the conviction that every nation, as Jean Jacques Rousseau says, contains within itself all the resources that can make living a reality in it without prejudices to its external relations. It all needs a great determination; after all, people do not come to their perfection till disappointment has dropped some hundred weights on their toes. Who would

---

22. *Ibid.*, 188.

know good horses if there were no heavy loads? African nations must pick up the pieces and work beyond the present disappointments and inaction within which they have settled. African intellectuals really need theoretical models to help African nations have a new grip on their socio-political life.

8

The Intellectuals' Attempts At Finding Theoretical Models[1]

What Prompted The Search For Defining Models

Many Africans and their sympathizers have been struggling to find intellectual landscapes under which the African person or reality in general could be comprehended. This is the quest for meaning and clarification within the borders of African philosophy. The politics of defining African philosophy or identity has traveled a long way. In the minds of the West, it first began with a total denial of humanity to the African. David Hume and G. W. F. Hegel were particularly negative about the humanity of Africans or the contribution of the Negro-African to civilization. The Western judgments or attitudes about Africa have been based on mere cultural bias, which "gradually grew into a formidable two-pronged historical reality: slavery and slave trade on the one hand, and academic expressions on the other hand."[2] Hume's essay, 'On National Character,' reads:

> I am apt to suspect the Negroes to be naturally inferior to the whites. There scarcely ever was a civilized nation of that complexion, nor even any individual eminent in action or speculation. No ingenious manufacturers amongst them; nor arts, no sciences. On the other hand, the most rude and barbarous of the whites, such as the ancient GERMANS, the present TARTARS, have still something eminent about them.... Such a uniform and constant difference could not happen...if nature had not made original distinction betwixt these breeds of men.[3]

---

1. See Francis O. C. Njoku, *Essays In African Philosophy, Thought and Theology* (Owerri: Claretians Institute of Philosophy, 2002), especially Chapters 1 to 6, and 15.
2. D. A. Masolo, *African Philosophy in Search of Identity* (Indianapolis: Indiana University Press, 1994), 2.

Hegel corroborates Hume's view, when he writes:

> The peculiarly African character is difficult to comprehend, for the very reason that in reference to it, we must quite give up the principle, which naturally accompanies all our ideas—the category of Universality. In Negro life, the characteristic point is the fact that consciousness has not yet attained to the realization of any substantial objective existence—as for example, God, or Law—in which the interest of man's volition is involved and in which he realized his own being. Thus distinction between himself as an individual and the universality of his essential being, the African in the uniform, undeveloped oneness of his existence has not yet attained; so that the knowledge of an absolute Being, an Other and a Higher than his individual self, is entirely wanting.[4]

It was really unfortunate that great philosophers such as Hegel and Hume wrote out of bias, reducing themselves to the position of armchair anthropologists. In this case, some scholars took the Humean-Hegelian sentiment as a missionary mandate.

Levy-Bruhl, a Hegelian scholar, believed that, since the African was not educated, he could not know God. No doubt then in giving his report to the Ethnological Society of London, Samuel Baker writes that without any exception African "are without a belief in a Supreme Being, neither have they any form of worship or idolatry, nor is the darkness of their minds enlightened by even a ray of superstition. The mind is as stagnant as the morass which forms its punny world."[5] Following Baker, in 1864 Richard F. Burton could write:

> The Negro is still at the crude dawn of faith-fetishism and he has barely advanced to idolatry…. He has never grasped the ideas of a personal Deity, a duty in life, a moral code, or a shame of lying. He rarely believes in a future state of rewards and punishment, which, whether true or not, are infallible indices of human progress.[6]

---

3. Quoted from E. Chukwudi Eze, 'Modern Western Philosophy and African Colonialism', in *African Philosophy: An Anthology* ed. Emmanuel Chukwudi Eze (Oxford: Blackwell Publishers, 1998), 214.

4. G. W. F. Hegel, *The Philosophy of History* (New York: Dover Publications, 1956), 93.

5. Samuel Baker, 'The Races of the Nile' in *Transactions of the Ethnological Society of London*, no. 5, 1867, quoted from Benjamine C. Ray, *African Religious Symbols, Ritual and Community* (New Jersey: Prentice-Hall, Inc., Englewood Cliffs, 1976), 2.

There is a belief, on the side of the West, that theoretical and religious knowledge must be accompanied by certain literary awareness.

However, at a point, a certain kind of allowance was made to grant some human attribute to the African. Actually, the intellectual exchange between Western discourses on Africa and Africans' responses have largely hovered around a "variety of topics and ideas depicting the individual's roles and impact in shaping and control of one's identity and destiny. At the center of this debate is the concept of reason, a value which is believed to stand as the great divide between the civilized and the uncivilized, the logical and the mystical."[7] The discussion on African philosophy, for some, rests on two great divides: that the West has a pride of reason and Africa has a preserve of emotions.

Areoye Oyebola, in Chapter one of his book, *Black Man's Dilemma,* gives an elaborate study of the various racial classifications of some scholars. Within the animal class, humans are identified, in contradiction to others of the animal group, as *homo sapiens. Homo sapiens,* according to the Swedish naturalist—Carolus Linneaus—in his racial classification in 1738, falls into four categories: *Americanus, Europeaus, Asiaticus* and *After* (African).

There are other significant classifications of race based on the color of the skin. In 1775, Otto Blumenbach came up with five racial groups, namely: Caucasian or white; Mongolian or yellow; Ethiopian or black; American or red, and Malayan or brown. Oyebola notes that Boyd's classification of races in 1950 was based on gene in which he also recognized five major races: European or Caucasoid; African or Negroid; Asiatic or Mongoloid; American Indian; and Australoid.

Although, it is difficult to say which racial classification is better than the other, anthropologists and scientists seem to settle generally for three major groups "based on geographical isolation," namely: Caucasians, Mongols and Negroes. Caucasians are said to derive from Europe and subsist in the present day Europeans. Mongols derived from Asia which major subdivisions are Chinese and Indians. Negroes derive from Africa, and they subsist in the people of West Africa. Without prejudice then, if one is asked who are the Caucasians or Mongols or Negroes, one can simply refer to people of a designated color point and to their respective geographical locations. So, under the geo-numerical identity, Izu Marcel Onyeocha articulates that Africa and all it contains is the world's second

6.   Richard F. Burton, *A Mission to Gelele King of Dahome,* 2d. vol. 2 (London: Tinsley Brothers, 1864), 199.

7.   D. A. Masolo, *African Philosophy in Search of Identity,* 1.

largest continent, covering "an area of 30,097,000 square kilometers (or 11, 617, 000 square miles)."[8] One who locates Africa on the map is rightly making a geographical designation and it will not be a mistake to call someone born in that geographically designated area an African.

But the question of who is an African goes beyond mere geographical location or designation. Although, Africans are grouped under Negroes or black people, not all black people are as dark-skinned as the people of West Africa who are said to typify the negroloid group. Negroes are not in one continent. Oyebola is aware of this designation of identity by geography and skin pigmentation when he observes that, although the home of the Negro race is the African continent, some found in it do not strictly belong to it, for the so-called designated black continent has other colors besides black or the Negro race. [9] In other words, a single characteristic such as color, ancestry or geography cannot settle the question of who is an African? or the problem of African identity.

Besides, racial classifications do not stop at a descriptive study/knowledge of the races and the geographical locations of the races studied. This can be seen in Carolus Linnaeus' division of human beings into four categories. Carolus Linneaus makes more than a descriptive statement, when he says that the *Americanus* are tenacious, contented, free, and ruled by custom; the *Europeaus* are light, lively, inventive and ruled by rites; the Asiaticus are stern, haughty, stingy, and ruled by opinion; and *Africans* are cunning, slow, negligent, and ruled by caprice. [10]

The question of African identity arose in the context of counter-assertions and polemics. In this regard, talks about races become instruments for exclusion, derogation and domination of certain groups or reinforce stereotypes about the African or the Negro as primitive, cunning, illogical, emotional, capricious and backward. These were tags that were given intellectual justification by Western scholars. Thus, certified that Negroes are backward and inhuman, and share no equality with the White race, Europe had no qualms of conscience in the exploitation of the Negro African through the instruments of ideological race classification. This image of the Negro as conceived by the West led to the inhuman treatment of the slaves. [11]

---

8.   See Izu Marcel Onyeocha, *Africa: The Question of Identity* Nigerian edition (Washington D. C.: The Council for Research in Values and Philosophy, 1997), 16.

9.   See Areoye Oyebola, *Black Man's Dilemma* (Ibadan: Board Publications Limited, 1982), 3.

10. *Ibid.*, 1

The allied evil of colonialism was parasitic on the image already bred in the slave trade. Since Africans were regarded as sub-humans, colonialism, by Europe, became a godly ordained task.[12] The Negro could be dominated and tamed alongside nature. Since, according to the thinking at the time, the Negro had no soul; he was simply another piece of matter.

The question of African identity, definition and re-definition, as a historical and intellectual problem, arose in the context of the experience of racial discrimination, slavery and colonialism. It is against this backdrop that one appreciates Langton Hughes' conviction that the new black generation is prepared to express its personality without apologies. [13]

At the conference of Negro-African Writers and Artists (Le Congrè des Ecrivains et Artistes Noirs), held in Paris in September 19, 1956, Alioune Diop noted: "it was due to the crisis which their cultures were now undergoing that the black intellectuals had come together. They were here to define and accept their responsibility, to assess the riches and the promise of their cultures and open, in effect, a dialogue with Europe."[14] To counter the image created by the West through intellectual bias, racial discrimination, slavery and colonialism, some Africans came up with certain images or projections of African identity or personality.

African Identity Recovered From History

Edward Blyden used the concept, 'African personality' in "opposition to any form of racial prejudice and racial chauvinism, and as a catalyst to a constructive solidarity among all Africans…and to form a dynamic political philosophy and a guide of action for the Africans who were beginning to make the first bold bases for the movement of national liberation."[15]

Blyden traces the history of Blacks to the sons of Ham mentioned in the book of Genesis Chapter ten; he claims that the city built by the descendants of Ham

11.   See Eric Williams, 'The Origin of Negro Slavery,' in *African Philosophy: An Anthology* ed. Emmanuel Chukwudi Eze (Oxford: Blackwell Publishers, 1998), 386-387.

12.   E. Chukwudi Eze, 'Modern Western Philosophy and African Colonialism', in *African Philosophy: An Anthology* ed. Emmanuel Chukwudi Eze, 213.

13.   See the Journal *The Nation* of June 1926, but quoted from D. A. Masolo, *African Philosophy in Search of Identity*, 3.

14.   James Baldwin, *Nobody Knows My Name* (London: Corgi Books, 1965), 26.

15.   T. Filesi, *Movimenti di Emancipazione Coloniale a Nascita dei Nuovi Stati in Africa* (Milano, 1971), 27.

was Egypt whose original descendants were blacks.[16] Blyden's argument is that Negro in ancient history contributed to universal civilization; and the Negro, even with experience of slavery, did not lose all knowledge of arts. Besides the inventions of ancient Egypt, even, after the slavery, Negroes continued to be inventive. One of the cases Blyden uses to make his claim is the *Vey* people of the West Coast of Africa, residing half way between Sierra Leone and Cape Mesurado, who invented a syllabic alphabet.[17] Against the background of glaring contributions by Negroes, Blyden refutes the allegation that Negroes are inferior and destined to be enslaved. He insists that people who built such great cities cannot continually be taken to be inferior.[18] It is the conviction of Blyden that black civilization was stolen and the Negro systematically degraded, and the history of human achievement and civilization was rewritten to the disfavor of Negroes. Blyden is not alone in the claim that Africa's legacy was stolen.

The stolen and rewritten history of black civilizations and achievements could be recaptured again, no matter how long it takes, according to Blyden. He believes that the black race is capable of this. But attention should be paid to the way the Negroes or blacks accept that they are different. The contribution of Negroes to civilization was universal; and their legacy, having been stolen, the West propagate that Negroes are different or peculiar to keep them away from their rightful place at the center of human civilization which they began. It is confirmed by anthropologists and archaeologists that the earliest signs of tool making and culture appeared in Africa.[19] Thus, if there is something peculiar about black, it is that of leading civilization; not a peculiarity that excludes him as inferior and unintelligent. This, for Blyden, is a false image created by the whites' distorted historical evidence and ideological theories, which are taught to date in Western schools.

---

16.   Edward Blyden, 'The Negro in Ancient History,' in *The People of Africa: a series of Papers on their Character, Condition and Future Prospects* ed. Henry M. Schieffelin, 2d. (Ibadan: Ibadan University Press, 1974), 8. (This article first appeared in Methodist Quarterly Review, January, 1869). Cf. also Luc Croegaert, *The African Continent: An Insight into its Earliest History* (Nairobi: Paulines Publications Africa) especially Ch 2.

17.   See Edward Blyden, 'The Negro in Ancient History,' in *The People of Africa: A series of Papers on their Character, Condition and Future Prospects*, 25.

18.   *Ibid.*, 26-27.

19.   J. Desmond Clark, 'The Prehistoric Origins of African Culture,' in *Papers in African Prehistory* eds. J. D. Fage and R. A. Oliver (Cambridge: Cambridge University Press, 1970), 1-3.

The Ethno-philosopher's Appeal to Cultural Roots and Values

Placid Tempels' *Bantu Philosophy* came as an attempt to assuage Western curiosity about Africa. Drawing from the categories of European philosophy, Tempels goes forth to prove that the African has some divine element in him: he has some reason, he can philosophize; he has some kind of philosophy. By studying the culture and life of the Bantu people, Tempels believes that he could derive a thought pattern.[20] He characterizes the fundamental principle of their philosophy as 'force,' which he identifies with being; hence he claims that without the element of force, "being cannot be conceived."[21] Thus, force moves all living beings, and values are judged according as whether they strengthen or weaken the vital force of the person.[22]

A correlative of Tempels' vitalist philosophy is the animistic concept of the world, which is applied to African thought. Animism is the so-called belief that there are spirits in everything. I have argued against the animistic epithet, noting that the claim that tree and stone and many other objects can be the abode of spirits, which the African tends to hold[23], is not a derivative of the imposed claim that everything has a spirit or a soul. This later view sounds very Aristotelian.

Tempels' study and many others, like J. Mbiti, Kagema, and Griaule who have fundamentally approached people's thought by studying their culture have been classified as ethno-philosophy.[24] Tempels' claim that 'vital force' is fundamental to the worldview of all the Bantu-speaking people of Eastern and Central Africa gives the impression that people who speak the same language, and share the same cultural values have the same philosophy. This genre of ethno-philosophy is called 'unanimism,' a belief that people have unanimous views about their culture and beliefs. This is not necessarily so. There can be multiplicity of worldviews coming from individuals of the same culture.

Ethno-philosophers have generally called our attention to the study of cultures within which people philosophize. Certainly, they have "transcribed into a written literature some of the oral accounts of traditional world views (their stories,

---

20. Placid Tempels, *Bantu Philosophy*, trans. Colin King (Paris: Presence Africaine, 1959), 40-41.

21. Placid Tempels, 'Bantu Ontology' in *African Philosophy: An Anthology* ed. Emmanuel Chukwudi Eze (Oxford: Blackwell Publishers Limited, 1998), 431.

22. *Ibid.*, 430.

23. See F. O. C. Njoku, *Essays in African Philosophy, Thought and Theology*, 125-141.

24. See *Ibid.*, 15-33.

songs and mythologies) and given us detailed ethnographies of ritual practices of African people. In this way, they have helped 'picture' Africa's past and contributed toward the conversion of African self-understanding from an oral to a written mode."[25] They have, however, been criticized for masquerading cultural and religious rites as African philosophy. Ethno-philosophy's attempt to define African identity is not discriminative enough in the materials it presents. As Paulin Hountondji points out, it gives the impression that people who speak the same language share the same philosophy. Moreover, the audience of ethno-philosophers is largely Western.

Like ethno-philosophers, the negritude movement tries to identify the common and fundamental elements that are specifically thought to be African or Negro-African. Leopold Sedar Senghor, the chief spokesman of this movement, emphasizes the uniqueness of race and cultural consciousness. He eulogizes the symbolic image; the melody of forms and movements, sounds and colors; and the rhythm of asymmetrical parallelism as the three elements of Negro aesthetic. Part of Senghor's poetic vision is encapsulated in the poem, Black Woman—the black woman whose color is her beauty and life. [26] According to Senghor, the end of Negro aesthetic is the rediscovery of the black Africa's fervent quest for the 'Holy Grail.' Senghor calls it "our Collective Soul."

Senghor uses the concept of *negritude* to symbolize what the black person stands for. Negritude conducts a journey of soul-searching. Senghor believes that Negro-cultural values have something to offer to the existing political system, but insists that the African has a different way of apprehending the world. It is different and contrasts with the western reason-based outlook that is largely discriminatory; the African conceptual scheme is sustained by an intuitive consciousness or reasoning-embrace:

> ...Negro-African speech does not mould the object into rigid categories and concepts without touching it; it polishes things and restores their original color, with their texture, sound and perfume; it perforates them with its luminous rays to reach the essential surreality in its innate humidity—it would be more accurate to speak of sub-reality. European reasoning is analytical, discursive by utilization; Negro-African reasoning is intuitive by participation.[27]

25. Richard H. Bell, *Understanding African Philosophy: A Cross-Cultural Approach to Classical and Contemporary Issues* (New York: Routledge, 2002), 24.

26. See Leopold Sedar Senghor 'Black Woman' in *Western African Verse: An Anthology* chosen and annotated by Donatus I. Nwoga (Harlow Essex: Longman, 1967), 96.

27. L. S. Senghor, *On African Socialism* (London: Pall Mall Press, 1964), 74.

Senghor prizes intuitive reason (emotion) as African, in which the subject participates in a knowledge situation through a symbiotic embrace. For Senghor, *negritude* is a "whole complex of civilized values—characteristic of the black peoples, or, more precisely, the Negro-Africa world.... In other words, the sense of communion, the gift of myth-making, the gift of rhythm, such are the essential elements of *Negritude*, which you will find indelibly stamped on all the works and activities of the black man."[28] With his concept of *Negritude*, Senghor claims that the Negro-African has something special and specific to offer in bringing about communion among the peoples of black race and beyond.

Senghor's views are said to be very romantic, and accomodationistic. He simply assumes the so-called negative attributes of the Negro-African (baptizes them as positive), and simply negotiates for a place along with others. He subscribes to the collapse of the African pluralistic consciousness into a single vital or unitary whole, thereby neutralizing the plurality of African cultures.

In fact, both ethno-philosophy and negritude movement are bogged down by some kind of cultural amnesia that ignores its internal workings. They tend to aim at satisfying an inattentive stranger only at the expense of exposing their own so-called inferiority complex. They raise awareness that the Afro-Negro way could be valid and satisfactory way, but they unconsciously assume, without arguments, the stereotypes that are imputed to the Negro-African. There is an imbalance in negotiating between the West and an ethno-philosophy or negritude movement.

The Critical Trend of African Philosophy

There are African philosophers we might call universalist or critical philosophers[29]; they think that African philosophy is more than what ethno-philosophy presents. Kwasi Wirendu, Paulin Hountondji and P. O. Bodunrin opt for the view that philosophy has a universal concern, thus African philosophy is not an exception. Wirendu claims that truth is truth; there are no privileged white truths or black truths. Non-scientific characteristics of traditional thought are not the preserver of any culture. Besides, the principle of rational evidence cannot be totally denied African traditional thinking.[30]

---

28. *Ibid.*
29. See F. O. C. Njoku, *Essays in African Philosophy, Thought and Theology*, 71-81.
30. K. Wiredu, 'On Defining African Philosophy' in *African Philosophy: The Essential Readings*, ed. Tsenay Serequeberhan (New York: Paragon House, 1991), 118-119.

Paulin Hountondji argues that philosophy is universal; he accuses ethno-philosophers of presenting a false image of what is thought to be African philosophy. He insists that philosophy, as championed by ethno-philosophers, is incapable of leading a coherent presentation of African definition. Oral traditions, according to Hountondji, cannot constitute philosophy. African philosophy, Hountondji believes, exists as "literature produced by Africans and dealing with philosophical problems."[31] What identifies writers as African, in Hountondji's conceptual scheme, is only their geographical origin. Thus, he argues that the objectivity and neutrality that apply in the area of science should also apply to philosophy.

Hountondji has been criticized for his assumption of Western literacy as a paradigm for philosophy. And he will lose his argument with scholars who insist on the African origin of Greek or Western philosophy. Sage philosophers will not accept that orality cannot constitute text in philosophical parlance. If we follow Hountondji's way in the call for identity, much worthwhile oral tradition will be compromised; and a valid text of African life and philosophy would have been lost.

P. O. Bodunrin departs with the conviction that philosophy is criticism. If we look at the Greek context, we discover that Socrates and Plato were opposed to popular beliefs. Thus, African philosophy should adopt the same posture towards tradition. According to Bodunrin, criticism is "rational, impartial, and articulate appraisal whether positive or negative."[32]

The sage philosopher—Henry Odera Oruka—regrets the claim that illiterate philosophy is non-scientific. After all, Socrates used his dialectic method to fashion philosophy out of narrative stuffs. Therefore, philosophy does not have to be written. Oruka believes that a distinction has to be made between folk sagacity and philosophic sagacity. Philosophic sagacity, according Oruka, is didactic wisdom, which is rational thought expounded by individuals with great or creative power of judgment.[33] Didactic wisdom issues from universal concern read from the text of oral tradition.

---

31. Paulin Hountondji, *African Philosophy: Myth and Reality*, 2d., (Indianapolis: Indiana University Press, 1996), 63.

32. See P. O. Bodunrin, 'The Question of African Philosophy' in Kwasi Wirendu, *Philosophy and An African Culture* (Cambridge: Cambridge University Press, 1980), 173.

33. H. Odera Oruka, 'Sage Philosophy: The Question of Methodology' in *Sage Philosophy* ed., H. Odera Oruka (Nairobi: African Center for Technology Studies Press, 1991), 33.

The Hermeneutical Reading of African Reality

The critical trend of African philosophy, in general, assumes that philosophy goes beyond the accumulation of anthropological and religious data. But it is not free from the charge that it is positing the Greek philosophical tradition as a paradigm for philosophy. Furthermore, its attempt at re-description, though it might be critical, has no program of action that can help diagnose and address Africa's socio-political problems.

There is the hermeneutical approach which, T. Okere claims, offers a more profitable ground for comprehending African philosophy. Hermeneutics is about meaning and interpretation. Anthropological and cultural presuppositions show that there is always an extra-philosophical material in philosophy. And philosophy is an exercise in interpretation or "an interpretative commentary on reality against the guiding, determining and suggestive background of a culture."[34] There is always a hand of non-philosophy, that is, elements of language, history, scientific, or other lore, religion, mythology, values and beliefs, social and individual experience" that serve as raw materials for philosophical reflection.[35] And in philosophers, such as Hegel and Heidegger, Okere could see the finger of non-philosophy at work. For example, besides building on the thoughts of his predecessors, Hegel's time and country's history, and Christian theology aroused the philosophical disquietude in him. Christian scriptures have had their hand in Heidegger's thought. Okere could deep hand further back to show that Greek mythology and religion gave background to Pre-Socratic and Socratic periods in Greek philosophy.[36] Therefore, philosophy and non-philosophy have always shared borders in the thoughts of individual philosophers, albeit philosophy is characterized by reflection and non-philosophy is taken to be an "unreflective baggage of cultural background."

Non-philosophy includes the pre-judgments or prejudices, individual and cultural presuppositions which the hermeneutical method wants to get beyond to reveal the real world structure. The ethnophilosopher's error, in Okere's conceptual schemes, is to assume non-philosophy as philosophy or to appropriate lifeworld without reflection. However, Okere is aware that reason cannot operate independent of us. The question of "truth of things" becomes as suspicious as it is unattainable, for we cannot know all about things and ourselves in advance.

---

34.   Theophilus Okere, *African Philosophy: A Historico-Hermeneutical Investigation of the Conditions of Its Possibility* (London: University Press of America, 1983), 81.
35.   See *Ibid.*, 82.
36.   See *Ibid.*, 107-108.

Okere summarizes his intellectual harvest by concluding that philosophy is context-bound; all philosophy involves a situated exercise, and extra-philosophical materials too:

> Philosophical reflection is the process of explicitation, an uncovering, a disclosure, an unfolding of the meaning and sense implied in those objectivations of life which are symbols. Reflection means *implicita explicare*—making the implicit, explicit. African cultures have their own symbols pregnant with meaning. A reflection on these symbols with a view to making the implicit meanings explicit would constitute African philosophy.[37]

Does African philosophy then exist? Okere answers that he does not quarrel with the *fact* of its existence but he worries over what *its existence* is claimed to be.[38] Given the hermeneutical intuition that the interpretation of cultural symbols provides an outlet for articulating both the individual's and communities' philosophy, Okere leans on Heidegger's line of thought to assure that African philosophy takes off from its environment of occurrence: "From Heidegger's philosophy of hermeneutics, one can validly infer that an African philosophy is a philosophy which gets its initial impulse and its nourishment from the African source, from African culture."[39] Africans have a philosophy that is original to them. Whereas, however, the sources of African philosophy will include traditional institutions, colonial and post-colonial experience, these cannot be uncritically assumed without questions. Symbols are context-bound, thus "a philosophical interpretation of the symbols of African culture would be African philosophy."[40]

The materials for philosophy are already there in the African environment waiting to receive philosophical reflection. What seems to be noticeable now is that African symbols are presupposed without being given critical reflection. An individual is situated in his cultural context; "it is by relating the elements of culture to himself that one creates and constitutes meaning and becomes a philosopher. The relation of culture to philosophy is explained from the structural constitution of man."[41] African philosophy exists, as Okere implies, and with this

---

37. *Ibid.*, 114-115.
38. See *Ibid.*, 114.
39. *Ibid.*, 118.
40. *Ibid.*, 115.
41. *Ibid.*, 116.

platform created by the individual's culture and the climate of opinion around him[42]; but it is not what ethno-philosophers are presenting.

The hermeneutical approach in African philosophy is strongly supported by Tsenay Serequeberhan, Marcia Towa and Okondo Okolo.[43] In these later authors, the hermeneutical school identifies the problem of a battered conscience: that the alienation brought by colonial administration is made worse by the politics of the new world order dominated by the United States and African elites who act as pawns in the hands of the super powers to oppress their own people. In the process of interpreting and sifting meaning from the internal and external rumbles in the midst of the African reality, the post-Okerean hermeneutic school claims that it is violence (colonialism) that should be confronted with another violence (a response from oppressed side).

The horizon of discourse is widened now, which in turn underlines Africa's speculative space. Thus, Serequeberhan says:

> In our case,...it is neither the theoretical exigencies of modern science nor the crisis of faith in confrontation with a foreign and aggressive piety that provokes thought. Rather, it is the politico-existential crisis interior to the horizon of post-colonial Africa, which brings forth the concerns and originates the theoretic space for the discourse of contemporary African philosophy. In each case, then, it is out of the concerns and needs of a specific horizon that a particular philosophic discourse is articulated.[44]

The present discourse, Serequeberhan speculates, should pay attention to Africa's specific concerns.

There is need for liberation from the evils of colonialism, but as Towa claims, Senghor and Negritude poets cannot lead the crusade neither would ethno-philosophers' obsession with the past stand as a palatable alternative. Whereas Towa accepts Hountondji's criticism against ethno-philosophers, he rejects Hountondji's reduction of philosophy to literacy. For Towa, oral tradition constitutes a text.[45] In this way, he acknowledges the sage philosophy of Oruka.

---

42. See Innocent Onyewuenyi, 'Towards An African Philosophy,' in *Readings in African Humanities: African Cultural Development* ed.; Ogbu U. Kalu (Enugu: Fourth Dimension Publishers, 1982), 247.

43. See F. O. C. Njoku, *Essays in African Philosophy, Thought and Theology*, 84-91.

44. Tsenay Serequeberhan, 'Philosophy and Post-Colonial Africa' in *African Philosophy: An Anthology*, ed., E. C. Eze (Oxford: Blackwell Publishers, 1998), 12.

45. Marcia Towa, 'Condition for the Affirmation of a Modern Philosophical Thought,' in *African Philosophy: Essential Readings*, ed., T. Serequeberhan, 197.

There are no apologies, in Okolo's thinking, regarding what Towa says about oral texts. For Okolo, "African tradition is the text of our reading," and it includes "verbal concatenations."[46] His message is that we need culture and historical experience in a creative manner if we must transcend the present limitations of Africa and look forward to a future that offers liberation.

The merit of the hermeneutical school is that it signals that both the home and foreign fronts can offer ambiguous perspective in the attempt to locate the enemy; hence the need for a seasoned clarification of meaning, taking on board the life experiences of African people. However, the explicit claim that the struggle of liberation involves matching violence with violence might pretend that the culprit is only the enemy from without. In fact, the hermeneutic school after Okere identifies the emotional basis for the struggle, but it lacks a sharpened and integrative intellectual framework that can be translated into a social praxis.

The Nationalist's Quest

There are also the nationalists[47] who feel that certain constants need to be identified and recaptured within the African tradition, constants that have been blurred by colonialism. It was Kwame Nkrumah's belief that traditional Africa was egalitarian, and egalitarianism can only be recaptured by divesting Africa of colonialism and its attendant capitalism. To achieve this return to the roots, a social praxis is needed, and a particular philosophical viewpoint has to be adopted. A social praxis gives the required training in political awareness, rule of action and how to deal with the evils of colonialism. The social praxis will involve a revolution that will put the Western and Islamic influences on Africa in their right perspectives:

> Social revolution must therefore have, standing firmly behind it, an intellectual revolution, a revolution in which our thinking and philosophy are directed towards the redemption of our society. Our philosophy must find its weapons in the environment and living conditions of the African people. It is from those conditions that the intellectual content of our philosophy must be created. The emancipation of the African continent is the emancipation of man. This requires two aims: first, the restitution of the egalitarianism of

---

46. Okondo Okolo, 'Tradition and Destiny: Horizons of An African Philosophical Hermeneutics' in African Philosophy: Essential Readings, ed., T. Serequeberhan, 204.
47. See F. O. C. Njoku, *Essays in African Philosophy, Thought and Theology*, 34-70.

human society, and, second, the logistic mobilization of all our resources towards the attainment of that restitution.[48]

Nkrumah calls his theoretical platform 'philosophical consciencism.' He defines consciencism as:

> the map in intellectual terms of the disposition of forces which will enable African society to digest the Western and the Islamic and the Euro-Christian elements in Africa, and develop them in such a way that they fit into the African personality. The African personality is itself defined by the cluster of humanist principles, which underlie the traditional African society. Philosophical consciencism is that philosophical standpoint which, taking its start from the present content of the African conscience indicates the way in which progress is forged out of the conflict in that conscience.[49]

What comes to Africa will then be evaluated; the good ones digested in such a way as to make them fit into the African personality. The new personality will undoubtedly emerge from a crisis of conscience.

Julius Nyerere believes that colonization has alienated the African. In addition, there are some forms of exploitation within the rest of society such as private ownership of the means of production, laziness, dishonesty and cheating. Thus, Nyerere, in his Arusha Declaration, presents the resolution of his party: the Tanganyika African National Union (TANU) as a way of fighting exploitation:

1. Every TANU and government leader must be either a peasant or a worker, and should in no way be associated with practices of capitalism.

2. No TANU or government leader should hold shares in any economy.

3. NO TANU or government leader should hold directorship in any privately owned enterprise.

4. No TANU or government leader should receive two or more salaries.

5. No TANU or government leader should own houses, which he rents to others.

---

48. Kwame Nkrumah, *Consciencism: Philosophy and Ideology for Decolonisation and Development with particular reference to African Revolution* (London: Heinemann Educational Books Limited, 1964), 78.

49. *Ibid.*, 79

6.   For the purpose of this resolution the term 'leaders' should comprise the following: members of the TANU National Executive Committee, ministers, etc.[50]

To eliminate exploitation, certain ways of doing things will have to be abandoned especially the capitalist mentality. Capitalism thrives on the basis of creating the *haves* and *have-nots*, exploiters and exploited, millionaires and non-millionaires, where the millionaire pretends that his wealth is "the just reward for his ability or enterprise."[51]

Nyerere insists on a kind of society that takes the needs of all on board, when he writes:

> For when a society is so organized that it cares about its individuals, then, provided he is willing to work, no individual within that society should worry about what will happen to him tomorrow if he does not hoard wealth today. Society itself should look after him, or his widow, or his orphans. This is exactly what traditional African society succeeded in doing. Both the 'rich' and the 'poor' individual were completely secure in African society. Natural catastrophe brought famine, but it brought famine to everyone—poor or rich. Nobody starved, either of food or of human dignity, because he lacked personal wealth; he could depend on wealth possessed by the community of which he was a member. That was socialism. That is socialism. There can be no such thing as acquisitive socialism, for that would be another contradiction in terms. Socialism is essentially distributive. Its concern is to see that those who sow reap a fair share of what they sow.[52]

African socialism, according to Nyerere, is not antithetical to a person's wanting to be rich; but it simply rejects wealth for the purpose of exploitation. Wealth, as means of exploitation, is a capitalist mentality. It contrasts with African socialism that took care of all its subjects. Therefore, a different attitude is needed. This different attitude is what *ujamaa* embodies and tries to convey. *Ujamaa* "is an attitude of mind needed to ensure that people care for each other's welfare."[53] It is an expression of the African sense of family:

---

50.   Julius Nyerere, *Ujamaa: Essays on Socialism*, 36. Cf. also Matthew I Nwoko, *The Rationality of African Socialism* (Rome 1985), 83.

51.   Julius Nyerere, 'Ujamaa: The Basis of African Socialism' in *I am Because We Are: Readings in Black Philosophy*, eds., Fred Lee Hord and Jonathan Scott Lee (Massachusetts: University of Massachusetts Press, 1995), 66.

52.   *Ibid.*, 66-67.

The foundation, and the objective of African socialism is the extended family. The true African socialism does not look on one class of men as his brethren and another as his natural enemies.... He rather regards as his brethren—members of his ever-extending family. That is why the first article of Tanu's Creed is *'Binadamu wota ni ndugu andgu, na Afrika ni moja'*—'I believe in Human Brotherhood and the Unity of Africa.'

Ujamaa, then, or 'Familyhood' describes our socialism. It is opposed to capitalism which seeks to build a happy society on the basis of exploitation...(It) is opposed to doctrinaire socialism which seeks to build its happy society on a philosophy of inevitable conflict between man and man.[54]

This familyhood is the justification or rationality of African socialism, and it contrasts with Western colonial capitalism that makes the individual acquire wealth at the expense of the other. In J.D. Okoh's words, "Nyerere's objective in stressing the dissociative element of *ujamaa* was to provide a new structure of value organization which would predispose his people to effect a change of attitude at a philosophical level."[55] It leads the crusade towards the recapturing of a certain traditional attitude of mind or orientation. Included in the cluster of attitude under *ujamaa* are the attitude of mind, the attitude of self-esteem, the attitude of co-operation, and the right attitude towards wealth.[56] Nyerere wanted a new nation, a new people, and a new individual to bring about a new state of affairs. It is against this background one can set alongside the convictions of Nyerere's TANU principles, Ojukwu's creation of the 'New Biafran.' The new Biafran is patriotic, he is his brother's keeper; he must be honorable, truthful, responsible, brave and courageous, law-abiding, freedom loving, progressive and industrious, resourceful and inventive.[57]

However, part of the reason why *ujamaa*, in spite of its great insight, suffered tremendous setbacks was that Nyerere over-estimated the so-called African communal spirit, and underrated inherent human selfish elements. Most people think

---

53. Julius K. Nyerere, *Ujamaa Essays on Socialism* (Nairobi: Oxford University Press, 1968), 1.

54. *Ibid.*, 11-12.

55. J. D. Okoh, 'Julius Nyerere's Philosophy of Ujamaa: A Model for Emergent African Nations' in *Academia: A CIP Journal of Philosophy* 1 (June 2003), 30.

56. See *Ibid.*, 29-36.

57. See Chukwuemeka Odumegwu Ojukwu, *Ahiara Declaration: The Principles of the Biafran Revolution (June, 1, 1969)* with the Declaration of Independence, speech before exile, the Cessation Declaration, call from Exile, and The Biafran National Anthem ed. Obi Harrison Ekwonna, 47-48.

that they are better off and fulfilled doing their own things. *Ujamaa* has great emotional and social appeals, but it has no cohesive conscience.

The attempt at re-description and founding African identity has to be rooted from within. There is no doubt that the first generation of African nationalists, especially Nkrumah and Nyerere, opened our vistas to the evils of colonialism and the need to tackle it against a framework of a philosophical standpoint. However, the nationalists fought against colonialism from without, but their tools were not sharpened for 'colonialism' from within. The evils African leaders have inflicted on their countries seem to outweigh that brought by colonialism. The continual brooding over colonization by African leaders has become unconvincing and a mere tool for diversion.

Senghor, like the nationalists, toed the line of seeking traditional forms of aesthetics in negotiating for a space in a world filled with prejudice against the Negro-African. However, the Negro-African problem was not solved when he was sympathetically conceded a space to sing and dance his black music. In all, a new theoretical tool is needed to address the African problem from within the larger context of sharing an existential plain with others. The present African re-description needs a tool that is adoptable, both from without and within, to its discursive terrain and existential interdependence. It is the author's belief that a philosophy of right will offer a description in a better light.

PART III

Towards A Philosophy of Right

9

Clarifying the Basis for a Philosophy of Right

An Approach Towards A Philosophy of Right

We need to clarify the basis for a philosophy of right. Man, in the African universe of being, has been described as the epi-center of cosmic reality. He has claim 'on himself' in the sense that he expects his biological or physiological components to function properly in order to help him survive meaningfully. He equally has claims on his environment, for he desires a favorable atmosphere for living his life. Wherever he finds himself, as he moves along in his existential facticity, he has to respond to the demands and duties of his being. By 'responding to the demands and duties of being' is intended to emphasize that the individual has an unquestionable claim to be in harmony with himself and the other person, God and the environment (family, nature, society and state). Duty is the claim one has to expect another to perform certain functions.

A right is a legitimate claim, be it on the part of the person or the group, to that which belongs to their persons, either by the sheer fact of their being as epi-center of existence or as what others are obligated to grant to their person as members of political society. Within the societal structure, people discover that they have rights. In other words, there are rights, which predate the political society. Within the political community such rights are protected and further rights are created in order to help people protect and change the socio-legal positions of one another. Therefore, the society is a framework within which right-claimants respond to themselves.

This part of the book will attempt to propose a philosophy of right,[1] within an African environment. Such a philosophy is expected to be of interest to any one who wants to assess a socio-political structure of a less sophisticated set-up. The approach here will be phenomenological in the sense that the data of African experience will be largely taken into consideration; such an experience will be rationalized along some theoretical framework. In other words, this attempt does not pretend to give a history of African experience; it simply claims to take on board the data of African experience and give some critical and theoretical foundation to it.

The philosophy of right intended here will be carved out certain theoretical backgrounds, namely: the philosophy of dialogue and complementarity, and the understanding of life as communion within covenant social relations. The concept of covenant is preferred because it is not foreign to the phenomenon of experience of African peoples. Thus, as a concept from within, it serves as an effective theoretical tool for interpreting aspects of African socio-political experience. In addition, a covenant-necessitated understanding of rights will be used to propose some models of leadership/governance in Africa.

Philosophy of Dialogue and Complementarity

A dialogue is, first and foremost, an encounter between persons. In this encounter, meaning and harmony are sought in the diversity of those walls and worlds that appear to separate potential interlocutors in word and action. Dialogue is a conversation, a communication, a talk, a meeting between minds in the midst of the riches of diversities. Richard H. Bell is right to acknowledge that in Africa, diversity, not symmetries, is the basis of dialogue.[2] The dialogue environment includes the subject, the common world and a medium (that is, speech and action = communication).

But speech is not necessary to this communication; hence Martin Buber writes:

> Just as the most eager speaking at one another does not make a conversation (this is mostly clearly shown in that curious sport, aptly termed discussion,

---

1.   The construction of an African philosophy of right has been attempted in an earlier book. See Chapter eleven of Francis O. C. Njoku, *Essays in African Philosophy, Thought and Theology* (Owerri: Claretian Institute of Philosophy, 2002), 176-192.

2.   Richard H. Bell, *Understanding African Philosophy: A Cross-Cultural Approach to Classical and Contemporary Issues*, 13.

that is, 'breaking apart,' which is indulged in by men who are to some extent gifted with the ability to think), so for a conversation no sound is necessary, not even a gesture. Speech can renounce all the media of sense, and it is still speech.[3]

Buber is talking about something that happens when people begin to exist in each other's confidence, which is technically called communication. Sometimes the diversity of our individuality constitutes a causal traffic in public relations. Claims and counter-claims are made in the forms of disputations. Our views become contested. However, that our views may be contested is not an argument in favor of the other side of the debate neither does it negate the possibility of a certain core of meaning in our understanding. No doubt Buber insists:

> The life of dialogue is not limited to men's traffic with one another; it is, it has shown itself to be, a relation of men to one another that is only represented in their traffic.
>
> Accordingly, even if speech and communication may be dispensed with, the life of dialogue seems, from what we may perceive, to have inextricably joined to its minimum constitution of one thing, the mutuality of the inner action. Two men bound together in dialogue must obviously be turned to one another, they must therefore—no matter with what measure of activity or indeed of consciousness of activity—have turned to one another.
>
> It is good to put this forward so crudely and formally. For behind the formulating question about the limits of a category under discussion is hidden a question which bursts all formulas asunder.[4]

A philosophy of dialogue departs from a certain conception of reality or humans as linked to one another. Humans depend on one another. This is not exploitative economic dependency projected in the dependency theory of development. Human dependency is not simply the composition of the dependent population at any given time; it is rather a fact of the human condition that humans at various stages of their lives depend on one another just as the human race also depends on its natural and social environments.

Reality is not an isolated monistic system condemned to the eternal regulation of its own solipsistic operations. Philosophy of dialogue believes that there is an interconnectedness that renders the being of any entity efficacious. This is a situation where beings or entities exist in each other's mutual embrace. While this

---

3.   Martin Buber, *Between Man and Man* trans. Ronald Gregor-Smith (London: Routledge & Kegan Paul, 1947), 3.

4.   *Ibid.,* 9-10.

understanding does not see reality as a continuum, it does reject the understanding that reality is made up of separate unconnected entities or existing monads. Writing in the early 1960s the Fathers of Vatican II noted:

> One of the most striking features of today's world is the intense development of interpersonal relationships due in no small measure to modern technical advances. Nevertheless fraternal dialogue is advanced not so much on this level as at the deeper level of personal fellowship, and this calls for mutual respect for the full spiritual dignity of men as persons. Christian revelation greatly fosters the establishment of such fellowship and at the same time promoters deeper understanding of the laws of social living with which the creator has endowed man's spiritual and moral nature.[5]

To understand a philosophy of dialogue, one needs to appreciate how it is inserted within the ambient of the philosophy of complementarity.

Complementarity is a view that the picture of reality cannot be exhausted from one point of view. A balanced understanding of it is that parts of reality reinforce or complement each other. The mountain, for example, is not made up of rocks and their physio-chemical materials, its nature as much as its environment comprehends the slopes, the trees and grass around it. The body is not only made up of kidneys and heart. There are arteries, veins and lungs, eyes and ears and so on that inter-depend on one another for the total and effective functioning of the whole body mechanism. Sometimes, to express the interdependence in bio-social spheres the Igbo say that '*imi bewaa anya e bewa,*' that is, 'when the nose begins to cry, the eyes follow as well.' Human beings function in the social atmosphere as interconnected wholes for their flourishing. Mary Ann Glendon is right to remark:

> Paradoxically, the concepts of the human person that are prominent in social science and social policy both over-emphasize individual self-sufficiency and under-rate individual human agency. The image of the free, self-determining individual exerts such powerful attraction for modern imaginations that we tend to relegate obvious facts about human dependency to the margins of consciousness. Nevertheless, human beings still begin their lives in the longest period of human dependency of any mammal. It is a fact that circumstances can catapult anyone at least temporarily from a secure to a dependent position. It is still a fact that almost all persons spend much of their lives either as dependents, or caring for dependents, or financially responsible for depen-

---

5.   *Vatican II Council, Gaudium et Spes* (Pastoral Constitution of the Church in the Modern World), 7 December, 1965, no. 23.

dents. It is still a fact that we all depend on the earth for resources that make life possible.[6]

The unique mission of human beings is mutual completion, for it is the reason why humans come together. However, this coming together, according to Johannes Messner, is possible by two factors or characteristics: the fact of equality in essence and the fact of inequalities of bodily and sensory natures.[7]

The fact of equality in essence insists that humans are alike in their essential nature. They possess body and soul. The existential ends of humans require equal moral responsibility from all. This equality in humans rests upon the equality of their spiritual and moral nature. In short, God has created humans equally and endowed them with equal essence. Human essence is the fountain of the individual's sense of inalienable rights dignity, compassion and love.

The fact of inequalities of bodily and sensory natures indicates that humans are not equally endowed in their individual natures, given their diverse qualities and faculties:

> Consisting of a unity of body and spirit, human nature is individuated by particular qualities and faculties, which make completion possible. By virtue of this individual inequality in powers and identity of the ends proper to their essential nature, men are predisposed to combine their qualities and powers to co-operate in order to attain to the integral human existence implied in these ends. Thus, man's social nature is rooted in the special character of his nature as a unity of body and spirit.[8]

Human nature is endowed with faculties of comprehending the worlds of truth and values, of ascertaining principles of law in the external world, and of utilizing these in the effort to realize the values in which civilization consists—"to rise in will and understanding into the world of the absolute and its cause, the divine nature, so that self-transcendence is a fundamental feature and a fundamental impulse of man."[9] A human being attains integral human existence by striving after values and culture engendered by his/her spiritual nature and

---

6.   Mary Ann Glendon, 'Final Report' on the First Plenary Meeting on Intergenerational Solidarity, Welfare, and Human Ecology held at the Pontifical Academy of Social Sciences May 2, 2004, 9.

7.   See Johannes Messner, *Social Ethics: Natural Law in the Western World* rev. ed. (London: B. Herder Book Co., 1965), 98.

8.   *Ibid.*

9.   *Ibid.*

encompassing the sensory, the moral and the external worlds. Life is essentially possible in the company of the other, for nature has burdened humans with many necessities.[10] Human deficiencies are reduced to their barest minimum through the co-operation of others,[11] for men have seen that the advantage of conjunction of forces in society.[12] Therefore inequality of sensory organs disposes humans for company.

The equality of essence and inequality of sensory organs help us to look at the reasons for human association from positive and negative perspectives.

Positively, human nature is disposed for complementation because the variety of beings adds to the harmony of creation. Thus, complementation or complementarity is part of the order of the body or universe or association. Although, every being is individually separated from others and true to itself, its truth and beauty inter-depend in the harmony of all beings or entities. In this way, it is an intrinsic bond that beings complement each other, not necessarily out of lack but essentially as part of their harmony within their existential communion. This is an indwelling in the common, existential and environmental space.

Negatively, people seek the way of complementarity to make up for their lacks. Although man and woman are ontologically complete as existential beings, they can only function well as humans in the social sphere by complementing their individual gifts. The rest of the part is in the other.

Dialogue and Complementarity: Process of Self-Donation

Dialogue is a process of self-donation in the sharing of meanings. We should come out of ourselves to others. And to have a complete picture of the world, we must look into others and ourselves:

> We must look into ourselves and to what others are saying of themselves and put together those links from what we have seen and heard, from what we have experienced and already understood. The *understanding* is something that an individual *does* and is tied to the particular self-reflective 'life-view' a person has within his or her own community.[13]

---

10. David Hume, *Moral and Political Philosophy*, ed. Henry D. Aiken (London: Hafner Press, 1948), 55-56.
11. See *Ibid.*, 56.
12. *Ibid.*

It should not be taken that humans are not naturally disposed for dialogue. Hobbes thought that humans were naturally anti-social; hence he concluded that only the Leviathan was needed to prod them to the way of peace and order. His view has company among those who give a genetic or evolutionary interpretation of social reality; it is a claim that conflict is in-built in the human process, and only the fittest survives, as in Darwin's evolutionary view.

If Hobbes' state of nature was unbearable and conflictual to the inmates, Jean-Jacque Rousseau's was quite the contrary. For Rousseau, humans were endowed by nature with living in peace with great respect; only the artificial being—the state or commonwealth—corrupted them. Although Rousseau believed that the action of humans acquired moral nobility in the civil society, he did not think that humans in the state of nature were as brutish as Hobbes painted them; they were rather noble savage.

Humans had right to everything as Hobbes thought, but natural right, John Locke pointed out, implied, in itself, a sense of respect or restriction. The civil society, in Locke, only oversees the natural rights as an umpire, not the creator of those rights.

Whether the resolution of conflicts dragged humans into civil society (Hobbes) or they found a greater and nobler existence in social society (Rousseau), the point is that humans are capable of getting along with others in dialogue and mutual complementation by chance or design. It is through dialogue and complementary interaction that humans effectively open up to their fellows. Certainly, the possibilities of misunderstanding are there, so also are those of understanding.

Grounds For Dialogue: A Common Humanity

The basis upon which humans come together in confidence to dialogue is a belief in a common-humanity. We have partly indicated this when we talked about the equality of essence.

Interlocutors in dialogue are subjects. Subjects are persons; persons are embodied spirits who posit themselves in the movement of word and action as irreplaceable subject at once interacting with others and conserving their specificity.

---

13.   Richard H. Bell, *Understanding African Philosophy: A Cross-Cultural Approach to Classical and Contemporary Issues*, 11.

There are no pre-conditions for dialogue in terms of color, language or belief except common humanity or personhood. Personhood is the only *a priori* condition that creates the common horizon for communication. To communicate, it is sufficient to recognize through the simple human instinct that the other is a human being.

Buber talks about the three ways "in which we are able to perceive a man who is living before our eyes,"[14] namely: observing, looking on, and becoming aware. Observing and looking are disinterested positions, which one can adopt towards the other. Becoming aware is a conscious involvement.

Humans possess reason that sets them apart from animals. Rationality is an instrument of cognition and discernment. Through the instrument of reason, humans are able to welcome, discover, assess and give response to actions and words discharged by others in the world of communication.

Chief Instrument Of Dialogue

Philosophers, social and philosophical anthropologists agree that humans are naturally ordained for society. Society is a willed group necessary for satisfying the existential ends of humans. It is in this regard that Messner restricts the use of the word 'society' to family, nation and state. Animals do not have society. If we must apply the word 'society' to them, it must be in an analogous sense. Even when such an instinctive organization is realized in more or less complex forms, the resulting co-operation can only be called 'social' in the wider sense, "for the individual member of animal society is already made by nature to fit into the whole almost as a part into a machine: its allotted function is part of its compelling instinct."

Like animals, pure spirits such as angels are incapable of social life in the human sense, since their nature is fully equipped to realize or attain their proper ends.

Dialogue partners give themselves to each other through the medium of language. The human language is a medium of self-donation for subjects, an instrument that opens one up to the other. It communicates inner sentiments as it fashions the world in the company of the other in the movement of action.

One of the greatest instruments the human language has produced is the *word*. With the word, the other says who he/she is, and creates an awareness in the human horizon that a human being is around. However, while the word is a

---

14.   M. Buber, *Between Man and Man*, 10.

very effective instrument of communication, it is not necessary for communication because there are other instruments in human language. People communicate through signs and symbols. Two women found themselves in a house, each trying to express her gratitude to the other but limited by the word. They looked at each other, but do not know how to say to each other what they felt; then they smiled at each other, drew closer and embraced each other. They smiled, laughed and nodded to each other in satisfaction. To communicate, words are sufficient but not always necessary. But to communicate it is necessary to recognize a sign or a certain presence (material or immaterial); signs, here, comprehend words and action. Whereas words make us aware of a presence, signs locate specific spots of human existential circumference. Dialogue then is communicative; it is enhanced by speech but not limited or enslaved by it.

Dialogue As Sharing Of Meaning: Language

People come to the dialogue arena carrying their chest of experiences. They come to discover each other in their root metaphors or meaning structures, that is, on the grounds that animate their words and actions. The subject's equality of essence guarantees that dialogue-partners have an equally unprejudiced ground to uphold themselves in their axiological signification. This rules out any attempt to manipulate the grounds within which, and in the context of which, meanings are shared.

To argue for a liberal basis for encounter, Richard Rorty has proposed a conversation philosophy within which meaning is pluralistically sought. The mistake Rorty makes, however, is to take dialogue partners as contingent, even asking them before hand to privatize some of their experiences, meanings, beliefs and values. His rejection of some *a priori* epistemological or metaphysical basis indicates his aversion for *a priori* foundations for human experience, that is, his attempt to raise non-foundational/contingent principles as enduring attitudes of mankind. Rorty's metaphysics treats people as transit truths, contingent constellation of experiences and mere instruments of the social process, without perduring identities. His pretence to get people on his side in the dialogue arena through the process of persuasion is only a political and social propaganda.[15]

Contrary to Rorty's attempt, partners are not there, first and foremost, to be persuaded or convinced to join the side of the other partner by way of rhetoric.

---

15. See Francis O. C. Njoku, 'Rorty On Post-Philosophical Culture: Shaping Our Culture With Our Thoughts in *WAJOPS* 3 (Dec. 2000), 88-110.

Subjects must be appreciated in their unique ontology and diversity of experiences. They are there to understand one another, to share meaning. Meanings are laid bear in the world of communication.

When dialogue partners begin to share their views or meanings, each listens and attempts to understand. It does not matter yet whether the partners' views are stupid, interesting or strange. I can understand why you love dogs more than cats; it could be that you prefer coffee to tea. So you take your coffee, I take my tea. It is understandable that B cannot stand the presence of dogs, thus, he prefers pigeons. If we know peoples' histories, beliefs and experiences, we can understand, to a large extent, some of their behavior patterns, values and preferences. The human horizon makes allowances for peoples' diverse preferences and values. Thus, diverse values are not necessarily irreconcilable, opposed or antinomies. Dialogue necessarily succeeds as an avenue for understanding patterns of behavior that emanate from different root metaphors or meaning-structures. This understanding already elicits com-passion, that is, steeping into the feelings or worlds of others.

D might see all Zs as enemies and crooked people. Through the process of dialogue, he might understand better that he may have misjudged a group or a person or a certain state of affairs. An enlightened dialogue resolves the impasse for better communion.

In certain circumstances, dialogue reveals that the situation is such that nothing can be done. Suppose that E hates human beings and prefers snakes. This is certainly strange. Humans ordinarily prefer humans to snakes; thus the person who consistently prefers snakes to humans will either be sick or abnormal. So we understand.

Dialogue is a movement in the sharing of meanings. Sometimes we succeed in understanding, and empathizing with the meaning of the other. Through an enlightened dialogue people can be laid to change or modify their views or adjust their axiological orientations. Dialogue also reveals how far apart we can stand on some issues. The point remains that dialogue opens the gate, other things being equal, by showing that a certain understanding can lead to better assessment of the situation.

Of A Certain Conception of Life As Communion

An African philosophy of right is based on an understanding of life as communion in its complementary signification. I will not undertake an elaborate treatment of life as communion since it has been done in previous works.[16] Life is a communion among the living and the dead. Everyone lives and moves around 'our life,' which owes its origin from God transmitted through our ancestors and maintained in communal respect by all. The closest people want to get in social relations is to approximate the closeness that exists among brothers and sisters for all life traces back to God. Against this backdrop, people relate to one another as children of God and relate among themselves as brothers and sisters. There is then an ontological bond that holds together all humans. Writing about life in Africa, Marie de Paul Neiers says:

> Man and...(his) environment interpenetrate each other by a kind of osmosis, in an intimate fusion...cosmic unit, personality stretches itself out beyond bodily venture and echoes all that surrounds it, vibrating intensely in its contact with the world and with other personalities.... The being and its milieu form a totality of which the break would leave the being rent and mutilated.[17]

In communal unions, there is a kind of 'marital-intentionality,' where knowing is not dichotomized from loving, as the traditional African reaches out to his object of knowledge in a 'rational embrace' or an 'impassioned reason' or 'communion.' According to Leopold Sedar Senghor, the subject and the object live in a symbiotic embrace.[18]

Even among the Christian Churches on African soil, some think that it is high time they learnt to allow the African understanding of life as communion permeate their lives; hence, Oduyoye asks:

> Can African Christians contribute new symbols and myths for the promoting of justice and reconciliation? Can covenant meals, symbols of sharing and of acceptance of communal responsibility begin to happen more meaningfully in the Church? Can more people 'break bread' together not only on their knees but in their homes, sharing in the homes, sharing the utilization of national resources?[19]

---

16. See Francis Njoku, 'An Understanding of Life within the Perspective of African Theology,' in *Encounter: A Journal of Life and Religion* 1, 1 (1992), 44-57; *Essays in African Philosophy, Thought and Theology* (Owerri: Claretian Institute of Philosophy, 2002), Ch. 10.

17. Marie de Paul Neiers, *The People of the Jos Plateau of Nigeria, their Philosophy, Manner and Customs* (Frankfurt: Peter D Lang, 1965), 117.

18. See Leopold Sedar Senghor in *African Socialism* (New York: Preager Press, 1964), 72-73.

Among the acts that attempt to establish a closer union between people, the ceremony to evoke intimate friendship or blood brotherhood among the Nyoro of Western Uganda is very significant in the way it highlights the grounds for a committed brotherhood. During the ritual ceremony, the ritual-elder makes some incision on each of the pairs of the abdomen and over the heart position of each of the partners. Some blood is let to gush out from these incised areas. Then, the ritual-elder breaks up a coffee bean, smears the halves with blood of the initiands, and each is given the other half of the bean to swallow. The friends thereafter make a resolution in the following words: "As we have become friends, let the stomach of whoever cheats his friend swell. When I visit you, at any time, you will not send me away. If I become poor you will not discard me. We will never do anything to harm any of our relatives and friends. May our ancestors be our witnesses. May God ratify our friendship, our brotherhood."[20] These words of the resolution show that ancestors are invoked as witnesses and God is appealed to as the sole guarantor of the pact. What is stressed in this pact is not the material reality of blood but the fact that participants will to be bound together in a closer relationship typical of brothers and sisters.

19.   Mercy A. Oduyoye 'The Value of the African Religious Beliefs and Practices for Christian Theology,' in *African Theology En Route* eds., Kofi Appiah-Kubi and Sergio Torres, 111.

20.   Anatole Byaruhanga Akiki, 'African Traditional Religious Values are to be used as a Force for Human Development,' in *African Theology in Progress*, eds., J. T. Agbasiere and B. K. Zabajungu, vol. 2 (AMECEA Publications), 56-57.

10

Dialogue in African Context as Process of Construction of Reality

The Importance Of Oral Narrative

Social anthropologists constantly refer to the phenomenon of palaver in African societies as a method of social construction of reality. The palaver is at once an arena and a process of dialogue in social construction of reality. As Richard Bell indicates, dialogue is a great component of an oral narrative:

> The village model in Africa is a model of free discourse for the purpose of making good judgments and for doing justice for individuals and the community. These narrative situations force dialogue and give rise to human reflection, and they are far from uncritical. Each dialogue situation has earmarks of the Socratic enterprise; each is formative of the values characteristic of that community; each dialectically serves to move a community from injustice to justice, from wrong to right, from brokenness to wholeness, from ignorance to truth.[1]

The dialogue situation is an occasion of critical evaluation of values. Bell insists in his new book:

> The ordinary struggles of human life are played out in these narrative situations—popular views are expressed, disputes are put forward, and human concerns are voiced. A narrative situation, if it is to be of some philosophical interest, will generate discussion leading toward alternative views, resolutions to the disputes, or just solutions to expressed human concerns.... Each new situation that forces such dialogue in a critical fashion is the narrative 'stuff' of philosophy.[2]

---

1. Richard Bell, 'Narrative in African Philosophy,' in *Philosophy* 64 (1989): 373.

People come to the palaver ground to dialogue, and report back to their families and kin. Dialogue continues until an agreement is reached. Dialogue permeates every aspect of African life nurtured in the village palaver. This method of
seeking answers and counseling in the face of life riddles is employed in land disputes, marriage negotiations and in many other ceremonies by the community.
Through the palaver or 'council model' communities do not only come to better
judgments, "each community re-evaluates its life in terms of new external factors,
it can critically evolve its traditions to meet modernity,"[3] and satisfy its sense of
relevance. To reach an agreement does not mean that everyone agrees to a particular line of action, although most of the time there was this kind of agreement in
traditional African society. The strength of the palaver lies in the fact that everyone has had the opportunity to express his or her views. The views expressed help
the community or the group to assess its own line of action and position as a
group. Whether the opinions in a discourse are for or against, they all contribute
to the construction of the resultant community-accepted view. This is a consen-
sual democracy, not necessarily the modern Western democracy that prides on
numerical advantages. The line of action adopted in consensus democracy
becomes the product of opinions/judgments to and fro. Reality is first and foremost fashioned in words through dialogue: the assessment of opinions and
counter opinions. A lot of injustice can be done if there was no proper dialogue.
Injustice disrupts the equilibrium of the community and persons.

The Igbo are known for their use of the palaver method in discussion embodied in the organization of the community and the resolution of disputes. George
E. Ekwuru has indicated that the palaver method encapsulates the spirit of *Igbo-
kwenu* (the Igbo-concordance assent in a communal dialogue):

> From the socio-political and linguistic level of consideration, the symbolic res-
> onance of Igbo-Kwenu, more than simply signifying a mere form of greeting,
> symbolizes a respectful invitation to listen and reason along with the speaker.
> It is a formal way of taking permission to speak, whereby one creates around
> oneself a mobile platform, a focal point that draws the attention of the whole
> assembly of the *Umunna*, thereby insinuating the much-valued dignifying
> aura of esoteric silence. Within a culture where both respect and dialogue are
> valued as essential elements of a socio-political life, *Igbo-Kwenu* represents a
> conscious customized mode of being and saying.[4]

---

2.   Richard H. Bell, *Understanding African Philosophy: A Cross-Cultural Approach to
      Classical and Contemporary Issues* (London: Routledge, 2002), 112.
3.   *Ibid.*, 113.

The participation in the palaver method is a making of, and participation in, the text. In this regard, Samuel O. Imbo rightly points out that "texts are constructed not in the medium of writing but in memory, and fixed in parables, myths, art, music, and so on."[5] The reality of dialogue in the African context is a great argument in favor of the fact that orality is a valuable text, and that social construction has a communal context.

> In an oral situation, philosophical texts are composed in a social context that emphasizes dialogic encounters and the social construction of meaning. No individual participant pretends to know the truth, and thus each couches his or her opinions, beliefs, and suspicions in the rhetoric of proverbs, aphorisms, and myths of the community. In this activity the individual merges his or her voice with that of the community. By retreating into the oral culture, the individual acknowledges being part of a larger enterprise and also acknowledges being a socially situated participant who is an agent in the construction of knowledge as well as an agent in an interpretative process that is creative. The rhetoric of oral traditions depends on the involvement of the audience, their participation in interpretation and judgment. Multiple interpretations by agents steeped in the oral tradition give the text a life of its own, and the final product is one whose author-ity is difficult to fix.[6]

The authority of a text may be difficult to fix where we consider authority as one person or unitary source. Many agents contribute to the making or interpretation of the oral text within the community. The palaver is a participatory way of molding individuals, the community and their values. What constitutes as authority or authoritative is truth, whichever way it is arrived at. Participatory encounter in the palaver is only an inquiry or journey into the discovery of truth. Authority is not person or source-centered but truth-centered.

The Role of Master-clarifiers

The dialogue arena is not a collection of rubble that recklessly shouts and haggles with one another. Opinions expressed in palaver are heard and interpreted collec-

---

4.   George Ekwuru, *The Pangs of An African Culture in Travail: Uwa Ndi Igbo Yaghara (The Igbo World in Disarray)* (Owerri: Totan Publishers Limited, 1999), 135-136.
5.   Samuel Imbo, *An Introduction to African Philosophy* (Maryland: Rowman & Littlefield Publishers Inc., 1998), 106.
6.   *Ibid.*, 106-107.

tively. But alongside the community participatory interpretation are masters of the oral text:

> An important consequence of orality is the social significance of literature in the face-to-face situations of traditional societies which provide the context of its realization. We need to take account of specialized workers, 'masters of the word.'…We may apply to this special category of individuals the well-known term 'Griot.' The social role and significance of the Griot in traditional society is of the first order….[7]

The Nzonzi and the Griot are masters of clarifications. They act on the spot as the guardians of the word. They perform a function that is at once aesthetical and dialectical, by acting as the Socratic midwives, guiding the palaver to a just and wise conclusion.

The written and spoken words have different evidentiary structures in negotiating for relevance, fact and truth. For example, Senghor appeals to the active brand of language when he stresses emotion as an important knowing process in the Negro-Africa's worldview:

> Speech seems to us the main instrument of thought, emotion and action. There is no thought or emotion without a verbal image, no free action without first a project in thought…. For the human being, speech is the living and life-living breath of man at prayer. It possesses a magical virtue, realizing the law of participation and by its intrinsic power, creating the thing named.[8]

Presence and thought are largely reified by speech. Speech embodies the social life of the group.

An oral presentation is always tested as it is presented. It is always the work of master clarifiers or philosophic sages to guide the reality sought in words.

The word is used to articulate the being of the community: its aspirations and life. The basic ethical fabric or foundation of the community is live and let live, or as expressed in the Western articulation of the basic principle of natural law: do good and avoid evil—bonum est faciendum et malum vitandum. By maintaining harmony in oneself and in the community in all its individual and social ram-

---

7.   Abiola Irele, 'The African Imagination,' in Research in African Literatures 21 (Spring 1990): 56.

8.   Cf. Parker English and Kilbujjo M. Kalumba, eds., African Philosophy: A Classical Approach (Upper Saddle River, N. J.: Prentice Hall, 1996), 48.

ifications, one is doing good and doing justice too. In the thought expressed by the *word*, one is indeed doing right.

The African traditional structure or order of life, it is said, centers on persons as community-beings who embody the conscience of the community. It is in the community that one's conscience is formed. Regarding conscience brought about through the magic of the community word, Benezet Bujo says:

> It is about talking with and listening to one another. The ear, which has a similar function as that of the female sexual organs, takes in the semen of the word and lets it penetrate deeply into the human person. In the human depth, the word is turned into life or death according to the inner state of the individual. The word, which was transformed in the depth of the human person, has to prove itself true and be successful in confronting other words, expressed by different members of the entire community. The word of the individual has to prove its innocence in public. During the process of talking and listening to each other, the word, which brings death is rejected, whereas the one which promotes life is confirmed and integrated into the service of the community. What community refuses or confirms through palaver, with the active participation of those concerned, merits respect, lest the individual should expose him/herself and the community to death.[9]

The individual who refuses to accept the community's position on an issue is branded a rebel or an 'individualist,' to use Bujo's term. However, the problem of the community-centered conscience building is how to handle individual freedom. It will be argued later in this book that a reading of the African community from the point of view of philosophy of right can help address the deficiencies of the collectivist's view of person in society or in the community.

---

9.   Bénézet Bujo, *The Ethical Dimension of Community: The African Model and the Dialogue Between North and South* (Nairobi: Paulines Publication Africa), 78.

11

An African Philosophy of Right

The Problem Of Analysis Of Rights In General

Sometimes one is questioned whether one is allowed to do a particular thing. If John is allowed to enter the property Z, then he has right to do it; whether or not he is in a Black or White territory does not arise. This is a claim that can be seen as an example of an institutional right. As Howard Davies and David Holdcroft write, "we have many institutional rights, among the most important of which are of course the legal rights conferred by statutes and the decision of courts, such as the right to make a will, to dispose of property that is lawfully owned, and to stand on a picket line when on strike, etc."[1]

There are moral rights such as right to freedom of speech or worship: although they may be recognized by a constitution or a legal system, they do not owe their existence or authority to a constitution or a legal system. People have moral rights whether or not they are recognized by the legal system or the constitution: "Such rights have a special value as they rest on a moral conception of persons as separate individuals equal in worth," who must be treated as ends in themselves and not as means. Immanuel Kant has articulated this principle in his deontology: "So act as to treat humanity, whether in thine own person or in that of any other, in every case as end withal, never as means only."[2] This principle, for Kant, implies an instance of a universal law.[3] Moral rights have been variously described as natural, fundamental, background and so on.

A utilitarian might find a reason to violate institutional rights on welfare grounds. For example, it is better to expropriate Mr B in order to build a park for

---

1. Howard Davies and David Holdcroft, *Jurisprudence: Text and Commentary* (London: Butterworths, 1991), 230.
2. Immanuel Kant, *Fundamental Principles of the Metaphysic of Morals* trans. J. K. Abbot (New York: Prometheus Books, 1988), 58.
3. *Ibid.*, 49.

the community. Thus institutional rights can be trumped on consequential grounds. But most people will not allow the violation of rights where the rights in question are fundamental rights. If to maximize welfare will involve the violation of fundamental rights, then we would not do it. It is in this regard that utilitarianism cannot give a justified explanation of fundamental rights.

Ronald Dworkin's rights thesis of law holds that fundamental rights put constraint on collective goals, that is, arguments of rights have precedence over policy-arguments; the violation of fundamental rights cannot be justified on grounds of utilitarian arguments. Courts are there to enforce existing rights.

By separating moral rights from the rights guaranteed by political societies, conflicts still exist in the analysis of rights. In general, there is everywhere in liberal societies a catalogue of conflict of right: the young against the old, one race against another, men against women, rich against the poor; the rights of the weak conflict with the strong, the developed with the underdeveloped. Sometimes we can refer to documents in which rights are catalogued; hence L. W. Sumner writes:

> The advantage of a catalogue is that the rights it contains are more general than those standardly invoked in particular public issues, thus raising the promise of verifying narrower claims by subsuming them under some broader category. Presumably we would then be entitled to reject as spurious any putative specific right, which could not be derived from some abstract and general right. A rights catalogue would thus enable us to ascertain the authenticity of rights in somewhat the way in which a stamp catalogue does so for stamps. It would serve as an authority.[4]

Arguments from authority generally succeed in telling us who has been granted rights; they do not always show us the basis of such rights. Thus, the controversy about rights is not resolved yet. And it is beyond the scope of this book to investigate at present.

Objections To Preferring A Philosophy of Right in An African Context

Some people think that, so far as the African context is concerned, we should be talking about justice and compassion instead of right. They believe that the ques-

---

4.   L. W. Sumner, *The Moral Foundation of Rights* (Oxford: Clarendon Press, 1987), 4.

tion about right leaves out of the picture issues of justice and compassion. Richard H. Bell writes:

> The moral issues are, first, the relationship of individual identity and community and emergent views of justice surrounding liberal individualism and communitarian thinking. The discussion explores whether there is a different sense in which the concept of 'justice' in the African context is being used, distinguishing between individual 'right-based' and more communal 'compassion-based' moral thinking and implications of each for rethinking civic order. The second set of moral issues has to do with the philosophical significance of suffering and poverty in African context, and how these two concepts affect our thinking about justice and human development.[5]

Those who prefer the moral category of justice claim that much insistence on rights forgets the community context; hence they believe that the moral category of justice argues for a community-based identity. In a multi-cultural milieu such as Africa, the issue of rights divides communities, the view holds:

> Values such as generosity, compassion, reciprocity, mutual sympathy, cooperation, solidarity, and social well-being continue to shape the moral practices of Africans and are generally held to be of more importance than the value of individual rights. From such communitarian values should flow both a sense of responsibility of individuals to their community and obligations to one's society.[6]

Bell accepts Kwame Gyekye's claim that too much emphasis on rights and privileges fragments social values, social relationships and the integrity of the community itself. The fear about insisting on the moral category of right seems to stem from the supposition that the category of rights enthrones individualism, and exaggerates the value of self-respect. Thus, identity is largely to be formed with "one's collective associations" within which the individual lives his life.

Even Gyekye would want to take a step further to separate justice from compassion because it is rooted in right-arguments:

> In the communitarian moral universe caring or compassion or generosity, not justice—which is related essentially to a strictly right-based morality—may be a fundamental moral category. In a moral framework where love, compassion, caring, friendship, and genuine concern for others characterize social relation-

---

5.   Richard H. Bell, *Understanding African Philosophy*, 59.
6.   *Ibid.*, 66.

ships, justice—which is about relations of claims and counter-claims—may not be the primary moral virtue.[7]

The reservation with the category of right, according to compassion-based argument, is that a right-based argument is not rooted in communitarian-based tradition. Bell recognizes Gyekye's concern, which Simone Weil had earlier expressed. Weil has argued, leaning on the experience of World War II, that "to place the notion of rights at the center of social conflicts is to inhibit any possible impulse of charity on both sides."[8] Weil believes that the notions of justice and right do not go far enough in addressing the source of hurt in community: "The notion of rights is linked with the notion of sharing, of exchange, of measured quantity. It has a commercial favor, essentially evocative of legal claims and argument. Rights are always asserted in a tone of contention; and when this tone is adopted, it must rely upon force in the background, or else it will be laughed at."[9] She holds that, because the question of right is rooted in the question of justice, it concentrates on addressing and redressing legal harms or claims, since it attempts to address the disequilibria between who has got more and who has got less. This state of affairs blurs the attention that should be given to the question: "Why am I being hurt?" This question, in Weil's thinking, is a matter of love. And only a sense of justice cemented in love can cherish it. In other words, obligation driven by a sense of compassion, Weil believes, takes precedence over that of rights.[10] The issue of justice to which the subject approaches from the point of view of compassion, according to Weil, puts into perspective the human situation of suffering or affliction and its roots, for justice rooted in compassion and love may discern obligations where considerations of rights are not evident. In this light, Bell supports the preference of Gyekye and Weil for compassion and loved-based intuitions:

> In a 'right-based' society the moral values of love, generosity, and compassion are seldom thought to be 'intrinsic.' If, in fact, we could assume such values as intrinsic, then the moral practices of the people would, indeed, be different. There would be a greater sense of concern or care for the well-being of one's fellow society members and a greater sense of civic responsibility.[11]

---

7. Kwame Gyekye, *Tradition and Modernity: Philosophical Reflections on the African Experience* (Oxford: Oxford University Press, 1997), 70.

8. Simone Weil, *Selected Essays: 1934-1943*, trans. Richard Rees (Oxford: Oxford University Press, 1962), 21.

9. *Ibid.*, 18.

10. See *Ibid.*, 28-30.

One could say that it is the fear of not knowing how to found right-based identity or argument within the community that makes Gyekye, Weil and Bell feel that it does not go to the root of addressing issues of poverty and suffering in the African situation. But I think that right-based arguments can be posited, and right-based identity successfully re-captured; without ejecting the sense of love and compassioned embedded in the community.

However, we should be reluctant to found human well being simply on the feeling of compassion by the other. We need a foundation where the human person can flourish as a justification of his own existence, independent of the other's emotional dispositions, whether or not such dispositions are good.

Hurdles On The Way to Constructing An African Philosophy Of Right

In order to create a basis for a philosophy of right within African conceptual schemes, it is important to note some hurdles on the way of such a project.

i) Ambiguities in emphasis: Sometimes one notices a lopsided shift of emphasis in an African environment. At one time, emphasis is laid on the individual and, at another, on the community. In general, however, the emphasis on the role of the collectivity as the ultimate dominant and determinant force seems to override. The resulting effect is that individuals who make up the communion suffocate in the process. Thus, the individualist and collectivist reasons set themselves in opposition to one another.

ii) The inability to reach a compromise: An African society may recognize that rights can be overridden; but the problem is that, most of the time, it is individuals that relinquish their rights. Can the community ever be made to know that persons may have a priori rights before which the community itself must bow?

iii) The problem of the super-structure created by the elite and priest-craft: This type of state of affairs confuses the model of relationship that exists between individuals and their rulers—men who have some pronounced social roles to perform. A major part of this confusion stems from the ardent interests of rulers to manipulate the social structure. Allegiance to such structures may largely be sustained, among other reasons, by ignorance, lack of education or fear of religious or social retribution.

iv) Lack of equitable theoretical background: There is a lack of reflection or conceptual framework on what should constitute a reasonable basis for better

11.   Richard H. Bell, *Understanding African Philosophy*, 71.

interaction in society. In other words, there is an evidential absence of a principled conceptual basis to effect genuine actions regarding legitimate claims. This seems to be part of the reason why J. Obi Oguejiofor has argued that traditional moral values in Nigeria are not universalizable.[12] Social judgments and interactions are conditioned by family, group and clan affiliations.

v) Dealing with mass morality: Sometimes one notices a situation in which what is right is what everyone is doing. One who takes a contrary view to what is happening in the *status quo* seems to be running backwards. What everyone is doing is taken to be what is right.

vi) Some negative reminders: There are some models of understanding or reconstruction that are antithetical to building a balanced philosophy of right within an African environment. Patrilineal societies are known to place emphasis on a male-constructed and male-ruled universe of meaning. The values of courage, wit and spirit of achievement may be underlined, but their inherent defect is a pretext to be always capable of dictating on every activity in the environment. Members of chauvinistic groups create a framework of meaning, approbation and disapprobation that is propagated by their class. While insiders of this group, who may respect the claims of their co-members, impose a world vision or a way of life which, in the final analysis, may diminish the persons of individuals outside of their group, the model of rights that comes out of this group, in relation to outsiders, is the offshoot of a male-dominated structure mostly translated in commands or societal imperatives. Certainly, this understanding of right fails to provide an equitable ground for society to create and change the positions of others within the conditions guaranteed by natural and socio-legal rights.

vii) There is the problem of the ancestor model of authority: since the forefathers had said it, it is taken to be correct. This seems to be an unchangeable creed. Thus the authority evoked in the name of an ancestor acquires a 'presbyterious' stability. What the elders or seniors have said is taken to be necessarily right whether or not is correct or reasonable. One earns another's allegiance and/or what one says acquires authority by simply pressing to the assembly that one is a senior. There is not much dialogue on the basis of critical reflective attitude. The ancestor model of authority has come to survive in the Afro-Nigerian political scene as an affair known as 'control by the godfathers.' Control by the godfathers has become a debilitating social and political phenomenon in Nigeria. To have a

---

12. J. Obi Oguejiofor, 'Non-Universality of Traditional Moral Values and Corruption in Nigeria,' in *Philosophy, Christianity and Science in the Third Millennium* ed. Francis O. C. Njoku (Owerri: Claretian Institute of Philosophy, 2000), 120-137.

political career or be recognized, one has to have or align oneself with one godfather or another, who at once manipulate the state machinery and divert its resources for their own selfish-ends.

The Community-Orientedness

By right is meant what an individual or person is entitled to claim by virtue of the provisions of natural and social justice. The demands of natural justice are rooted in the nature of man, the claims demanded by his nature as man without which he would be less than a man or person. For example, man is an embodied spirit—body and soul. In distinguishing himself as a rational and unified entity, he has claims to maintain himself, and the means to sustain himself through food, clothing and shelter. He has the right to be educated and protected through the co-operation of others; thus, he attains his full humanity in the social group. Any statement of affairs that flouts his rightful realization as an undivided entity and as a member in social association will be infringing on the basic rights of his person. The community-orientedness of the African life has been strongly championed by Julius Nyerere.. We recall his statement:

> For when a society is so organized that it cares about its individuals, then, provided he is willing to work, no individual within that society should worry about what will happen to him tomorrow if he does not hoard wealth today. Society itself should look after him, or his widow, or his orphans. This is exactly what traditional African society succeeded in doing. Both the 'rich' and the 'poor' individual were completely secure in African society. Natural catastrophe brought famine, but it brought famine to everyone—poor or rich. Nobody starved, either of food or of human dignity, because he lacked personal wealth; he could depend on wealth possessed by the community of which he was a member. That was socialism. That is socialism. There can be no such thing as acquisitive socialism, for that would be another contradiction in terms. Socialism is essentially distributive. Its concern is to see that those who sow reap a fair share of what they sow.[13]

Nyerere's socialism insists that African traditional society takes care of its members. It is based on some kind of distributive welfare or justice. M. I. Nwoko corroborates Nyerere's views in the following words:

---

13.   Julius Nyerere, 'Ujamaa: The Basis of African Socialism' in *I am Because We Are: Readings in Black Philosophy*, eds., Fred Lee Hord and Jonathan Scott Lee (Massachusetts: University of Massachusetts Press, 1995)., 66-67.

African traditional society is a society where the individual is always considered a free integrated member of his community—a communion person. It is a society where individualism is a taboo, and where the member takes up the interest of the community as his own. His pride is in *igwe-bu-ike* (the community is power). The more united to the community, the stronger and more secure he is. He feels the community as a direct extension of the family.[14]

In other words, the community is the center of gravity. The gravitational force largely pulls individuals to the communal center. Consequently, individuals are like spokes organized around the hub—the community. A disruption in any part of the circular structure or collectivity creates a malfunction in the whole set-up. It is said that, if a rung of the societal ladder is removed, the line of the societal life force is jeopardized. The emphasis on the collectivity as determining the 'person' of the individual prides itself as an ontological unity which creed is 'I am because others are, or I am because we are.' The sense of community and extended family spirit got into the United Nation Regional Advisor on Social Policy and Training, Economic Commission for Africa:

In rural Africa, the extended family and the clan assume the responsibility for all services for their members, whether social or economic. People live in closely organized groups and willingly accept communal obligations for mutual support. Individuals satisfy their needs for social and economic security merely by being attached to one of these groups. The sick, the aged and children are all cared for by the extended family. In this type of community nobody can be labeled as poor because the group usually shares what they have. There is no competition, no insecurity, no big ambitions, no unemployment and thus people are mentally healthy. Deviation or abnormal behavior is almost absent.[15]

Communalistic views maintain that the African is ontologically predisposed to care for the other, that is, individuals have an attitude of care towards each other. Kwame Nkrumah branded the attitude of care as 'egalitarian'[16] and Julius Nyerere articulated it as an '*ujamaa.*'[17] In the world of cultural encounter with Europe

---

14. Matthew I. Nwoko, *The Rationality of African Socialism* (Rome: Tiop-Litografia Aurelia, 1985), 71-72.

15. See John Iliffe, *The African Poor: History* (Cambridge: Cambridge University Press 1989), 3.

16. See Kwame Nkrumah, *Consciencism: Philosophy and Ideology for Decolonisation and Development with particular reference to African Revolution* (London: Heinmann Educational Books Limited, 1964), 78.

and America, Leopold Sedar Senghor captured the lively African spirit with the concept of *Negritude,*[18] the predisposition for care by the African as a posting of the self in a free and symbiotic embrace with the other. Within the theological parlance, Eugene E. Uzukwu sharpened the egalitarian or care-attitude as 'hospitality'[19] that can serve the Gospel to inculturate itself within the African socio-religious matrix. The end value of the egalitarian understanding of African societies is the insistence on communion among members of African breed.

There is a merit to the view that the community gives individuals their 'being.' To be 'maintained' in 'being,' one must conform to community's injunctions and ways. The ethics of such a life is that 'I am not alone in the social game—in the world.' What I do touches the other. The 'other' is understood as another person or a natural environment or God or any other symbol. The 'we-identity' has been used to explain the social being of the African as a positive value by African authors or writers on African values.

Reservations About The We-Identity-Claim

The community-centered argument implies that community dies or survives with the co-operation of others. In the collectivistic community of meaning, what claims one has do not derive from one's ontological constitution as an irreplaceable and incommunicable being but from the label placed on one as constituting a part in the whole. Evidently, the community in the African sense presents itself as the greatest infallible judge and distributor of resources for social living. Rights are then community-sanctioned. If we translate this world-view in positivistic terms, a collectivistic understanding of African societies will tend to recognize only socio-legal rights. The dispenser of community goods, whether symbolized in the sole authority of the individual or some collectivity, will be the imperative speaker who makes social labels, places them on items, making them have, and become, what their labels have imbued in them. It is significant to note, as

---

17.   See Julius Nyerere, *Ujamaa Essays on Socialism* (Nairobi: Oxford University Press, 1968), 1.

18.   See Excerpts from a speech delivered by Senghor at Oxford University in October 1961. See also Leopold Sedar Senghor, 'Negritude: A Humanism of the 20th Century' in *I Are Because We Are* eds. Fred Lee Hone and Jonathan Scot Lee Massachusetts: University of Massachusetts Press, 1995), 45.

19.   See E. E. Uzukwu, 'Missiology Today: The African Situation' in *Religion and African Culture, Inculturation—A Nigerian Perspective*, ed. E. E. Uzukwu (Enugu: Spiritan Publications, 1988) 158-169.

observed by Johannes Messner, that "the social theory of all collectivist systems...begins with the social entity as the absolute primary value, but never
reaches the full reality of the human person with its supra-social ends and its
value ranking above that of the society."[20] Much emphasis on the community
devalues the person standing as an incommunicable entity in-charge of his own
conscience and author of his co-operation as an existential personality.

But how realistic then is the claim that egalitarianism reinforces the attitude of
care or hospitality or communality to which the African is inherently and ontologically predisposed?

Challenging The Community-centered Claim

It is really time to critically probe into the so-called communitarian claim about
African families or societies. Did rural or traditional society take care of all its
members, especially the poor, as Nyerere and the rest claim? Actually, the various
African families have a social inclination or orientation as to what class of people
or poor the society protected. Depending on the group, compassion is not always
shown to the widow or her children. Some African cultures that allow the dis-
inheritance of the woman or wife after the death of her husband will not be said
to be compassionate or, perhaps will indeed be said to have a very different
notion of compassion! The general assertion that traditional Africa is very egalitarian and caring has to be demythologized. Some times, the family perpetrates
poverty and social discrimination. In this regard, one appreciates Iliffe's remark:

> Equally important, however, is the fact that Africans lived in different kinds of
> families, from the Yoruba compound with scores of related residents to the
> elementary households of Buganda. Each kind of family had its particular
> points of weakness and excluded its particular categories of unsupported
> poor—orphans in one case, barren women in another, childless elders in a
> third. Moreover, family structure was not an immutable ethnic characteristic
> but could change to meet changing needs. The intimate connection between
> poverty and family structure has been neglected by historians of Europe and
> may be Africa's contribution to the comparative history of the poor.[21]

---

20. Johannes Messner, *Social Ethics: Natural Law in the Western World* rev. ed. (London:
     B. Herder Book Co., 1965), 4.
21. John Iiiffe, *The African Poor: History*, 7-8.

African communalists and their sympathizers seem to ignore how poverty, social exclusion and oppression are maintained within African traditional set-up or families.

The people whose ideas reigned in the clan were the domineering or influential individuals. There was an obsessive fear of the juju man, the rich, the strong wrestler, the man with immense physical strength, the medicine man, the man who knows the way to the house of the medicine man, and so on. It will be great remiss to ignore the element of priest-craft in shaping social, political and religious realities. While one does not deny that African traditional societies had their sense of justice, it should be acknowledged that most of the time, because there was no organized jural system, there was a miscarriage of justice for the balance was apt to be tilted to suit the dictates of some influential individuals. In fact, because, the intellectual intuition of the society or individuals constituting the influential group was shortsighted and sickly redolent with suspicion, many talents were simply ignored, suppressed or minimally tapped. Without much equivocation, it is not an off-hand statement to say that traditional African society largely suffocated the private world of the individual; its formulated social constructs or recipes were largely codified mode of communication safe-guarding the interests and world views of the clever members of the group. In short, one can argue that there was no egalitarian society therein but a society of projected interests of some individuals who could exert their influence and impose the longings of their 'ideological' conscience as the social creed.

Bénézet Bujo has attempted to defend the community-centeredness of the African person by insisting that the name given to an individual safeguards his or her independence. He claims that within the community the individual is a historical being responsible for his or her action amidst the social web. Thus, Bujo insists:

> Because there is interdependence between the community and the individual, the community must not subordinate what is particular, but should promote and support it, because without the individuality of the single members it would totally disintegrate. Interaction, within the African context, makes it clear that the individual is an incomplete being who is basically dependent on the community.[22]

There is no doubt that individuals are given names, and there is interdependence between the community and the individual. And names individuate: iden-

---

22. Bénézet Bujo, *The Ethical Dimension of Community*, 148.

tify and isolate in the midst of the social rubble. However, what Bujo fails to do is to state how an allowance for the private world of the person in a society dominated by community-centered sanction could be made, where individuals simply bear the conscience of the community creed. Thus, until a theoretical basis is established for guaranteeing a free space for the individual in the socio-communitarian atmosphere, it will be difficult to talk about rights and freedom of the individual. We cannot simply evade the question of the individual-free space within the community by chorusing that in Africa—in contradistinction to the West—property rights of parents and others are never private.[23]

With the failure of a rigorous account of a collectivist approach to African socio-political worldview, can we recast such an account in individualistic terms?

An individualistic social theory lays stress on freedom of the individual over and above that of the social group. The individual is the epi-center of cosmic action; he champions the course of history by his self-determination. How free was the individual in the traditional African society? Not many were free.

The mechanism of a traditional society, as we pointed out above, was controlled by a few—the influential ones, whose major creed was the acquisition of greater power, force and wealth at the expense of others. One recalls Bantu's ethics that the social strength of a man is measured by how much he could increase his force. There is the saying among the Igbo of Onitsha area of Eastern Nigeria that *azu na-erighi ibe ya etobeghi*, that is, a fish that has not eaten a fellow fish has not grown up yet.

A man who went to his farm daily, ate at his home with his children and so on, would think that he was free! It would be difficult for him to see himself as a robot in the society, controlled and monitored by invisible forces or the societal superstructure. He lived like a domestic animal in the farmyard of the community that could be used for sacrifice when the owner desires.

The common man had many taboos to observe, and many daily rituals to perform, either to appease the community or the divinities. If he was not an indirect or unconscious slave of the dominant conscience, he held perpetual allegiance to one divinity or another. If he was 'free' with men, he was not free with nature or his environment. Suppose community and environment allow him to live his life with fewer burdens, he would still have to pay the debts owed by his past ancestors! He may still prefer to follow the uncritical way of his forefathers to spare himself the trouble of reasoning or evaluating the present situation. The individual in traditional Africa was living in bondage or slavery but was only free proba-

---

23. See *Ibid.*, 149–155.

bly by virtue of his ignorance of the conditions under which he lived. In an inclusive consideration of pre-colonial, colonial and post colonial Africa, we should realize that the so-called influential individuals, even with their acquisition of Western education, in the present scheme of things, still remain great actors in an environment either dominated and enslaved by natural, environmental forces or outside influences.

In my judgment, the attempt to give account of the African society in terms of strictly individualistic or collectivistic terms has not succeeded. A few selfish minded individuals, who incapacitated the social order as a whole, largely dominated traditional African society. Such a restricted vision of society did not lead to the individual's free doing and independence to secure means that could, without much danger, achieve the individual's self-enhancement: the means of livelihood and social action was restricted to some. What actually has come to be exposed in our scrutiny of traditional Africa is that it was a closed society, secretive in its empirical manifestations and largely chauvinistic in its operation.

Towards A Re-constructive Interpretation Of The Ontological Basis Of African Society

One's life-world in traditional societies was very limited to one's immediate family. Let us extend this life-world to the clan. By clan here is meant a group of families that traces to one ancestral blood relationship. Life outside of this cycle was almost as precarious as it was hostile. Beyond the family-clan axis, life out there was a *not-me, not-us*. Whatever they are out there, they are not of us and for us, and we are neither of them nor for them. Therefore, we must be protected against them. While I do not solely intend to align myself with Thomas Hobbes in his hypothesized claim that man in the state of nature was very brutish, it is important to note that the view that traditional African society was peaceful, just and egalitarian must be restrictive and qualified. One assumes that peoples' primitive or undisturbed peace and life were immediately linked to their immediate families, which were their immediate environment of occurrence. Persons outside of this environment were as mysterious and suspicious as the mountains, hills, big trees, rivers and forests out there. Any thing outside of me or of us was a *numen*—an object either of fear (superstition) to be kept at arms length or magic (coerced for one's selfish purposes). But how was conviviality brokered among individuals and their environment?

With persistent wars and conflicts families began to enlarge their hold or control over the territories they occupied and those of others. By arbitrary and peaceful settlement of inter-family or clan differences, different communities began to lay down their arms at the altar of tolerant conviviality or communion.[24] Sometimes, such solutions of conflicts were not the most justified but were the best less evil that could result in the name of peace and furtherance of group progeny. The transition from interpersonal and family conflicts to community or societal conviviality was mostly wrought by a *covenant*, establishing peace among persons and groups.

---

24.   See Francis O. C. Njoku, *Essays in African Philosophy, Thought and Theology*, 169.

12

The Concept Of Covenant and Philosophy Of Right

Briefly, a covenant is a pact between two or more entities.[1] *The Reader's Digest Oxford Wordfinder* defines a covenant as (1) an agreement; a contract; (2) Law (a) a contract drawn up under a seal, especially undertaking to make regular payments to a charity; (3) in Biblical terms, the agreement between God and the Israelites. Lexically, a covenant is an agreement that is strongly binding on the parties involved. The idea of covenant in Biblical and extra-biblical sources is that it is a commitment made through a promise. It is against this backdrop that G. E. Mendehall defines covenant as a "solemn promise made binding by an oath, which may be either a verbal formula or a symbolic action. Such an action or formula is recognized by the parties as the formal act which binds the actor to fulfill his promise."[2] The act of people binding themselves together through a solemn promise dates back to ancient times as excavated treaty formula of Hittite empire has indicated. Thus, covenant has a secular character, and the Israelite covenant conforms to the secular character.

In specific African context, "a covenant group is a ritually established blood related group/people whose being is by a common consent rooted in a spiritual anchor."[3] It is effected in the environment of communion or binding together of lives that attempts to establish a closeness of relationship typical of brothers. Thus, through covenant, persons and groups arrive at peace. On the other hand, the basic idea of covenant itself has a negative chord to it. Covenant making is a

---

1.   See my previous article: 'An Understanding of Life Within the Perspective of African Theology' in *Encounter* 1-1 (1992), 44-57.

2.   G. E. Mendhall 'Covenant' in *The Interpreter's Dictionary of the Bible* A-D, George Arthur Buttrick ed. et al (New York: Abingdom Press, 1962), 714.

3.   Francis Njoku, 'An Understanding of Life within the Perspective of African Theology,' in *Encounter: A Journal of Liffe and Religion* 1 (No. 1, 1992) 49.

product of conflict-situation. The goal in covenant ritual, in Africa, is to establish a blood relationship. People who are already blood-related have, strictly speaking, no need of making covenants. If people are blood-related, they cannot be any closer than members of the same family.

Through covenant or a socio-religious pact, persons or families who were not in any way related by blood come to establish a blood relationship or something like it in which they commit themselves to the pursuit of their well-being as members of the same blood-related family. Within the covenant framework, participants share the same meaning-structure in the same community of life. Covenant is a willed act or pact. By it, a willed meaning-structure ensues—a community of the sameness of meaning that should not be conceived in terms less than family-bond. Covenant is rooted in blood or family spirit. The family, as a relationship of blood-pairs, is the closest association nature has endowed humans with, right from the womb through birth to the development of one's personality. All social relations tend to approximate a closeness that is founded on family or the sameness of brotherhood.[4]

Deriving Covenant-Based Rights Within African Environment

When people are involved in a conflict situation and want or desire to create a lasting relationship or rebuild a broken relationship, they invariably want a guaranteed atmosphere of safety and good will. They want an environment of trust to exercise and give effect to their willingness to belong to a common family-hood (paternity or maternity, group, society, and political set-up). Such goodwill on the part of persons or groups or families involved is symbolized by a covenant ceremony. Within the family cycle, other things being equal, suspicion or lack of trust is not a common place. The horizon of blood relationship is an ambient of trust and communion in the same life-bank. And when persons and communities

---

4. In reviewing my book, *Essays in African Philosophy, Thought and Theology* in *West African Journal of Philosophy* (WAJOPS) 5 (December 2002), 112-115, Alfred Emeka Nwoye has objected to the covenant model. He thinks that we should substitute the family model for covenant model. I do not really think that the covenant model is in opposition with the family model, as I have pointed out in my earlier articles prior to the publication of the book. The unity of relationship that is sought in covenant is typified by family spirit. In covenant, people who were formerly strangers come together to bind themselves in a relationship, seeking a closeness that is typical of brothers and sisters. That closeness is an appeal to familyhood.

make a ritual pact, they are expressing, in a symbolic manner, their commitment to the same blood-hood of meaning and life as members of the same life-stock. We have seen an instance of this in the making of blood brotherhood among the Ugandan people, where covenant partners commit themselves to the welfare of one another and their peoples in an atmosphere of true compassion for each other and their relatives.

Persons who were not originally related, but now accept or commit themselves in relationship as brothers, as a family, make a covenant commitment. For, even among people of the same blood relationship, there are ways of invigorating strained relationship, hence oath-taking among the Igbo of Southern Nigeria. The oath-taking ceremony allays one's fear or suspicion in communion in the same life. In like manner, *Nsi-oriko* (a ritual for re-establishing confidence among members of the same family) among the Igbo also is a way of prodding couples or persons of the same family to bury their differences and return to communion in the same life.

Covenant making is characteristically public. To say that covenant making is 'public' does not mean that every covenant has to take place in an arena where every single member of the public will see it. Certainly, it ought to be seen but is fundamentally a public act because it is an intra-personal, inter-family or communitarian act. It involves *the other and me*. The world between the other and me or *I* and *thou* is a public world, an inter-subjective world belonging to all, but eventually to none.

Furthermore, the act of making covenant is public in another significant way; it involves a 'third entity.' The third entity could be a person, any symbol, or God or a juridical entity. The 'third' is a witness to a covenanted relationship. On the metaphysical level, it is God himself who is the Absolute Guarantor of all human and cosmic relationships and ordering. In making a covenant, a person, a tree, a deity or anything could be invoked as a witness. Children could be called to witness the rebuilding of the strained relationship between their parents. The court could be a guarantor in the resolution of personal or intra-family feuds. On the whole, God is invoked as an invisible guarantor to keep on track a new or restored relationship. The covenant world is not dualistic, as there are more than two individualities involved; thus, the chances of ideological manipulation, on the part of participants, are minimized. Covenant poles, therefore, are triadic/tri-dimensional: there are *you, our world and I*. Covenant relationship embodies these three essential poles, as against a relationship based simply on mere compassion, which easily lends itself to manipulation without control.

The Ontology Of Human Subjects In The Movement Of Word And Action

I shall assume, without arguments, that covenant relationship between persons in the light of an African philosophy of right should be understood in terms of a parity treaty—a covenant between equals. It may be a reasonable assumption of an African metaphysics of experience that everyone is created at the same time: God willed everyone at the same time. When God created human beings as men and women, he created everyone as persons[5]; but individuals came into being as willed by God and particularized and temporized entities in their cycle of life. By the same token, the first time individuals see or know of themselves is the first time they begin to exist in each other's temporal frame and existential axis. Their equality stems from the fact that they are willed and created by God at the same divine instance. Differences of periods of birth are differences in temporal instantiation. Within this understanding is buried an ontological truth concerning subjects in a covenant situation: covenant subjects are not the cause of each other. They exist to themselves at the same temporal instance as potential covenant subjects. As subjects in the horizon of perception and realization of their existential ends, they depend on each other for their temporal flourishing. The dependence here, which I call 'complementary flourishing,' is a positive dialectic resulting from their physical and spiritual limitations. Because human beings are not ontologically creators of themselves, they are essentially limited. Because their existence and action, in the midst of communication, are limited by time, place, perception and knowledge, their being is existentially complementary; hence they are naturally candidates for company and co-operation.

---

5.   This conviction is replete with meaning in Judeo-Christian tradition and philosophical anthropology referring to man and woman as persons created in the image of God. What is secured in the Western concept of person I will speak of as *human beings* in Igbo. A human being (whether man or woman) is by its name '*nma-ndu or mmadu*,' meaning the beauty of life or the beauty of all. In the linguistic import of 'human beings' or persons is a manifestation of their metaphysical essence: humans are the beauty of earthly life, and as a home of beauty, they represent the totality of all as an expression of this beauty. They are persons by virtue of being endowed with beauty at creation. Their personhood is not socially acquired or to be decided by a court of law but they are naturally persons that are presented at creation as the beauty of their creation and Creator. Humans are the place of beauty where their Creator is beheld. So the words 'human beings and persons' mean the same here.

When people come together in a covenant situation, since they are not the cause of each other, they are equal in dignity and essence by virtue of being products of the same eternal instance. Since the subjects of covenant encounter are bound to give committed action to their will, they depend on each other. The action symbolized by covenant acts, as expression of the will of the subjects of action, is interpersonal; hence public. Subsequently, the resulting world of encounter is a *common world*. As a common world whose existence is equally supra individual, it is a justification of its own existence—superimposing its demands on the subjects whose will it is. A common world that belongs to all but to none of the encounters in dialogue has come into being. There is an ethics of encounter that derives from the world created by the willed action of covenant subjects as persons sharing a community of life and meaning. The ethics of encounter is a product of a common world—a community. This community is instantiated in the being of individuals, and maintained by their wills. The environment of encounter, in turn, transcends the isolated claims of its members. So the community subsists in the individual in as much as individuals subsist in the community. Therefore, persons and their communities co-penetrate.

The Juro-Ethical Order Of Covenanted Wills: The Legal Axis

When covenant subjects express their unified bond for a greater communion in the same community of life and meaning, in the presence of the third, the resultant order is at once communitarian and juridical. Juridicality stems from the fact that covenanted wills are clothed in norms whose validity and gratuity are rooted in objective facts or phenomena of common experience apprehended by all as nomologically and morally justified in the natural and communicative movement of subjects. The emerging rights of the juro-ethical order are positive. The word 'positive' is not to be understood here as something commanded or granted by the superior to the inferior, in which there is an implicit separation of morality from the juridical order. Juro-ethical rights are neither solely conferred by individuals nor by the social order. They are not rights decided upon after claims and counter-claims. They flow from the being of members as part of the definition of their ontological roots. Juridico-ethical rights derive from the ontological signification of covenant subjects and their environment of encounter. Rights, understood in the conceptual schemes of legal positivism of the brand of theories of Jeremy Bentham and John Austin, Hans Kelsen's pure theory of law and H. L. A. Hart's conceptual alternative to the command theories, will sacrifice the natural morality embodied by covenant subjects and in their environment of encounter at the altar of socio-legal authentication.[6] Such an understanding in imperative terms will diverge from the being or facticity of covenant as an activity between equals. The 'positivity' of 'positive' rights of juro-ethical order is based on the conviction that the resulting effects between covenant partners are children of their will in the existential order. The existential order, as has been indicated, bears the imprint of an empirical experience of the metaphysical nature of the partners in dialogue and their environment of encounter. The resulting effects freely bind partners, embracing their legitimate claims, and at the same time, transcend the isolated claims of their individual wills.

---

6. Jeremy Bentham and John Austin proposed the imperative theory of law, which claims that there is a separation between what law *is* and what it *ought* to be. For them, positive law deals with what the law is. Law is a posited fact. But in their analysis, they accepted the principle of utility as the only principle that should guide both legislators and common citizens alike, thereby endorsing utilitarian morality as the morality for social acting. Such a morality is essentially legal.

    Kelsen attempted to follow the line of separation between law and morality toed by Bentham and Austin. He claims that no morality is allowed at all in law; hence he excludes the issue of justice. Kelsen proposes his 'pure theory' of law whose orientation is the study of law as a social technique. A just law, according to him, is still a valid law; injustice ensues when the law is not applied equally. If there is any morality in law, for Kelsen, it is here that it comes in. Such an understanding of morality will be simply legal.

    Hart's theoretical alternative to command theory of law recognizes that law and morality have some specific content in common: the minimum contents of natural law, given survival as an aim in society. However, Hart maintains that the relationship between law and morality on the basis of minimal content is contingent in such a way that the law need not extend such provisions; thus, a law that does not contain them will still be a valid law; hence Hart argues that morality is not intrinsic to the quality of law as law. The validity of law is different from the question of morality of law. Therefore, the morality, which Hart allows in law, is the minimal content and the moral intuition, which the judge may invoke in hard cases; but ordinarily there is no necessary relationship between law and morality. The morality of law, for Hart, in the final analysis, lies in treating like cases alike.

Covenant As A Conceptual Frame For Embodied Humanity

The bonding together of persons in a covenant situation creates a new outlook in human relationship. Partners come to be recognized, not as things or someone meeting somebody, but covenanted entities, taking their stance in dignity before the other. Their development will always be person-centered. A closeness of the type in blood relationship desires much respect, as it is sacred. This being the case, the bonding of covenant subjects has theoretical and practical aims. It prescribes a conceptual framework for conceiving the identity of subjects in relationship and praxis as to how subjects stand and respond to each other's expression. Expressions are effects (words and deeds) of mental operation discharged in the common world of being. The environment of such expressions is humanity/ nature. Partners should act or respond in such a way that their expression should not endanger the flow of their life (persons and their property)—the constituted blood-relationship; subjects should act in a way that will always enhance the flourishing of all: stability in peaceful and truthful living and the growth of their common humanity and nature. The covenant axis is a horizon of values for human flourishing, environmental and developmental sustainability. Any development that does not aim at an embodied humanity will be incomplete.

Covenant subjects are conceived in all their internality and externality: internality refers to their spiritual and moral well-being as persons; and externality refers to the ownership of property they have claim to in the world which derives from their identity as I-subjects extended in time and space; hence covenant partners are embodied spirits. They own themselves as auto-determinants and property, which are extensions of them. The first property people have are themselves. Therefore, personhood and property are part and parcel of the internal and external constitutions of covenant subjects, not caused by them, but realized and dependent on a common world for their flourishing. No doubt then the Igbo existential creed—*Egbe bere Ugo bere* (let the kite perch and the eagle perch)—is at once a profession of unity and peaceful co-existence in the common world and a re-affirmation of the founding belief of the community. It is because of the sacredness of life that the Igbo conceive life to be an attribute of communal stability that they add a caveat that: if the kite or the eagle does not allow the other to perch, let its wings rupture—*Nku kwaa ya*. A bird without wings not only has lost its identity but is as good as dead. The import of the Igbo proverb is simple: we all have the right to live, that is, we are created to live and to have space to exercise. Life is action, and action implies ownership in the sense of what you have done or achieved or claimed. Thus every action brings into being some material or immaterial property. We have the right or claim to property, that is, to that which is our own. 'Own' here encompasses the right and place to exercise. In short, humans are conceived along with their property—their personality.

An African philosophy of right should then pay attention to the issue of property. Talks about property are the present utterances about land ownership in many places. The contemporary outlook on property presents itself as part of the tension in the job or labor market. It is difficult to pretend to care for people or to be their political leader or spokesman in an environment in which they have claim to property, without paying attention to how they realize their humanity and communality. An imbalance in labor relations or property rights is a sign that some members of the covenant relationship are cheating on others. Within the covenant or inter-personal relationship, we all have rights to our personhood, property and the preservation of our common humanity.

I still think that the lack of a proper analysis of the framework of communal living and property, and an enlightened basis for personal and community claims are sources of continued tension in many African states, where citizens still see themselves as *a mass of people amalgamated together*. They prefer to bewail or brood over their arbitrary amalgamation instead of accepting their togetherness as a framework for establishing good and lasting political union based on the vision to create or discover their common humanity. Humanity is one. What matters is that people scratch where it itches them in their environment, while uniting their experience with the universal patrimony of human quest for meaning and truth. African philosophy, like European or American strands of philosophy, is an attempt to make sense of human life by a people whose experience is at once particular and universalizable.

13

Authority In Covenanted Socio-Politics

Who Has Authority?

Quite often people ask: who is the leader? How can we identify one? It is common to say that a leader is someone specified by the constitution or someone appointed or elected by the rule or people to lead them. In this regard, the leader (he/she) has a legitimate power, having certified certain conditions, to issue rules/law (and commands), which bind acts. Thus, Thomas Aquinas writes that law is "a rule and measure of acts, whereby man is induced to act or is restricted from acting."[1] He defines law as "nothing else but a dictate of practical reason emanating from the ruler who governs a perfect community."[2] A legitimate authority issues law; the end of law is to realize the common good, and its effect is to make men good.[3]

It is normal for civil societies to lay down rules or conditions as to who will become their rulers or leaders or authorities.[4] In H. L. A. Hart's rule theory of law, therefore, a leader or an authority within law is one appointed and certified according to the rule of recognition.[5] A ruler commands obedience from others simply because the rules say so. Such obedience owed to the leader is reasoned on the basis of the fact that the rules recognize and regard him/her as having author-

---

1. St. Thomas Aquinas, *Summa Theologica*, First Complete American Edition in three volumes. Literally trans. by Fathers of the English Dominican Province, (New York: Benziger Brothers, Inc. 1947), Vol. 1; Pt. I-II, q. 90; a. 1.
2. *Ibid.*, q. 91, a. 1.
3. See *Ibid.*, q. 92, a. 1.
4. For an elaborate treatment of the views of Hart, Raz and Finnis on reason and authority see Francis O. C. Njoku, *Philosophy in Politics, Law and Democracy* (Owerri: Claretian Institute of Philosophy, 2002), Ch. 8.

ity. He has a legal authority, and this may be quite independent of the fact whether or not he is a good person. His utterances present themselves as authoritative legal reasons for action. So far as he rules according to the rules of the system, he remains legally correct. The morality of the rules he is issuing, as far as they certify the criterion of recognition or legality, is not the issue. The morality of rules in the Hartian model is not co-extensive with legality or validity.

Certainly part of the expectation of citizens is that the leader appointed under the conditions set by the rules direct accordingly. But who becomes the ruler where there is no provision for saying who is the leader? Or who becomes the leader where the rules are silent? This is the problem, which is not clarified by Hart's model of rules. Whoever the law certifies, through the appropriate means, as legitimate leader, is the leader whether or not he is a good person. Thus, in the absence of stipulated rules by the system, the members of Hart's society will be in a lot confusion.

Joseph Raz explains authority in terms of having reasons for action and being able to cancel protected reasons. He believes that reasons are used in explaining, evaluating and guiding people's behavior,[6] although they are not always co-extensive with the facts:

> Only reasons, understood as facts, are normatively significant; only they determine what ought to be done. To decide what we should do we must find out what the world is like, and not what our thoughts are like. The other notion of reasons is relevant exclusively for explanatory purposes and not all for guiding purposes. It is precisely this which shows that this purely explanatory notion is the secondary one presupposing the other and not being presupposed by it.[7]

The reasons understood as facts are normative. The facts referred to here may not be empirical in the sense of being verified by the other person; it is enough that they are the state of affairs the agent believed to exist; hence Raz insists that the special feature of the reasons of the first kind is that "they explain the agent's behavior in terms of his beliefs as to what he should do, in terms of his own

---

5. 'Rule of Recognition' belongs to the category of Hart's secondary rules that validates all other rules. It is a power imposing rule clarifying how new rules come into existence and how people can change the legal positions of one another. See H. L. A. Hart, *The Concept of Law* (Oxford: Oxford University Press, 1961), 93.

6. See Joseph Raz, *Practical Reason and Norms* (London: Hutchinson & Co., 1975), 15-16.

7. *Ibid.*, 18-19.

assessment of the relevant reasons (in the primary, normative sense) which apply to him."[8]

What then is authority in Raz's own understanding? Raz writes:

> A person has effective or *de facto* authority only if the person over whom he has that authority regard him as a legitimate authority. This would usually, though not necessarily always, imply that he claims legitimate authority for himself. It is enough that others regard him as legitimate authority. This condition may have to be weakened. It may be unnecessary for the relevant population genuinely to believe that the person having effective authority is a legitimate authority; it is enough if, for whatever reasons, they avow such a belief.[9]

If the hearer of an utterance avows belief in the authority of the speaker, it means that all does not depend on the speaker, as Raz may want to claim! However, his reason-based explanation is intended to underline that the hearer of an utterance has also a basis on which to assess what he has heard. It is not enough that an authority has just uttered something, largely in accordance with the rules; therefore, he is to be obeyed, as implied in Hart's claims. At this juncture Raz inserts a reason, from the part of the hearer, to serve as ground for believing what the speaker said. It does not matter whether the speaker has a legitimate claim to the authority he/she claims; it is enough that people have reason to believe that he/she has such an authority. The insertion of a reason within the context of his treatment of authority throws light on Raz's explanation that part of the unique feature of reasons as types of explanation is that "they explain behavior by reference to considerations which guided the agent's behavior."[10]

There are reasons that empower us to act and also reasons that debar us from acting for a reason. Raz states: "I shall call a reason to act for a reason a positive second-order reason. There are also negative second-order reasons, that is, reasons to refrain from acting for a reason. I shall call negative second-order reasons exclusionary reasons."[11] From the point of view of the addressee, there may be many reasons for or against performing an action. As Raz claims, "…sometimes the same fact is both a reason for an action and an (exclusionary) reason for disre-

---

8.   *Ibid.*, 19.
9.   *Ibid.*, 28.
10.   *Ibid.*, 16.
11.   *Ibid.*, 16-17.

garding reasons against it. I shall call such facts protected reasons for an action."[12] In this light, Raz defines a normative power as *ability to change protected reasons:*

> A man has normative power if he can by an action of his exercise normative power. An act is the exercise of a normative power if there is sufficient reason for regarding it either as a protected reason or as canceling protected reasons and if the reason for so regarding it is that it is desirable to enable people to change protected reasons by such acts, if they wish to do so.[13]

People can yield to their protected reasons being changed. The reason of the addressee in Raz is still subjective, since my reason for regarding B as an authority may not convince D to so regard B. Why should another have the gut in the public arena, other things being equal, to regard B rather than D, for example, as the leader/authority albeit one has various reasons? If I do not succumb to the dictator's demand, he might make life difficult for me. So I have a reason to obey him or her as an authority. Yes, there may be various reasons for regarding someone as an authority, but Raz does not specify which reasons are really genuine reasons.

John Finnis has provided, above the rule and reason-based conceptions of authority of Hart and Raz respectively, the justifiability of exclusionary reasons for action before an authority. Authority, for Finnis, has reference to co-ordination problems associated with the common good. The considerations about the common good are based on moral grounds.

Finnis agrees that something is treated as authority where one has a sufficient reason for treating it so, even though ordinarily one may not see good reason for so believing:

> A person treats something (e.g. an opinion, a pronouncement, a map, an order, a rule...) as authoritative if and only if he treats it as giving him sufficient reason for believing or acting in accordance with it *notwithstanding* that he himself cannot otherwise see good reason for so believing or acting, or cannot evaluate the reasons he can see, or sees some countervailing reason(s), or would himself otherwise (i.e. in the absence of what it is that he is treating as authoritative) have preferred not so to believe or act.[14]

---

12. See *Ibid.,* 18.
13. *Ibid.*
14. John Finnis, *Natural Law and Natural Rights* (Oxford: Oxford University Press, 1992), 233-234.

Finnis understands sufficient reasons in terms of Raz's exclusionary reason, that is, "a reason for judging or acting in the absence of understood reasons, or for disregarding at least some reasons which are understood and relevant and would in the absence of the exclusionary reason have sufficed to justify proceeding in some other way."[15] For Finnis, to justify authority, its limits and proper operation, reference must be made to the common good, which includes justice and human right.[16] Here Finnis leads us beyond the strict legal validity and unspecified reasoned-based foundations of authority in Hart and Raz respectively.

The root of legal authority derives from the ability to solve co-ordination problems. This is a requirement of the common good, [17] which, in other words, is a moral requirement. To achieve the common good demands a morally coordinated action. And one who adheres to this standard has authority within the human community; hence Finnis affirms that authority has primacy in the human community only with reference to co-ordination problems:

> Authority (and thus the responsibility of governing) in a community is to be exercised by those who can in fact effectively settle co-ordination problems for that community…
>
> The *fact* that the say-so of a particular person or body or configuration of persons will in fact be, by and large, complied with and acted upon, has normative consequences for practical reasonableness; it affects the responsibilities of both ruler and ruled, by creating certain exclusionary reasons for action. These normative consequences derive from a normative principle—that authority is good (because required for the realization of the common good)—when that principle is taken in conjunction with the fact that a particular person, body, or configuration of persons can, for a given community at a given time, do what authority is to do (i.e. secure and advance the common good).[18]

One who can settle co-ordination problems has authority. If we find one who can harmonize human resources in a particular human environment for the good of all, we have reason to regard him as an authority. In like manner, since legal orders are geared towards the realization of the common good, in Finnis' thinking, they are authoritative.

---

15. *Ibid.*, 234.
16. *Ibid.*, 236.
17. See *Ibid.*, 244.
18. *Ibid.*, 246.

Even if we have a society of perfectly virtuous people, there will still be a need for authority to co-ordinate. This need arises not so much from the fact that people will not be acting out of character in such a perfect condition such that laws prohibiting harmful behaviors will be useless; there will still be need for authority, at least for particular determinations of projects. Why? Finnis answers within his Thomistic theorizing:

> It is because, as the theory of *determinatio* implies, many problems of social life can be solved in more than one, perhaps many, different *reasonable* ways. So, in relation to this wide range of problems, agreement that some form of co-ordination is required will be much easier to reach than agreement about what the appropriate form of co-operation is. Even if disagreement about appropriate form of co-operation could in practice be settled by some other means, it rarely could be settled peacefully and fairly without an authoritative decision.[19]

There may be various reasons or motives for obeying an authority some of which may be more reasonable than others either absolutely or at least in a given situation. Finnis insists that within the borders of practical reasonableness, an understanding of the authoritativeness of a ruler is rooted on the sheer fact of effectiveness that is presumptively (not indefeasibly) decisive.[20] And it is on the basis of this that the laws made by an authority will be morally binding on the people; this moral authority is consequent of the promotion of the common good[21]:

> The authoritative decision, whether legislative, executive, or judicial, and whether by formal institutional decision or the informality of customary practice, will not result in co-ordination unless it is accepted as settling the question, accepted even by those who would have preferred a different form of co-ordination, a different decision, a different law. To treat the law as authoritative in one's practical deliberations, i.e., as morally binding, is to treat it as settling the question how to co-ordinate with others in one's actions and forbearances in the relevant area of conduct; or how to deal with others in one's judgments, orders, and actions as judge or administrator.[22]

---

19. John Finnis, *Aquinas: Moral, Political, and Legal Theory* (Oxford: Oxford University Press, 1998), 269.
20. John Finnis, *Natural Law and Natural Rights*, 247.
21. John Finnis, *Aquinas: Moral, Political, and Legal Theory, 269.*
22. *Ibid.*, 270.

There is, in the social life, the need for an authority that respects the laws and takes seriously the realization of the common good, in order that individuals may instantiate the good in their actions.

Generally then, the rules can invest a person with authority in order to solve co-ordination problems; at other times, a person may assume authority in the circumstances in order to bring about the public good. Authority or leadership is scored according as it is used to secure the common good, that is, the values of human flourishing in their integrative signification. It is against this background that laws and rules make appeal to practical reasonableness. Finnis suggests that, in practical terms, a reasonable subject will identify an authority where he/she sees one. And the subject of the law has a moral responsibility to obey such an authority. Bearing in mind that Finnis endorses the focal meaning of law, without disregarding the ordinary or non-focal meaning of the law, he affirms that his theoretical interest in explaining the concept 'law' is

> to develop a concept for use in a theoretical explanation of a set of human actions, dispositions, interrelationships, and conceptions which (i) hang together as a set by virtue of their adaptation to a specifiable set of human needs considered in the light of empirical features of the human condition, and (ii) are accordingly found in very varying forms and with varying degrees of suitability for, and deliberate or unconscious divergence from, those needs as the fully reasonable person would assess them.[23]

It is, thus, Finnis' argument that law has reference to the common good of persons and communities from which the fundamental principle derives that "one acts in the way that respects this basic good—'the common good." This fundamental principle finds its way into legal formulae, which

> have their specific intelligibility from the fact that they are self-consciously designed not only to fit into the recalcitrant citizen's sanction-dominated practical reasonings, but also and most characteristically to fit and to give a special conclusory force to the practical reasonings of those who see and are generally willing to act upon the need for the common good for authority.[24]

---

23. John Finnis, *Natural Law and Natural Rights*, 278-279. Finnis' distinction between focal and non-focal meaning of law leans on Aquinas' understanding of law in terms of its primary import: that law ought to be just in order to be *simply* law. In its primary sense, law has to be just, as distinguished from its aberration where it retains some good in a particular sense, albeit unjust.

24. See *Ibid.*, 317-318.

Finnis believes that the fundamental point that urges one to act in a way that respects the common good, which enters into legal formulae, demands morality or moral obligation to obey each law.[25]

Derivation Of Some Leadership Models From Covenant Intuition

Leadership against the background of a philosophy of right based on covenant recognizes a basic public attitude that motivates people to enter into covenant relations: the need for peace/stability/protection of life. Peace, stability of possessions and protection are common good—in an atmosphere of familiarity typical of brothers or people sharing the same life. People want to progress or develop; they want to flourish. The cause for covenant relations is stability of life as brothers, that is, as the same people sharing equal and mutual conditions of life; thus the reason or cause of covenant relationship is life in its extensions and ramifications. One intends something if that which is done is part of the agent's reason for acting or is in the agent's plan of action. Therefore, the reason for covenant coming into being is part of the justification of its existence.

A leader or an authority in the pact model can be explained in two major ways: the *first* and *third* person perspectives respectively. The first-person perspective is that of an insider—a member of the covenanted wills—who is invested with authority to foster the cause of the covenant; he is to protect covenant wills of which he is a member, to safeguard emergent rights, according to the rules which are the offshoot of the reality of covenant of which is a part of. As an insider, the person has legislative authority, which is acquired by the consent of members of the covenant. It is to be noted that by investing legislative authority in one of their members, members of covenanted wills do not relinquish their freedom or rights of property, but only administrative rights in so far as the leader directs according to the rules of the covenant.[26] Beyond this, the members of the covenant have the right to depose the leader, if he has become a cheat. By not

---

25. See *Ibid.*, 318. We shall not be detained here by Finnis' implicit claim that there is a moral obligation to obey each law; for a discussion on moral obligation to obey the law see Ch 7 of my *Studies in Jurisprudence: A Fundamental Approach to the Philosophy of Law* (2000).

26. John Locke's foundation of civil society is very relevant here. People do not relinquish their freedom; the community/leader/authority only acts as an umpire.

paying attention to the foundations or conditions of the association nurtured around covenant, he becomes a saboteur. The legislative authority of covenant, from a first person perspective, only fosters that which is invested in the leader by covenant agreements. The reason for covenant is human flourishing for all. A leader who fails to secure it loses adherence and consequently the moral obligation to be obeyed.

There is the third-person perspective. It is modeled on the *third* that is invoked to safeguard covenant relations, although it is not strictly speaking a member of the covenant. The 'third' in a covenant is only a guarantor, and is there to moderate the excesses of legislative authority and the individual's isolated claims, making sure that no one cheats the other. The 'third' has stood as the court that makes sure judgments or adjudications about human affairs are done according to justice. Many African countries have been battlegrounds for claims and counter claims because of evidential lack of an impartial adjudicator. People appoint the 'third' or 'witness' or guarantor; hence the 'third' is not to be manipulated by the executive or legislature who makes second-order binding rules.

In other words, executive authority can be invested with one who is not a member of the covenanted wills. He carries out the rules laid down by partners of covenant, and accounts to them. In this way, the 'third' will act as the *podestà* in the early modern political Italy, who was invited from outside to take an administration of a city so as to give justice to all and foster peoples' liberty. The concept of *podestà* evolved from the rules of consuls who were elected by people desirous of liberty to carry out their affairs. Against this background, Quentin Skinner writes:

> The rule of consuls came to be superseded by a stabler form of elective government centered on an official known as the *podestà*, so called because he was invested with supreme power or *potestas* over the city. The *podestà* was normally a citizen of another city, a convention designed to ensure that no local ties or loyalties should interfere with his impartial administration of justice. He was elected by popular mandate,...The *podestà* enjoyed comprehensive powers, since he was expected to act as the city's supreme judicial as well as administrative officer, and to serve as its leading spokesman on its various embassies. But the crucial feature of the system was that his status was always that of a salaried official, never that of an independent ruler. His term of office was customarily restricted to six months, and throughout that time he remained responsible to the citizen body, which had elected him. He had no authority to initiate political decisions, and at the end of his tenure he was required to submit to a formal scrutiny of his accounts and judgments before

he could gain permission to depart from the city, which had employed him (Waley 1969, pp. 68-9).[27]

The third-model of authority in covenant relations emphasizes the fact that an authority in covenant-modeled ruler-ship ought to be impartial and accountable. The operation of an authority is limited by the term of contract; that term is defined by the intentions of members of the covenant community, and the intentions are the reason for the covenant or authority coming into being in the first place.

The ancestor model of authority loses its continuous grip on people's consciousness before covenant models of authority/leadership. An ancestor model of authority thrives on the claims that the forefathers already determine everything; its cognate view is that because the elders or political godfathers have said it, it is presumably right. This understanding interprets African societies as if they are closed. It has to be maintained that authority is good only in so far as it pays attention to the terms of the covenant, that is, the furtherance of integral development—the common good for which reason authority comes into being and deserves to be respected and sustained.

---

27. Quentin Skinner, *The Foundations of Modern Political Thought Volume One The Renaissance* (Cambridge: Cambridge University Press, 1978), 3-4.

14

The Democratic Bent of Covenanted Leadership

The Basic Problem With Representative Democracy

Democracy has been defined as government of the people by the people for the people. People want a government which people at once own and participate in. In the other words, democracy is the government where people are the sovereign. To be sovereign implies the unrestricted ability to make laws. Even Plato and Aristotle, who took democracy as a government by mob, and a degeneration of the best type of government, saved its existence where the best is absence and the worst form intolerable. And what stabilizes democracy as a government of the people, even among its Greek disclaimers, is that it is organization of the people for law in order to rule themselves. In a democracy then, the people are sovereign, having the power to make laws that will govern them.

The act of governing has become sophisticated because society has become complex. It is not easy to get the whole people sitting in the same place and deliberating; hence the need for representative democracy. Representative democracy claims to be a system of democracy where people govern through their elected representatives.

Modern representative democracy claims that when people elect their representatives, in fact the power to make laws or changes in the laws passes over to the people's representatives. The implication then is that the power to make laws and changes in the law gradually slips away from the people's hands. What we have in the present day modern democracy is a situation where politicians or representatives make laws and impose them on the people. People are led to obey laws that they neither initiate nor make or generally promote their welfare. If they want to tell the truth, many politicians (senators and representatives alike) will admit that the first thing that immediately comes to their mind in making decisions is everything but the welfare of the people.

Representative democracy creates a dichotomy between the people and their representatives, between their interests and the interests of their representatives. Instead of the process of initiating laws coming from the people, it now comes from the representatives. The sovereign (the people) now become the subject, obeying laws imposed on them by the representatives (their subjects). Even if people surrender their sovereignty in aristocratic and monarchical governments, it is not in democracy. The modern representative government has become a travesty of democracy. Infrequently, what the people want or the laws they want in place contrasts with what the so-called representatives want. To bridge the gap between what the people want and the ideological wishes of their representatives, a different model of democracy must be re-invented. This corrective I call *initiative-covenanted democracy*.

Initiative-Covenanted Democracy

The first-and-third person perspectives of covenant models of leadership indicate that representative government is a reality. Members of the covenant can call on others to direct their affairs, which may include appointing one of their fellows to initiate laws on their behalf, determining how they want to live. They initiate laws, which then are passed by various levels of government that represent and carry out their wishes. It is important that the procedure of initiating laws come from the people—the Sovereign. However, in representative democracy, this procedure plays out, as a kind of referendum issued by the representative government, letting people to support or endorse what the leaders or the government wants.

Initiative democracy takes the opposite course in terms of the source and authority of the laws. The people initiate the laws, which the politicians will administer. Who are the people? Ojukwu once responded: "The farmer, the trader, the clerk, the business man, the housewife, the student, the civil servant, the soldier, you and I are the people."[1] The people are the master, and are supreme. Power and laws come from the master—the people. The leader is a servant, and he who despises the people—the sovereign, is not worthy to lead. The advantage of initiative-covenant democracy is that there is a partnership between

---

1. Chukwuemeka Odumegwu Ojukwu, *Ahiara Declaration: The Principles of the Biafran Revolution (June, 1, 1969)* with the Declaration of Independence, speech before exile, the Cessation Declaration, call from Exile, and The Biafran National Anthem ed. Obi Harrison Ekwonna, 24.

the people and those they have elected to man the machinery of government. While the people concede the power of administration to their elected leaders, they retain the power of making laws, that is, the power of saying how they want to live. In talking about the Legislature in the New Biafra, Ojukwu stated:

> Ideally, all the people should be involved in the actual process of law-making. As a matter of fact, in our traditional society all adults who had attained the age of reason were directly involved in discussion, debate and decision-making on all things affecting the whole people. That was the original government by consensus. That was possible when the community was small and compact. With the emergence of the nation-state, which is larger and heterogeneous, this ideal procedure became impracticable. Therefore, the process of delegation of power was evolved to meet a practical need. But this does not invalidate the original principle that power belongs to the People. A man who is delegated by the People to represent their interests, therefore, is acting on behalf of the People and ceases to act for them the moment they withdraw their mandate.[2]

The people have the supreme power and whoever represents the people does so because the people have duly mandated him or her; and the will of the people must prevail over his or hers. It is against this background that in a participatory or initiative democracy, the principle of delegation of power encourages democratically organized groups of youths, traders, women, farmers, professionals bodies, managerial and business groups to participate actively in public and political discussions. They should initiate the ways they want to live, and the laws to bring about the desired socio-political order. The principle of the primacy of the people is at the center of initiative-covenant democracy, for the people "are the bastion of the Nation, the makers of its culture and history."

The Nigerian Analogy: A Bad Example of Democracy

The call, for example, in Nigeria for a national conference to discuss how Nigerians want to live, is an indication that their so-called representatives in representative democracy are out of touch with the people—the sovereign. Some of the laws made in the federal and state houses of government generally protect the interests of the politicians than those of the people. Instead of people presenting to politicians what laws they want, politicians impose laws on the people to safeguard everything but public interest.

---

2.   *Ibid.*, 35.

Representative democracy in Nigeria has become a mockery of, and an insult to, the people's sovereignty. A politician who is at the federal or state level of affairs, when making decisions has the following considerations almost in the order of priority:

He thinks first of himself and his interests;

He thinks of the ways of maintaining his stronghold in power;

He thinks of his re-election;

He considers his political godfathers;

He thinks of his party because if his party is in control, power easily flows down to him. He many think of some public good or interest in so far as it could be used as an instrument for safeguarding his interest or bringing about his re-election.

The bottom line is that no senator, representative or congressman at the federal and state levels of government, at least in Nigeria, honestly thinks of public good or interest as first priority. How then can we make power flow back to the people in Nigeria?

- There is need for the people to sit down and write a constitution, stating in clear terms the origin of their laws and the process of their promulgation and abrogation; the power to initiate laws belongs to the people, and such power is non-negotiable. The people have absolute right to say what they want.

- When people decide what they want, their view is made known to their so-called representatives to endorse it or be aware of it, (if need be). I really hesitate to use the word 'endorse.' A law does not have to have the endorsement of the people's representative for it to be law. Endorsement here serves for the records as a matter of procedure, not a fact of validity. It is better to say that they inform their representatives or make them aware of it.

- Then, the representatives send back to the people the initiative presented to them by the people for confirmation. (In some cases, this can be re-presented to the people as a referendum; but the people must always make sure that what comes from them and goes to their representative and comes back to them actually represent what they want. The people should always look with suspicion at that referendum that is not traceable to their own initiative).

- The people then vote upon the initiative. (The voting here is direct. Initiative process of democracy or law making avoids such distractions or intermediaries as parties). Partisan politics has created an unwanted intermediary between the people and their servants. Partisan politics turns servants into sovereigns and sovereigns into servants. It can dangerously hijack the process of governance or come in-between the people and the government, as it is noticed, albeit unfortunately, in the present structure of Nigeria's government.

Until there is a good and accountable partnership between the government and the people with whom sovereignty resides and through some process of direct dialogue and initiative, a few individuals will continue to present their ideologies and selfish interests as national creed, thereby eroding the powers of the people. The so-called bunch that claims to represent the people has become arrogant, fraudulent, abusive, oppressive and out of touch. It is time to re-invent the people's initiative in the affairs of government. The power of re-definition, as always, lies with the people, as history can testify. Let the people defend their covenant—their democracy, their sovereignty.

15

Revisiting Development Within Covenanted Perspective

Person-Centered Development

Development is about people in their structured end in society. Common humanity unites all in covenant. What is sought is to establish a relationship where all will see themselves as people of one family. Family is the first school of socialization and human flourishing. Subjects of the covenant want to be maintained in being as a community that shares the same meaning. The end of all is full humanity in the shared effort and collaboration of all.

The family spirit of covenant bonding implies a certain environment: harmony of all with all—humans and non-humans like. Man lives in an environment in which he co-penetrates with others. Man, plants, animals, seas and rivers co-penetrate and co-mingle with one another. This is a certain bio-cosmic indwelling. Harmony or peace is an environmental and existential commodity. It permeates all the spheres of the ecosystem. To realize a better and sustainable human development, attention will have to be paid to indigenous knowledge system in managing life and agriculture in Africa. Indigenous knowledge builds persons, communities and environment from within. The covenant model pays attention to the sustainability of humans and the conservation of biodiversity: For example:

> From the Eggon in Nigeria to the Mandra mountain farmers in Cameroon to the Engaruka irrigation in Tanzania, the adaptation of the population to the environment in scientific instances was at the center of the success each achieved.
>
> .... If indigenous knowledge and sustainable development take hold to determine and implement planning and economic development, the use of indigenous knowledge and success of sustainability will be based not merely on the knowledge and sustainable aspects of development but on the decision-

making process involving the participation of the participants, not merely that of the decision makers.[1]

One does not advocate a rural way of life here; but a development that has a human face and at the same time biosystemic. It gives priority to humans and their concerns, developing them without destroying them or their environment. Sustainable development widens people's judgment and social realities without uprooting their cherished values. It unfolds from within, where growth is still part of the unfolding process and actualization of humans and their environment.

Co-existence within a covenant understanding underscores the fact that mutual respect through the observance of laws guiding each state of life and being ensures mutual flourishing.

People must be allowed to develop in the perspective of actualization of their potential in the midst of other existences. Such development is integral and eco-systemic.

The community that results from the bonding together of covenanted wills is built on personhood. The Igbo word *mmadu* translates the beauty of all or the totality of all, which the English word *person* poorly translates.

Covenanted persons are subjects in the midst of word and action that found the community itself. The common personhood of members is the justification of the community of persons. The covenanted ambient is a horizon of values, values that nurture humans in all their ramifications; development then brings up the best in humans for the development that emerges in and around the individual is person-and community-centered.

Problems do sometimes result in a covenant situation. Humans are the major participants in dialogue-covenant relations. When as human beings covenant partners drift away from their interpersonal and ritual commitments, they have something to fall back on: a conscience, a witness or a guarantor. They can avail themselves of the infinite possibility of renewals, re-enactments and re-commitment to the initial cause, for they are not gods. The covenant ideal recognizes human weakness and insures the attendant risks in their humanness. In this way, we say that the pact model is robust in making allowance for the legitimate claims, pretences and possibilities that can crop up within the communication situation. The many ethical and juridical features of man as a subject in word and action are, to a large extent, recognized in their predictable possibility. Like other

---

1.   Terrence J. Lamb, 'African Economic History and Its Planning Potential: An Investigation of Source,' in *Sustainable Development in Third World Countries*, ed., Valentine Udoh James, 141.

people, Africans know that there is an infinite possibility for breaking a covenant and an infinite possibility for dialogue, appeasement and pacification.

To the African, a covenant with a human being is a covenant directly or indirectly with the earth. An offence against a human person also contradicts one's relationship with God, the other and the earth. One then understands the preoccupation for the interdependent nature of the earth, our home, in the *Earth Summit* in Rio de Janerio (Brazil, June 1992) as contained in the twenty-seven declaratory articles on Environment and Development, already quoted at length: the first of which insists that "human beings are at the center of concerns for sustainable development, they are entitled to a healthy and productive life in harmony with nature." Michael Grubb et al criticize the conference for not insisting more on a serious sustainable development ethic that should recognize the intrinsic value of the natural world, irrespective of its value to human beings. However, at least, it suffices that the *summit* was aware that any mishandling of the earth rebounds on humans; hence the integrative view of development called by the participants at Rio de Janerio.

Development has to be integral, sustainable and co-penetrative. And it is by respecting the order and stability in nature that truth and excellence are attained following the order and laws of things, whose creation and preservation derive from the same God.[2] This is an understanding the covenant model of relationship offers or aspires to offer. The material and religious or spiritual aspects of man and his universe must be taken on board in the attempt to improve his world by his activities. In this respect human advancement in the world becomes well integrated with the craving of humans for salvation.[3]

The call for an integral living extends to technology, which is human self-expression. This human self-expression can no longer ignore human dignity, rationality and destiny. Thus, technology—a human activity in a material universe, that is, a sensible manipulation of nature—should not shy away from blending the material with the spiritual in an integral whole. Technology has no rationality except in relation to human destiny and good. Hence M. I. Nwoko rightly argues that technology has to face ontology, ethics and ecology in discussion. Technology is ambiguous if it is left to criticize itself. Any model of development that ignores ecology and creative stewardship will not be doing any good to human life. Any model of leadership or development that is modeled on power

---

2. *Vatican II Council, Gaudium et Spes*, no. 36.
3. See Francis A. Sullivan, T*he Church We Believe In: One, Holy, Catholic and Apostolic* (New York: Paulist Press, 1988), 133.

and domination will be very controverted. Process theologians have given us an inspiration of another side of God in relation to creation. Denis Carol says:

> Rather than stand over and against creation, God enters it, is part of it, draws it upwards and forwards. All things have their inner (cognitive) and their outer (quantitative) aspects. They retain their freedom and their purposiveness even in their relation to God. God is the persuasive lure of their inner life. In this view, God feels with the universe in its pain, in its failure, in its joy. Not only does God give life and love, God is responsive to that life and love.[4]

To achieve an integral vision of humans, human development has to be compenetrative—blending the material and the spiritual. No aspect of the human person should be left out of the picture of development.

The Common Good of Covenanted Wills

A good is a value for humans because it enhances and promotes their welfare as humans. It is common because it includes all humans or persons in so far as they are creatures of God endowed with dignity and nurturing this dignity in association with others. Humans realize their best then by being-with and collaborating with others. Common good is a set of values discerned by intelligence as constituting the weal of human flourishing. Johannes Messner articulates certain existential ends of society thus: i) self-preservation, including bodily integrity and social respect (personal honor); ii) self-perfection physically and spiritually, including the development of one's faculties for the improvement of the conditions of one's life and provision for one's economic welfare by securing the necessary property or income; iii) the enlargement of experience and knowledge; iv) Marriage and the rearing of children; v) interest in the spiritual and material welfare of one's fellowmen as human persons and equal in value; vi) social fellowship, to promote common utility, which consists in the maintenance of peace and order and in opportunity for all members of society to attain full human existence by sharing proportionately in the welfare of society; and vii) the knowledge and worship of God and the ultimate fulfillment of man's destiny through union with him.[5] These are values or goods sought and instantiated in the lives and actions of persons and communities.

---

4.   Denis Carroll, *Towards a Story of the Earth* (Dublin 1: Dominicans Publications, 1987), 168.
5.   J. Messner, *Social Ethics*, 19.

Messner's 'existential ends' could be referred to as consisting common good; they are realized through the conduct of persons. On the whole, the specifically human conduct is the conduct of rational nature; the ends designed in the physical and psychical instincts of their nature indicate the conduct demanded of humans by the full actuality of their nature. Messner's use of "existential end" pays attention to the existing jural order in the various spheres of social life or what, in the ethics of St. Augustine, is called "temporal ends." With the notion of existential ends, the *idea of end* remains at the center of the natural law theory. Man is understood in his nature as an individual as well as a social being.

The common good, then, is not a piece of pie in the sky or a piece of cake at the center of government out there to which people scramble and stumble over in greedy pursuit. Regarding the common good, Maritain rightly writes that it is the good of human life of all, embracing the totalities of the material and spiritual in their communal and liberating manner; it is the enhancing of the totality of the person in all its flourishing.[6] The common good is a horizon of values and responsibilities to be realized and tasks to be done in the mutual complementation and development of members of society or state. Political leaders err a lot when they do not sit down to discern the values to be realized that constitute the common good in true human development. Values are not co-extensive with facts yet they reveal themselves in the factual and existential situation of covenant subjects. Thus, they are self-evidently grasped by intelligence by those who are practically reasonable and can discern the things that are significant and relevant for the building up of persons and human communities.

Covenanted subjects come to life because people want to bring out the best in themselves and to create the best conditions within which their flourishing can be realized. The common good of covenanted political communities and persons is an ambient of values (life, health, property, education, peace and security, etc.) which individuals and communities desire by the sheer fact of their nature as a community of persons bound together to foster their integral development and well-being. In other words, actions of leaders and the led alike are judged good or bad, right or wrong according as they foster or impede the common good or human development.

The covenant group is not a crowd or an aggregate. Collectively and singly, covenanted subjects are the embodiment of effective wills in which the powers of self-donation and withdrawal, self-transcendence and autonomy reside. The consistent manipulation of the people of Africa in political matters even by their own

---

6.   See Jacques Maritain, *The Rights of Man*, 8-9.

leaders has led some people to deny the existence of a political entity called people. It seems to me that an appreciation of politics of the right model, that respects the dignity, humanity and identity of covenant subjects, can redirect the understanding of African leaders in political affairs. At present, what goes on mostly in the continent is a politics of manipulation and dehumanization of the people by their leaders. A frightened, maimed, displaced, dejected and disadvantaged bunch cannot offer itself freely in the movement of word and action. Government so far goes on without the people. People have no hope in any form of organized authority that claims governance. Government is blocked from hearing the cries of the people. Consciously or not, the right of persons and communities to determine their own future has been ripped off by the political elite whose jargon and insensibility the people do not understand. In a country such as Nigeria, whatever government it had been so far, is a government of mutual exclusion between the governed and their leaders, even when the political climate wears what is mistakenly called *democratic*. A democracy without a human face and sense of respect and care for the governed unfortunately passes as a legally enthroned kleptocracy. It under-develops people rather than develop them.

16

Political Economy of Development in the Philosophy of Covenant

What Economic Development implies

The aim of this Chapter is to attempt to rationalize political economy of development along the line of philosophy of covenant. In Chapter One of this book, we said that development was a process towards fuller and better status of being or state of affairs. A development is termed human when that process leads humans to flourish in all their internal and external dynamics. In this way, development implies a passage of time.[1] By 'passage of time' is meant that development is a process, a movement, a growth in human and institutional transformation. It involves humans, their institutions and environment. Economics is a system of production and distribution of goods and services in the awareness that the goods and services are scarce and have alternative uses. Development in economic terms pays attention to the joint increase and capacity of members of the group to deal with their environment. With an eye on economics and passage of time, Robert Bates sees development as "the growth of per capita income and...transformation of social and political systems."[2] Here we want to focus on how humans as actors bringing about development within their social, political and economic environment; hence the discussion on political economy of development.

Two theoretical tools or concepts will help our focus: economics (as referring to the formation of capital), and violence (in terms of politics or use of force). In the area of economic development, economists compare the National Per Capita

---

1. See Robert H. Bates, *Prosperity and Violence* (New York: W. W. Norton & Company, 2001), 20.
2. *Ibid.*

189

in the distribution of income. In other words, the major factor on economic development is the formation of capital. To grow humanly and economically, individuals, groups want to accumulate and distribute or share wealth. Thus, in the formation of capital, people try "to secure the increased possibilities for consumption that investment makes possible. They make present sacrifices in order to secure future gains."[3] Against this background, two major problems, I think, face Third World countries such as Nigeria, namely: the formation of capital (economic power), and the distribution or management of capital (political power or the use of violence).

The Formation of Capital

There is an erroneous understanding that capital is simply the money I have in my pocket or in my bank or the quantity of stocks I may have. This understanding is sister to another erroneous reasoning, especially in Nigeria, that the common good is just like money stored in the closet or bank for all or a beautiful piece of cake decorated at the seat of government for which people queue or stumble over one another to get their own share, and from which the government, as an entity with privileged position, distributes and helps itself at will. This is not what capital is all about.

Capital, as we have said, is a major component in production. It can be the money I have in my pocket or bank or the money I have put in to buy or produce something. However, capital means more than physical cash: it includes talents, skills, abilities and sacrifices; hence Bates rightly points out:

> Capital can take the form of a bridge or canal or industrial plant. It can also take the form of a bank account or financial portofolio. But capital need not be physical or monetary. It can also take the form of a skill or a mode of expression, which may itself be costly to acquire. Time that could be spent in pleasure may instead be devoted to study, such that the person can later gain the rewards that accrue to proficiency and attainment. Classrooms, universities, and apprenticeships: these, as much as banks or industries, constitute loci for the formation of capital.[4]

The lack of understanding of what capital means is shown in the way Third World countries have neglected areas that can help its formation. The flooding of

---

3. *Ibid.*, 21.
4. *Ibid.*, 21-22.

their markets with foreign goods and technology to the neglect of major areas of education and rural upliftment is only one example among others. Capital formation implies a horizon of vision and co-ordination of tasks. If we train good engineers now, we may have better bridges and good road network in the future; if we invest in our young people now, we will have a viable and responsible nation; if we invest in education, we will have less ignorant people in the future; if parents train or invest in their children, they are likely to have support materially and financially, thereby insuring for old age; if we have a good neighborhood watch and look out for one another's goods and treat persons with respect, we will minimize the risk of attacks on our goods and on our persons, and then on loss of capital. If the government responds promptly and have good environmental plans, we will reduce the risk of famine and draught. In this way, there will be less dependence on foreign importation of goods that could have been produced locally at a cheaper rate, thus save money for other projects. The patience, sacrifice and good planning in the present in harnessing talents, creating vibrate institutions with good well-trained personnel might translate into better future for a country. Capital formation, therefore, implies investments in human resources in their varied forms: persons, projects and institutions, especially where people have the right attitude towards their welfare. The sum total of the harnessing of human and economic resources results in economic growth:

> By opening up new lands or purchasing new plant or machinery, or by investing in skills or improvements in the mechanical arts, people can secure higher levels of output per capita and thereby increase the quantity of goods or services they can consume. Economic growth also results from increase in the productivity of land, labor, and capital: by investing in the creation of new technologies, people can increase the level of output they secure from a given quantity of each resource. Equally as important, economic growth results from changes in the manner in which people organize the process of production.[5]

People should know what they want, and then organize themselves in the best manner to achieve maximum output for their holistic growth. A well-organized agricultural economy will yield stable income, so also a well-organized household that effectively co-ordinates the interaction and cooperation of its members or units will flourish. The way and manner persons and units organize their work place will affect the output. The attitude of persons, groups and units towards the common project or goal will also affect output. Since there is division of labor

---

5.   *Ibid.*, 22-23.

going on in every sector of the socio-economic life, the conduct of one person or unit greatly impacts on others, for all the units inter-depend:

> Increases in output result not merely from the sum of the efforts devoted to production, but also from the complementarities among them. Such forms of organization can thus generate increases in output that are more than proportionate to increases in the quantities of inputs. The form of organization itself becomes a source of growth.[6]

Better co-ordination among the segments of the whole helps bring about the required output. Thus, there is need for teamwork from the sub-specialized units to the broader management of economic or productive activity. As Bates rightly insists:

> Hazards as well as opportunities result from interdependency within teams. Not only can a member of a team enhance the performance of those about her, she can also sulk, withhold effort and harm the performance of others. If only for this reason, teams possess managers who can inspire, cajole, or coerce, and so impose discipline. Like sport teams, economic organizations also require governance structures. Firms require managers to co-ordinate relationships, ensuring that the conduct of one unit of the team enhances, rather than impedes, the performance of others.
>
> The creation of capital provides one source of growth. So too does the formation of economic organizations. To form economic organizations, those who possess power must delegate it to private hands. They must place it in the hands of those who will govern productive relationships and secure the benefits that can be produced by the complementary efforts of those who employ land, labor, and capital to produce goods and services.[7]

However, it is one thing to form capital but is another thing to distribute and re-distribute wealth. People who engage in politics specialize in the use of power; thus their power is better used for redistribution of wealth, but not in the creation of wealth.

---

6. *Ibid.*, 24-25.
7. *Ibid.*, 25.

The Distribution of Capital (Political Power or the Use of Violence)

Power in politics must be used in a creative way to distribute wealth and reduce inequalities or diffuse those frictions that will not make conducive the environment for the production of wealth. Bates calls the instrument of politics at the level of distribution of wealth, violence. We may also refer to it as legitimate or distributive politics, and the competence of wealth creation as "power of wealth creation." At the level of capital formation, some units of production and interaction are needed, so also those whose job it is to create, organize and direct such units so that life could flow. One has in mind individuals, groups, firms, communities and corporations. They hold the economic base, create wealth and maintain it. Not only will they enhance wealth, but will be able to discipline anyone from within the group who might have dangerous impact on the rest. Within the economic base—the formation of capital, the group should be able to provide insurance against acts of individuals and those of nature. For the economic base to flourish, not only that the co-operation of members is highly needed, those who specialize in distributive politics or the 'use of violence' should provide a system that is capable of safeguarding property and restraining adverse behavior. In other words, development within political economy has two major wings: economic and political. It involves the "formation of capital and the organization of economic activity." As Bates argues, "politically, it involves the taming of violence and the delegation of authority to those who will use power productively."[8]

The use of violence or the power to distribute wealth (politics) must not be mistaken for the power to create it (economics). Before the formation of civil society, every individual tried to feign for his or herself: producing goods and protecting his or her property at the same time. Since it was a state of might was right, the stronger dominated the weaker person, group or community. The goat that had borders with the lion had no incentive to procreate; it was not secure for Mr Jack to cultivate because the goats of the 'mighty man' were always on parade beside his farm. Where the land was unproductive, environment unsafe with a feeling of insecurity with surrounding neighbors, people invested little or nothing. Thus, the power of violence may thrive on accumulation, stealing or confiscation of wealth, but not in its creation. The accumulation of wealth in the environment of insecurity is as precarious as the conditions that brought it into existence.

---

8.   *Ibid.*, 29.

Thomas Hobbes was aware of the environment where everyone enforced their right of preservation without restrictions. In his *Leviathan*, Hobbes gives a description of human nature. The 'given' he finds in human nature is that human beings have "voluntary motions" or passions. From this given fact, Hobbes deduces the circumstances required for peaceful co-existence. He distinguishes between "voluntary motions" and "vital motions." Vital motions are products of such organs such as the heart and lungs. They are motions, which are generated to maintain life, as it were on their own accord. Voluntary motions or passions are instigated or initiated by *endeavors*. Endeavors, according to Hobbes, are small movements of the brain. An endeavor as a movement toward something is an appetite or desire; it is an aversion when it is a refraining from something.[9] Desires and aversions translate into love and hate.[10]

The natural condition, in which humans lived, according to Hobbes, was almost a condition of equality of power and abilities.[11] And the happiness or "felicity of this life" consists in continual success in obtaining one's desires. In any case, this life is far from being tranquil. Hobbes writes: "Life itselfe is but motion, and can never be without desire nor without feare, no more than without sense." In the state of nature, everyone was free to push his or her desires and wants, since it was a state of no property, no dominion: words such as 'mine' and 'thine' did not exist in the state of nature. What any man was able to grab belonged to him and so long as he could keep it. Hobbes also points out that our natural state was one in which we moved towards what we wanted; but as we did this to satisfy our desires, we collided with one another; hence the resultant conflict. Hobbes writes:

> So that in the nature of man, we find three principall causes of quarrell. First, competition; secondly, diffidence; thirdly, glory.
>
> The first, maketh men invade for gain, the second, for safety; and the third, for reputation. The first use violence, to make themselves masters of other mens persons, wives, children, and cattell; the second, to defend them; the third, for trifles, as a word, a simile, different opinion, and any other signe of undervalue, either direct in the persons, or by reflexion in their kindred, their friends, their nation, their profession, or their name.[12]

---

9.   See Thomas Hobbes, *Leviathan* ed. C. B. Macpherson (London: Penguin Books, 1968), Part 1, Ch. 6, 119. (Spellings and punctuation are left as in the original text).
10.   See *Ibid.*
11.   See *Ibid.*, Part 1, Ch. 13, 183.
12.   *Ibid.*, 185.

These principal causes of quarrels indicated that men were in the state of perpetual war:

> where every man is enemy to every man; the same is consequent to the time, wherein men live without other security, than what their own strength, and their own invention shall furnish them withall. In such condition, there is no place for industry; because the fruit therefore is uncertain: and consequent no culture of the earth; no navigation, nor use of the commodities that may be imported by sea; no commodious building; no instruments of moving, and removing such things as require much force; no knowledge of the face of the earth; no account of time; no arts; no letters, no society; and which is worst of all, continuall feare, and danger of violent death; and the life of man, solitary, poore, nasty, brutish, and short.[13]

Consequently, for one in the state of nature or war, words such as 'unjust,' 'right,' 'justice,' and 'injustice' had no place. Everyone had right to everything. Therefore, the ultimate outlook of a situation where violence is not properly channeled is described as a total breakdown of law and order. There will be no society, and people will live in constant fear and violent death, a situation that reduces man to a solitary, poor, nasty, brutish and short existence. Hobbes is very correct.

People want to preserve their life, and this too is a natural desire. There is also recognition by natural reason that people want the best conditions under which they can preserve their lives; hence the desire for peace. Thus, the natural human being is someone who desires security and peace, albeit he is perpetually engaged in conflict. He is naturally made to conflict with others as much as he naturally desires peace: the natural conflict signals a desire for the values of security (survival or each person, the protection of possessions) in co-existing with others in a non-warring atmosphere (peace). Hobbes resolves this state of affairs through the coming into existence of the Commonwealth.

The Commonwealth is an idea that employs the *passions* and the *reason* of the natural condition as the basis for an artificial structure:

> The passions that encline men to peace, are feare of death; desire of such things as are necessary to commodious living; and a hope by their industry to obtain them. And reason suggesteth convenient articles of peace, upon which men may be drawn to agreement. These articles, are they, which otherwise are called the lawes of nature.[14]

---

13. *Ibid.*, 186.

Hobbes finds a solution to a state of constant war in the idea of the Common-wealth, which will express a second nature, "that a man be willing, when others are so too, as farre-forth, as for peace, and defence of himselfe he shall think it necessary, to lay down this right to all things; and be contented with so much lib-erty against other men, as he would allow other men against himselfe."[15] The state of perpetual war will continue as far as everyone had right to everything and do everything. Peace comes where people are prepared to lay down their rights, that is, to divest themselves of their liberty and hinder others also the benefit of their own right. As Hobbes says, the end of renouncing and transferring of rights is nothing but the security and preservation of a man's life and his person in a peaceful way.

People enter into covenant to maintain peace and stability of life and prop-erty, thus ensuring mutual enhancement. With people inter-depending on one another, they secure better social and economic conditions and goods, which would not have been possible were they left to themselves unassisted by others; hence they decide to enter into covenant relationship. Covenant relationship is an outcome of a decision that lays down arms at the altar of mutual conviviality. It is a product of dialogue, sacrifices, concessions, tradeoffs, understanding, mutual acceptance, reconciliation and so on. Covenant is a reality brought about through the dynamics of social construction.

The dialogue within covenant relationship streamlines how power is to be managed so that the life and property of everyone will be secured in atmosphere of peace. The production of goods and services is usually in the hands of individ-uals, groups and communities. Authority is appointed to secure the environment for the flourishing of people and their property for that is the aim of authority coming into being in a covenant situation, and the end of covenant relationship itself.

The society is a community of mutual enhancement and support: it is not built on force but on mutual complementarities in the atmosphere of coordinat-ing human affairs. Thus, the palaver assembly constructs its social reality through dialogue in order to ensure the creation and protection of wealth. This is what Bates probably has in mind when he writes:

> The creation of parliamentary forms of government creates incentives for those who possess power to employ it in the interests of those who possess wealth. It provides assurances to those with capital that, should they

14. *Ibid.*, 188.
15. *Ibid.*, Pt. 1, Ch., 14, 190.

invest—and so increase the wealth of the nation—those who control the instruments of coercion will refrain from appropriating the value that they generate.[16]

Conditions should be created for people and groups to generate wealth; politician should not take advantage of their position or the state's monopoly of violence to embezzle and plunder wealth created by others. Such behavior and its consequent effects can plunge people back into the state of nature, that is, the state of strife, civil unrest, mutual distrust and suspicion. That is why in the dialogue situation that color covenant, tasks are shared, and the rules are specified through dialogue, consultations and weighing of opinions. There are those who have been appointed or elected to govern (those who have authority in political matters or in the use of violence) and those who guarantee the economic base of the community—the formation of capital. Individuals, groups and communities create wealth.

One recalls Ojikwu's characterization of the people. The people are the farms, the traders, the clerk, the businessman, the housewife, the student, the soldier, you and I. The people are both the economic base and the sovereign. Power and laws belong to the sovereign. They only delegate the power of violence to politicians for the purpose of their peace and flourishing; but this gesture of the people does not in any way set the politician above the people. The work of the government is to protect and create appropriate environment for all. The government should structure its policies in like manner:

> The creation of limited government may not be sufficient to secure high levels of investment, much less the growth of national economies. But assurances to investors surely are necessary to secure the formation of capital. Too often, in the developing world, politicians fail to induce the selection of policies that offer attractive prospects to investors. And institutions too rarely impose limits upon those who would use power to prey upon the wealth of others. The use of coercion for predation is too little checked; its use to promote the creation of wealth is too weakly motivated. Political risk therefore clouds the prospects offered to those with capital, thus hindering investment and retarding the development of nations.[17]

Governments should create safe bases for the formation of capital. People need to govern their lives as economic agents. The small cells in the social fabric

---

16. R. Bates, *Prosperity and Violence*, 106.
17. *Ibid.*, 107.

have their life, engineering social and economic life; thus, "the orchestration of complementarities, the building of teams and the organization of productive enterprises require that economic agents possess the authority to govern."[18] One then understands why the oil producing areas in Nigeria want to govern the products that come out of their land; they want to benefit from the fruits from their land so that the wealth of the nation can reflect in their lives and environment. However, it should be noted that authority at whatever level is there to take care of co-ordination problems. It is only in this regard that coercion is tamed and made productive. The art of taming force or violence is a schooling in prudence. Prudence is a moral and social virtue at the level of persons and groups and communities. Commenting on Aquinas, Finnis highlights that virtue is "the *perfection* of the human capacities involved in action, i.e. the powers of understanding and responding to intelligible goods and of choosing and carrying out one's choices well—a perfection which involves bringing those powers of intelligence, will, and (as sharing in rational choice and action) emotion into co-operative harmony with each other and with the human goods."[19] When coercion is disciplined, it not only integrates itself in the horizon of practical reasonableness but also enjoys in securing those goods that lead to the fulfillment of peoples and societies. When coercion is well tamed, it will discipline those whose will want to disrupt the well being of the society through what they do or fail to do. Like individuals or groups, governments can fail in doing what they are not supposed to do or in not doing what they are supposed to do.

The present day Nigeria democracy is everything but what encourages the formation of capital and the taming of violence. The government makes life insecure through its own greed and use of violence to appropriate not only wealth but use its power to destroy the economic base of the nation by ignoring investments on meaningful projects, education and encouragement of talents. It makes itself irresponsible thereby engendering irresponsibility in its own citizens.

---

18.   *Ibid.*, 108.
19.   John Finnis, *Aquinas*, 107-108.

Selected Bibliography

Achebe, A., *The Trouble With Nigeria* (Nigeria: 4th Dimension Publishers, 1983.

Ake, C., *Development and Democracy in Africa*. Ibadan: Spectrum Books Limited, 1996.

Akiki, A. B., 'African Traditional Religious Values are to be used as a Force for Human Development,' in *African Theology in Progress*, eds., J. T. Agbasiere and B. K. Zabajungu, vol. 2 AMECEA Publications.

Aquinas, T., *Summa Theologica*, First Complete American Edition in three volumes. Literally trans. by Fathers of the English Dominican Province. Vol. 1. New York: Benziger Brothers, Inc. 1947. Vol. 1.

Baker, S. 'The Races of the Nile' in *Transactions of the Ethnological Society of London*, no. 5, 1867.

Baldwin J., *Nobody Knows My Name*. London: Corgi Books, 1973.

Barongo, Y., 'Alternative Approaches to African Politics' in *Political Science in Africa:A Critical Review*, Yolamu Barongo ed., London: Zeb Press, 1983.

Bates, R. H., *Prosperity and Violence*. New York: W. W. Norton & Company, 2001.

Bell, R., 'Narrative in African Philosophy,' in *Philosophy* 64 (1989).

Bell, R. H, *Understanding African Philosophy: A Cross-Cultural Approach to Classical and Contemporary Issues*. London: Routledge, 2002.

Blyden, E., 'The Negro in Ancient History,' in *The People of Africa: a series of Papers on their Character, Condition and Future Prospects* ed. Henry M. Schieffelin, 2d. Ibadan: Ibadan University Press, 1974.

Bodunrin, P. O., 'The Question of African Philosophy' in Kwasi Wirendu, *Philosophy and An African Culture*. Cambridge: Cambridge University Press, 1980.

Buber, M., *Between Man and Man* trans. Ronald Gregor-Smith. London: Routledge & Kegan Paul, 1947.

Booth, J., *Writers and Politics in Nigeria*. London: Hodder and Stoughton, 1981.

Bujo, B., *The Ethical Dimension of Community: The African Model and the Dialogue Between North and South*. Nairobi: Paulines Publications Africa, 1998.

Burton, R. F., *A Mission to Gelele King of,Dahome*, 2d. Vol. 2. London: Tinsley Brothers, 1864.

Carroll, D., *Towards A Story of the Earth*. Dublin 1: Dominicans Publications, 1987.

Chaliand, G., *The Struggle for Africa: Conflict of the Great Powers* (1980).

Chris N. D. Anyanwu, C. N. D., *The Law Matters: Federal Republic of Nigeria 1999-2003* 3d. Nigeria: Craft International 1999.

Clark, J. D., 'The Prehistoric Origins of African Culture,' in *Papers in African Prehistory* eds. J. D. Fage and R. A. Oliver. Cambridge: Cambridge University Press, 1970.

Churchill, W., *The River War*. London: Eyre and Spottiswoode, 1951.

Croegaert, L., *The African Continent: An Insight into its Earliest History*. Nairobi: Paulines Publications Africa.

Curzo, V., 'The True Imperialism' in *Nineteenth Century and After* LXIII (Jan. 1908), 151-165.

Harrison, P., *The Third World Tomorrow: A Report from the Battlefront in the War against Poverty*. Middlesex: Penguin Books Limited, 1980.

Hountondji, P., African Philosophy: Myth and Reality, 2d., Indianapolis: Indiana University Press, 1996.

Davies, H., and Holdcroft, D., *Jurisprudence: Text and Commentary* London: Butterworths, 1991.

Darby, P., *Three Faces of Imperialism: British and American Approaches to Asia Africa (1870-1970)*. London: Yale University 1987.

Dorr, D. *Spirituality and Justice*. New York: Orbis Books, 1984.

De Salins., A and De Galhau F., V., eds., *The Modern Development of Financial Activities in the Light of the Ethical Demands of Christianity*. Vatican City: Liberia Editrice Vaticana.

Ekwuru, G., *The Pangs of An African Culture in Travail: Uwa Ndi Igbo Yaghara (The Igbo World in Disarray)*. Owerri: Totan Publishers Limited, 1999.

English, P., and Kalumba, K. M., eds., *African Philosophy: A Classical Approach* (Upper Saddle River, N. J.: Prentice Hall, 1996.

Eze E. C., ed., *African Philosophy: An Anthology*. Oxford: Blackwell Publishers, 1998.

Eze, O., 'Nigeria and Human Rights—Prospects and Problems' *Bulletin of Ecumenical Theology* 4 (Numbers 1-2, 1991).

_____ *Human Rights in Africa: Some Selected Problems*. Lagos: Nigerian Institute of International Affairs, 1984.

Filesi, T., *Movimenti di Emancipazione Coloniale a Nascita dei Nuovi Stati in Africa*. Milano, 1971.

Finnis, J., *Natural Law and Natural Rights*. Oxford: Oxford University Press, 1980.

_____ *Aquinas: Moral, Political, and Legal Theory*. Oxford: University Press, 1998.

Frieden, J. A., and David A. Lake D. A., eds., 3rd. *International Political Economy: Perspectives on Global Power and Wealth*. New York: St Martin's Press, 1995.

Fuellenbach, J., *The Kingdom of God: The Message of Jesus Today*. New York: Orbis Books, 1995.

Galilea, S., *The Beatitudes: To Evangelize as Jesus Did*. New York: Orbis Books Maryknoll, 1984.

Geyle, P., *Encounters in History*. London: Collins & Sons Co., 1963.

Gilpin, R., *Global Political Economy: Understanding the International Economic Order*. Princeton: Princeton University Press, 2001.

Grubb, M., et al eds., *The 'Earth Summit' Agreements; A Guide and Assessment:An Analysis of the Rio '92 UN Conference on Environment and Development*. London: Earthscan Publications Ltd., 1993.

Gyekye, K., *Tradition and Modernity: Philosophical Reflections on the African Experience*. Oxford: Oxford University Press, 1997.

Hart, H. L. A., *The Concept of Law*. Oxford: Oxford University Press, 1961.

Head, B., *Tales of Tenderness and Power*. Johannesburg: AD. Douker, 1989.

Hegel, G. W. F., *The Philosophy of History*. New York: Dover Publications, 1956.

Hume, D., *Moral and Political Philosophy*, ed. Henry D. Aiken. London: Hafner Press, 1948.

_____ *Enquiries Concerning Human Understanding and Concerning the Principles of Morals*, 3d., P. H. Nidditch (Oxford: Oxford University Press, 1975.

Iliffe, J., *The African Poor: History*. Cambridge: Cambridge University Press 1989.

Ikoku, E., *Self-Reliance: Africa's Survival*. Enugu: Fourth Dimension Publishers, 1980.

Irele, A., 'The African Imagination,' in *Research in African Literatures* 21 (Spring 1990).

Iwe, N. S. S., *Christianity, Culture and Colonialisation in Africa*. Port Harcourt: R. S. N. C.

John Paul II, *Africa, Apostolic Pilgrimage*. USA: St Paul Editions, 1980.

Kant, I., *Fundamental Principles of the Metaphysic of Morals* trans. J. K. Abbot. New York: Prometheus Books, 1988.

Lonergan, B. J. F., *Insight: A Study of Human Understanding*. London: Longmans, 1957.

Maritain, J., *The Rights of Man and Natural Law*. London: Geoffery Bless, 1958.

Masolo, D. A., *African Philosophy in Search of Identity*. Indianapolis: Indiana University Press, 1994.

Messner, J., *Social Ethics: Natural Law in the Western World* rev. ed. London: B. Herder Book Co., 1965.

Mohammad, S., and Edoh, T., eds., *Nigeria: A Republic in Ruins* (1986).

Muller, G. E., *Origins and Dimensions of Philosophy: Some Correlatives*. New York: Pageant Inc., 1965).

Mumford, L., 'How War Began' in *Adventures of the Mind* ed. Richard Thruelsen and John Kobler London: Victor Gollancz Limited, 1960.

Munck R., and O'Hearn, D., eds., *Critical Development Theory: Contributions to a New Paradigm*. London: Zeb Books Limited,1999.

Njoku, F. O. C., 'An Understanding of Life within the Perspective of African Theology,' in *Encounter: A Journal of Life and Religion* 1, 1 (1992), 44-57.

_____ 'Rorty On Post-Philosophical Culture: Shaping Culture With Our Thoughts in *WAJOPS* 3 (Dec. 2000), 88-110.

_____ *Essays in African Philosophy, Thought and Theology*. Owerri Nigeria: Claretian Institute of Philosophy, 2002.

_____ *Philosophy in Politics, Law and Democracy*. Owerri Nigeria: Claretian Institute of Philosophy, 2002.

_____ ed., *Philosophy, Christianity and Science in the Third* (Owerri Nigeria: Claretian Institute of Philosophy, 2000.

Nkrumah, K., *Consciencism: Philosophy and Ideology for Decolonisation and Development with particular reference to African Revolution*. London: Heinmann Educational Books Limited, 1964.

Nwala, T. U., *Igbo Philosophy*. Nigeria: Latern Books, 1985.

Nwoko, M. I., *The Rationality of African Socialism*. Rome: Tipo-Litografia Aurelia, 1985.

Nyerere, J., *Ujamaa Essays on Socialism*. Nairobi: Oxford University Press, 1968.
_____ 'Ujamaa: The Basis of African Socialism' in *I am Because We Are: Readings in Black Philosophy*, eds., Fred Lee Hord and Jonathan Scott Lee. Massachusetts: University of Massachusetts Press, 1995.

Obiora F. Ike and Ndidi Nnoli Edozien, *Development Is About People Business Is About Ethics*. Enugu: Catholic Institute for Development, Justice and Peace (CIDJAP), 2003.

Ojiako, J. O., *13 Years of Military Rule 1966-79*. Lagos: Daily Times Publication.

Okoh J. D., 'Julius Nyerere's Philosophy of Ujamaa: A Model For Emergent African Nations' in *Academia: A CIP Journal of Philosophy* 1(June 2003), 25-38.

Okolo, O., 'Tradition and Destiny: Horizons of An African Hermeneutics' in African Philosophy: Essential Readings, ed., T. Serequeberhan. *African Philosophy: The Essential Readings*. New York: Paragon House, 1991.

Onyeocha, I. M., *Africa: The Question of Identity* Nigerian edition. Washington D. C.: The Council for Research in Values and Philosophy, 1997.

Oruka, H. O., 'Sage Philosophy: The Question of Methodology' in *Sage Philosophy* ed., H. Odera Oruka. Nairobi: African Center for Technology Studies Press, 1991.

Oyebola, A., *Black Man's Dilemma*. Ibadan: Board Publications Limited, 1982.

Rapley, J., *Understanding Development: Theory and Practice in Third World*. London: Lynne Rienner Publishers, 1996.

Ray, B. C., *African Religious Symbols, Ritual and Community*. New Jersey: Prentice-Hall, Inc., Englewood Cliffs, 1976.

Raz, J., *Practical Reason and Norms*. London: Hutchinson & Co., 1975.

Rodney, W., *How Europe Underdeveloped Africa*. Washington D. C.: Howard University Press, 1982.

Sandbrook, R., *The Politics of Africa's Economic Recovery*. Cambridge: Cambridge University Press, 1993.

Schutz, A., 'Phenomenology and Social Sciences,' in *Phenomenology and Sociology* ed. Thomas Luckmann. New York: Penguin Books, 1978.

Senghor, L. S., *On African Socialism*. London: Pall Mall Press, 1964.

———— 'Black Woman' in *Western African Verse: An Anthology* chosen and annotated by Donatus I. Nwoga. Harlow Essex: Longman, 1967.

———— 'Negritude: A Humanism of the 20th Century' in *I Are Because We Are* eds. Fred Lee Hone and Jonathan Scot Lee Massachusetts: Universityof Massachusetts Press, 1995.

Serequeberhan, T. ed., *African Philosophy: The Essential Readings*. New York: Paragon House, 1991.

———— 'Philosophy and Post-Colonial Africa' in *African Philosophy: An Anthology*, ed., E. C. Eze. Oxford: Blackwell Publishers, 1998.

Shagari, S., 'Address to Nigerian Institute of International Affairs' in *Third World Diplomacy Press*, Winter vol. 1, 3d., (1982).

Skinner, Q., The *Foundations of Modern Political Thought Volume One The Renaissance*. Cambridge: Cambridge University Press, 1978.

Sowell, T., *Basic Economics: A Citizen's Guide to the Economy*. New York: Basic Books, 2000.

Soyinka, W., *The Man Died* (Prison Notes). England: Penguin Books, 1972.

Sullivan, F. A., T*he Church We Believe In: One, Holy, Catholic and Apostolic*. New York: Paulist Press, 1988.

Sumner, L. W., *The Moral Foundation of Rights*. Oxford: Clarendon Press, 1987.

Tempels, P., *Bantu Philosophy*, trans. Colin King. Paris: Presence Africaine, 1959.

_____ 'Bantu Ontology' in *African Philosophy: An Anthology* ed.,Emmanuel Chukwudi Eze. Oxford: Blackwell Publishers Limited, 1998.

Towa, M., 'Condition for the Affirmation of a Modern Philosophical Thought,' in *African Philosophy: Essential Readings*, ed., T. Serequeberhan, *African Philosophy: The Essential Readings*. New York: Paragon House, 1991.

Uba, A., *Fundamental Psychology of Childhood and Adolescence*. Ibadan: Claverianum Press, 1980.

Udoidem, S. I. *Values and National Development*. Lagos: African Heritage Research and Publications, 1992.

Uzukwu, E. E., 'Missiology Today: The African Situation' in *Religion and African Culture, Inculturation—A Nigerian Perspective*, ed. E. E. Uzukwu. Enugu: Spiritan Publications, 1988.

Weil, S., *Selected Essays: 1934-1943*, trans. Richard Rees. Oxford: Oxford University Press, 1962.

Williams, E., 'The Origin of Negro Slavery," in *African Philosophy: An Anthology* ed. E. C. Eze Oxford: Blackwell Publishers, 1998.

Wirendu, K., 'On Defining African Philosophy' in *African Philosophy: The Essential Readings*, ed. Tsenay Serequeberhan. New York: Paragon House, 1991.

Other Documents

Human Development Report 1992. Oxford: Oxford University Press, 1992.

Pius XI, *Quadragesimo Anno* (1931).

Soviet Monthly Digest August (19

The Mission of the Claretians Today: Document of the 19th General Chapter in *The Claretian Mission of the Claretians Today and the Claretian in Process of Congregational Renewal: Documents of the 19th and 20th General Chapters of the Congrega-*

tion of Claretian Missionaries, trans. Joseph Daries (Philippines: Claretian Publications).

Vatican II, Pastoral Constitution on the Church in the Modern World (Gaudium et Spes), 7 December 1965.

World Development Report 1991: The Challenge of Development. Oxford: Oxford University Press, 1991.

About the Author

Francis O. C Njoku cmf, Ph.D. was educated at the universities of Duquesne Pittsburgh, (Pennsylvania, USA); Gregorian (Rome, Italy) and Oxford (England, UK). He teaches philosophy at the Claretian Institute of Philosophy, Maryland, Nekede, Owerri, Imo State, Nigeria. He has contributed articles to scholarly journals, and his major works include: *Studies in Jurisprudence: A Fundamental Approach to the Philosophy of Law*; *Essays in African Philosophy, Thought and Theology*; *Philosophy in Politics, Law and Democracy*; *Empiricism and Causation in the Law*; and *The Reason Why a Human Being Should Act Morally*.

0-595-32949-7

www.ingramcontent.com/pod-product-compliance
Lightning Source LLC
Chambersburg PA
CBHW061354280526
45784CB00001B/258